THE
TWENTY-FOUR-INCH
HOME RUN

★

MICHAEL G. BRYSON

CONTEMPORARY
BOOKS

CHICAGO

Library of Congress Cataloging-in-Publication Data

Bryson, Michael G. 1942-
    The twenty-four-inch home run : and other outlandish,
  incredible but true events in baseball history / Michael G. Bryson.
      p.   cm.
    1. Baseball—United States—Anecdotes.   2. Baseball—
  United States—History.   I. Title.
  GV873.B7   1990
  796.357'0973—dc20   89-28099
                                                 CIP

All photos from the collection of Bill Bryson.

Published by Contemporary Books, Inc.
180 North Michigan Avenue, Chicago, Illinois 60601
Manufactured in the United States of America
International Standard Book Number: 0-8092-4341-5

Published simultaneously in Canada by Beaverbooks, Ltd.
195 Allstate Parkway, Valleywood Business Park
Markham, Ontario L3R 4T8 Canada

To Sherry,
my wife, my love, my best
and most cherished friend

CONTENTS

PREFACE

This book would not have been possible without the inspiration of—and some vital research by—my late father, William E. Bryson, a sportswriter and baseball historian for nearly fifty years. My father covered both major- and minor-league baseball for a midwestern newspaper and wrote thousands of baseball stories for national magazines. When he discovered his eldest son's keen interest in baseball, he began taking the kid along on baseball trips and interviews.

It was a thrilling experience for an impressionable youngster sitting in on discussions with such greats as Charlie Grimm, Burleigh Grimes, Rogers Hornsby, Satchel Paige, Dizzy Dean, Bob Feller, Charlie Root, Fred Clarke, and a host of other Hall of Fame members.

My father always had one rule when I sat in on these interviews: I had to remain quiet and unobtrusive while he conducted his work. Later there always seemed to be an opportunity for me to ask a question or two.

Charlie Root with author Michael Bryson (at age nine).

I'll never forget Hornsby telling me about his playing days when he refused to attend movies or even
read a book or newspaper for fear of damaging his
eyes, Fred Clarke recalling nearly sixty years later
the play-by-play details of baseball's first World Series, or Grimes, the last of the "legal" spitball pitchers,
explaining to me just how he threw a spitter.

And I'll never forget Charlie Root's face turning
beet red when I asked him about Babe Ruth's famous
"called" home run. Charlie, the pitcher who delivered

that homer toss, sat me down, put an arm over my shoulder, and without tarnishing my admiration for Ruth, patiently explained why the story was a myth.

Many of those stories that I heard in my formative years are included in this book. The rest come from the huge collection of anecdotes and generally unknown baseball stories that my father (and later I, when I became a sportswriter) collected over the years. My father and I shared a delight in offbeat baseball stories. Dad's interest in unusual baseball events was well known, and fellow sportswriters, the former curator of the Hall of Fame, and even people on the street were constantly sending him stories of baseball oddities.

I owe a heavy debt of thanks to several members of my family for their help in preparing this book. My younger son, Robert Bryson, a budding baseball expert, spent countless hours helping me go through files, aged clippings, and notes in selecting the stories.

Sherry Bryson, my wife, and Mary Bryson, my mother, two expert journalists, contributed valuable help in editing and proofreading the manuscript. I also owe a debt to my elder son, Michael Jr., for his strong encouragement on this project—and for taking time out of his busy life to help me comb through reference books in search of an answer to one question or another.

I'd also like to acknowledge the valuable help I received from Karen Schenkenfelder, who performed a marvelous job of copyediting this book, and my editor, Linda Gray, who contributed vital ideas and suggestions and whose enthusiasm made this project a work of joy.

INTRODUCTION

Baseball was first played by gentlemen, strictly amateurs. They had the idea, those New York aristocrats who made up the Knickerbocker Baseball Club, that the game for which they devised the first formal rules in 1846 would be the cricket of America.

It would be a game played by graceful and correct young men as a means of social relaxation, watched by genteel, tea-sipping, and quietly applauding spectators from the upper classes.

And so it was for a few years. But the Knicks developed a game that was too interesting. The common folk saw it, liked it, and began playing it. When the Civil War broke out, soldiers from the Northeast taught their compatriots from other sections of the country how to play this fascinating new game. Confederate prisoners of war mastered the sport while confined to Northern prison camps.

Less than twenty-five years after young Alexander Cartwright first paced off the base paths, athletes began earning their daily bread by throwing a ball

1

with remarkable accuracy or mightily pounding it with a lathed stick of wood.

People flocked to the ballparks to look at these emerging national heroes and our new national pastime. A number of reasons have been put forth for why the public continues to have a love affair with this rather slow-moving sport, even in this age of zestier and speedier games such as football and basketball.

One of the prime reasons may be that there is no other sport in which an individual—or a whole team for that matter—can do so many different things right—or so many different things wrong. No other sport has produced as many stories about oddities or strange occurrences.

The old saying is true: "Anything can happen in baseball." And that's what this book is all about—the daffy, dumb, and delightful things that baseball players and teams have done over the years, the things that have endeared this sport to all of its fans.

1
ODDS, ODDITIES, AND ODD MEN OUT

A WHALE OF A POSTPONEMENT

A professional baseball game was once officially "called on account of whale." Another game was suspended when a little dog swiped a baseball. A major-league game was forfeited because of a snowball fight, and, unbelievably, a minor-league game was called "because of sun."

It's literally a whale of a story that happened at Wilmington, North Carolina, one afternoon in the 1920s. It was the era before night baseball, and only about fourteen customers turned out for the midweek contest. Just as the game was about to start, a man came running into the park shouting that a whale had washed ashore. Virtually everyone in the park, including the players, rushed out to see the huge mammal. Umpire Art Knowles, left alone in the ballpark, called the game "on account of whale"—and that's the way it went into the record books!

The late John McGraw used to bubble with laughter about a minor-league game that was suspended "on account of canine." McGraw, in the early days of

3

his career, was playing with Olean, New York, in a game with Pennsylvania rival Bradford. The game was knotted in the fourteenth inning, when an Olean batter knocked a shot down the left-field line. Suddenly, from nowhere, a little black-and-white spaniel darted onto the field, picked up the ball, and started running.

The Bradford leftfielder gave pursuit but couldn't nab the speedy dog. The shortstop joined the chase, and minutes later the entire Bradford team was in pursuit of the pup, which still had the ball clutched tightly in its teeth. The chase ended unexpectedly when the frightened dog made a sharp turn and exited from the ballpark.

That forced the game to be suspended "on account of canine," because no other baseballs were available. All of the others that had been brought to the park had been damaged or knocked out of play earlier in the game.

The snowball fight erupted in 1907, when the New York Giants and Philadelphia opened the season at the Polo Grounds—despite a six-inch snowfall the night before. Huge piles of the white stuff ringed the field.

Philadelphia quickly built a big lead, and at the start of the eighth inning, several hundred disgruntled Giants fans left their seats, sauntered over to the piles of snow, and began flinging snowballs at the Philadelphia players.

Before long, a fierce snowball fight developed—so ferocious that the umpires had to call the game and award a 9–0 forfeit victory to Philadelphia.

A total eclipse of the sun produced a sudden disruption of a minor-league game in Ventura, California, many years ago, before the era of lighted games. The schedule makers neglected one important thing in slating the afternoon contest: Ventura was directly in the center of the area blacked out by the eclipse, and the game was halted when day suddenly became as dark as the dead of night.

In the early days of the National League, Louisville was a member of the loop, and Cincinnati used a riverboat to travel down the Ohio River to the Kentucky city. There were no reports of a legitimate shipwreck, but ancient records indicate that at least one game was delayed because the barge washed up on a sandbar.

Of all things, the sun forced postponement of a Babe Ruth League game in 1956 at Auburn, New York. The ump called the game after the fifth inning because the sun was shining in the batters' eyes.

PAL'S ACCIDENTAL HIT DEPRIVED ALEXANDER OF A NO-HITTER

Grover Cleveland Alexander once lost a no-hitter when a good friend accidentally got a hit off the future Hall of Famer with two out in the bottom of the ninth inning. The weird incident came early in Alexander's twenty-year career, when he was pitching for Philadelphia one afternoon at St. Louis.

"Old Pete," as he was later called, was in masterful form that day, blending his pitches with such perfection that the Cardinals didn't even come close to getting a hit. Alexander finally reached the bottom of the ninth and retired the first two batters.

That brought to the plate Artie Butler, a small shortstop who was not a particularly good hitter. More important, Butler and Alexander were the best of friends off the field.

Butler conceded years later that because Philadelphia had already erected an insurmountable lead, he had no intention of breaking up his friend's no-hit bid. Alexander delivered the first pitch, a bad one, and Butler swung weakly and missed. The same thing happened on the next pitch.

On the third pitch, which would have put away the no-hitter, Butler again simply went through the motions of swinging—but by *pure accident*, the ball collided with his bat and looped lazily over the second baseman's head, well out of the reach of any of the Phillies. Butler threw down his bat in disgust and virtually strolled to first, but he reached it before the ball was recovered.

Ironically, Alexander said later that he simply shrugged off the incident and soon forgot it; Butler said it produced many sleepless nights for him.

ENEMY SOLDIERS PLAYED CATCH BETWEEN BATTLES

One minute, the Union and Confederate soldiers were shooting at each other during the Civil War; the next, they were tossing a baseball back and forth between enemy lines.

A Sergeant Dryden, a member of an Iowa regiment, once wrote about baseball's strangest matchup. It happened during the long wait in the trenches at the siege of Vicksburg, Mississippi, when one day the Northern and Southern soldiers jokingly challenged each other to a baseball game. They didn't actually play a game, but Dryden reported that the men from his company and the enemy "played catch" from line to line.

"We were throwing and catching the ball belonging to our company team one day," Dryden related, when firing suddenly broke out and the men from both sides dived into their trenches. Dryden said there was "one big fellow named Halloran who, after we had got under cover, wanted to go over and whip the Confederate soldier who had stolen our ball."

But the next morning, "during a lull in the firing," Dryden said, "that Southerner yelled to us—and in a moment the ball came flying over" to the Union trenches!

SIX STRIKES AND YOU'RE OUT!

Oh, it's one, two, three strikes, you're out at the old ball game. Not necessarily so. It once took six strikes to retire Walter Missler, who played for the Lima, Ohio, minor-league team in 1939.

Missler was batting against Tiffin, Ohio, and ran up a two-and-two count. He failed to take a cut at the next ball, figuring it was a bad pitch—and he didn't hear any ruling by umpire Virgil Majors. The catcher tossed the ball back to the pitcher, who stepped to the side of the mound to tighten a shoelace.

Missler used the momentary pause to run over to the dugout to exchange his bat for a lighter cudgel, then returned to the plate. The next pitch was on target, and Missler swung heartily and missed. Assuming he was out, he started back for the dugout when he heard the ump exclaim, "Strike one!"

Missler was mystified but nonetheless returned to the batter's box. He fouled off the next pitch, then swung at the next pitch and missed—for his sixth strike.

It wasn't until later in the inning, after another Lima player had flied out, that Ump Majors discovered just what had happened—that Missler had been called out on strikes after the two-and-two count but didn't hear the call. Because he had gone back to the dugout to get a bat, the ump had assumed that it was a new Lima batter coming to the plate.

After mulling it over, Majors finally decided that Missler would have to be credited with two strikeouts in that one inning, and he ordered the Lima team to take the field.

WILLIAMS WOULD HAVE HIT .549 IN 1887

Anyone browsing through some old record books would be startled to see the .492 batting average credited in 1887 to J. E. (Tip) O'Neill of St. Louis in the

American Association, then a major league. The same year, Cap Anson led the National League with a .421 mark.

Rather lusty hitting? Actually there's a catch: that was the one and only year that pro baseball changed the rules to permit bases on balls to count as hits. The logic was that a walk was as beneficial for a team as a single. Fortunately, baseball executives quickly decided that their logic was illogical.

Had the same rule been in effect in 1941, Ted Williams would have batted an astonishing .549. With his .406 average that year, the Red Sox slugger was the last major leaguer to hit over .400. He had 185 hits in 456 official trips, but he also lured 145 bases on balls, which would have made his totals 330 hits in 601 attempts under the 1887 system.

Not even Babe Ruth would have beaten Williams's hypothetical 1887 average, even though the Babe drew 170 walks in 1923. Ruth had a .393 average that year by the customary methods of figuring. Converting his walks into times at bat and hits would make Ruth's mark .542 under the 1887 system.

Some modern baseball guides have modified these 1887 records by removing the walks-as-hits and listing the averages based on at-bats and hits.

TEAM WINS SIX GAMES IN ONE DAY

There have been a couple of instances where major-league teams have been involved in tripleheaders, but that's mere child's play compared to the finish of the 1899 New England League race—when a team posted six victories in one day!

The only way the Manchester club had a chance of catching league-leading Portland was to win six games on the final day of the season. Surprisingly, the Portland players and management went along with the idea of trying to play six games in one day.

They started at 9:00 A.M., and Manchester won two nine-inning games before lunch. After the brief lunch break, the teams played three more nine-inning games in the afternoon. Manchester won all three.

A sixth contest was started, but after two innings, Portland protested a decision by the umpire—and ended up trudging wearily off the field in protest. The umpire awarded Manchester its sixth victory by forfeit.

Unfortunately, the Manchester players later learned that they had expended a lot of energy for nothing. Newport took the league title the same day by scheduling a tripleheader with Taunton and won all three games, enough to propel Newport ahead of both Manchester and Portland.

Then league officials stepped in and threw out seven of the nine last-day games and permitted Newport and Manchester to be credited with only one victory each. That allowed Newport to hang on to the league championship.

• • •

For the record, the last tripleheader in the major leagues was on October 2, 1920, when Cincinnati and Pittsburgh were fighting it out for third place. The fourth-place Pirates were two and one half games behind the third-place Reds, but because of postponements earlier in the season, there were still three unplayed games between the two teams.

Pittsburgh could overtake Cincinnati by winning three times, and team officials appealed to John Heydler, league president, to play the tripleheader. Heydler granted the request, despite strong objections from Pat Moran, Cincinnati's manager.

The first game began at noon—and only one game was needed, because the Reds locked up third place with a 13–4 victory. Nonetheless, the other two games were played. Cincinnati won the second one 7–3 before the Pirates prevailed 6–0 in the third game, which was called after six innings because of darkness.

There was precedent for the tripleheader. In 1896, pennant-bound Baltimore won three games from Louisville on September 7—then swept a doubleheader from the Kentuckians the next day.

BEARLY BELIEVABLE TRAINING SCHEDULE

Walter Scott Brodie holds the record for the player who undoubtedly underwent the most rigorous and unusual training schedule in baseball history. Late in the winter of 1896, the hard-hitting outfielder of the Baltimore Orioles (then a National League team) wrote to club officials that he was getting into fine shape for the coming season by sparring and wrestling every day with a trained bear! He hastened to add that he wore a mask "to keep him from scratching me. I also wear a chest protector."

But this, according to Brodie's letter, was only a small part of his preseason training. "In addition to this exercise, I ride a bucking bronco pony thirty miles a day, and spend some time running and jumping hedges," he wrote.

The training must have been too much for Brodie. His batting average, .365 the year before, plummeted to .294 in 1896.

WEAK THROWING ARM? JUST MOVE THE BASE

Early in this century, a weak throwing arm ended the sixteen-year major-league career of shortstop Herman Long. But he wanted to continue playing baseball and caught on with Des Moines of the old Western League.

Unfortunately, his arm proved to be inadequate even in the minors, although his glove work was simply sensational. Mike Cantillion, then the owner of the Des Moines team, had a simple solution for the problem: he lengthened the distance from the plate to first base from ninety to ninety-two feet—just enough extra distance to permit Long's throws to beat the runners.

• • •

Matty Mathews was another aging veteran who used a moved base to prolong his stay in baseball. Mathews, who once served as a bullpen catcher for the New York Yankees, was well past his prime when he signed to play the 1914 season with Newport News. But opposition players soon caught on that Mathews's aged arm wasn't capable of stopping anyone from stealing second.

Mathews easily solved the difficulty by slipping into the park late one night and moving second base several feet closer to home. It wasn't until the end of the season that anyone discovered the subterfuge— while Mathews spent the summer consistently nabbing some of the fleetest base stealers in the league by a step or two at second base.

HOLDING RUNNER ON THIRD SUITED HIM JUST FINE

In the early 1900s, a Chicago clothier offered an expensive suit of clothes to the player who led the Chicago Cubs in home runs. This was an era when home runs were rare and there were no regular coaches. The players took turns coaching at first and third.

Catcher Johnny Kling was one home run ahead of Joe Tinker (of Tinker-to-Evers-to-Chance fame) and had drawn the third-base coaching duties. Tinker was at the plate and slammed a drive that caromed off the fence and ricocheted about the outfield. There was little doubt that it would be an inside-the-park home run. But as Tinker approached third, Kling held up his arms for him to stop—and later collected a fancy new suit.

KELLY STOLE FROM FIRST TO THIRD

In the early days of baseball, there was only one umpire—and that's how King Kelly of the old Chicago White Stockings got away with the most audacious base stealing of all time. King's most famous type of steal was from first to third—directly across the diamond. Under the old one-ump system, he repeatedly got away with it.

THE OUTFIELDER WHO DISAPPEARED

Portland, Oregon, baseball fans were dumbfounded one day when they watched one of the team's outfielders lope along after a fly ball—and then suddenly vanish into thin air.

"What an eerie feeling," said Bruce Hamby, who was a sportswriter for the Portland *Oregonian* and later sports editor of the Denver *Post*. Hamby, an eyewitness, said outfielder Rupert Thompson was running "along in plain sight—then he was gone! It was like the vanishing Hindu in that rope trick."

Startled fans and players gasped and leaped to their feet. The vanishing act was solved a few seconds later, when Thompson climbed out of a hole in the ground. According to Hamby, "There was an old cesspool out there, and it had been boarded up, with sod on top of it. The boards just gave way."

Thompson was shaken but escaped any serious injuries. The only damage to him was nothing that a hot, soapy shower didn't cure.

PITCHER LIVID BECAUSE UMP CALLED HIS DELIVERY A STRIKE

A pitcher was once tossed out of a major-league game for arguing with an umpire that he *didn't* strike out a batter! It was when Rogers Hornsby was managing the old St. Louis Browns, and the Rajah had one strict rule for his pitchers: if a hurler got two straight strikes on a batter, he was supposed to "waste" the next pitch. Failure to follow this edict would result in an automatic fifty-dollar fine.

One afternoon, pitcher Jim Walkup whistled two straight strikes past a batter. Remembering Hornsby's order (and the fifty-dollar fine), Walkup deliberately threw the next pitch high and wide. The umpire called it strike three. To the astonishment of umpire and batter, Walkup came roaring off the mound, screaming: "No! No! It was a ball!"

He wound up raising such a fuss about the strike that he was ejected from the game.

HIGH SCHOOL TEAM WINS NO-HITTER 109–0

The Atlantic, Iowa, high school team once beat Griswold, Iowa, 109–0 on a no-hitter. While the Atlantic pitcher was holding the opposition in check, his teammates slammed out 92 hits in 139 trips, including sixteen home runs, six triples, and twenty-three doubles. Atlantic scored thirty runs in the second inning and twenty-seven in the third. For obvious reasons, the game was called in the eighth inning.

PLAYER STRUCK BY PITCH DOESN'T GET FREE PASS TO FIRST

Billy Hunter, who had the dubious distinction of playing with five different teams during his six-year major-league career, once was struck by a pitched ball—but didn't get a free ride to first base. The reason? Hunter was in the on-deck batting circle when the very wild pitch conked him!

THE AMAZING LITTLE PITCHER THAT HISTORY NEGLECTED

Mention the name Dickie Kerr, and you'll probably draw a blank stare from even the most ardent of baseball followers. Yet this mighty little marvel, who stood only 5'7" and weighed 130 pounds soaking wet, tossed two of the most astonishing victories ever by a rookie in World Series history.

Kerr, you see, was one of the honest players on the 1919 Chicago Black Sox, and he earned his two victories even though eight of his teammates were involved in a conspiracy to throw the fall classic to Cincinnati in what turned out to be baseball's greatest scandal.

After Cincinnati had "won" the first two games, Kerr baffled the Reds 3–0 on just three hits in game number three at Chicago. Cincinnati then posted two more victories in the best-of-nine series before Kerr returned to the mound and *scattered* eleven hits in a 5–4 ten-inning victory.

Ironically, this young symbol of honesty was treated shamefully by the White Sox management. After posting a 13–7 record in his rookie year, Kerr was 21–9 in 1920 and 19–17 in 1921. When he asked for a $3,500 salary for the 1922 season, the White Sox turned him down flat. Disillusioned, Kerr dropped out of baseball. He did make one comeback attempt in 1925, appearing generally as a relief pitcher, but was battered badly in the thirty-six innings he pitched. Kerr then quit baseball forever.

PAY RAISE TURNED INTO A CUT

Outfielder Hugh Duffy had a spectacular season for Boston's National League team in 1894. He hit .438 and collected a league-leading 18 homers, 50 doubles, and 145 RBIs.

Duffy figured that kind of production merited a salary increase. Surprisingly, Boston's team officials refused to give in to his demands—and Duffy became baseball's first famous holdout.

When club officials finally realized that Duffy did intend to sit out the season, they capitulated and awarded him his salary increase: *$12.50 more per month*. But the club added a stipulation. Duffy had to serve as team captain in 1895 and assume responsibility for all of the equipment the team used.

The trouble was, at the end of the season, the owners added up the amount of equipment that had been lost and deducted the cost from Duffy's salary. That deduction totaled more than Duffy's salary increase, so in the long run, Duffy wound up taking a salary cut!

MCGRAW PLAYED FIFTY-THREE-YEAR-OLD IN TITLE GAME

James Henry O'Rourke undoubtedly holds the record for longevity in baseball participation. He began in 1867 and didn't hang up his glove for good until after the 1914 season, a span of forty-seven years.

That alone is unbelievable, but the smooth-talking Irishman performed a feat in 1905 that is equally amazing: he convinced tough old John McGraw to let him play in the New York Giants' pennant-clinching game against Cincinnati. At the time, O'Rourke was *fifty-three years old*.

O'Rourke came down from Bridgeport, Connecticut, to see the National League pennant-clinching game—and suddenly decided that he wanted to have a role in one last championship.

(The dapper Irishman had batted .327 for Boston's champions in 1876, the National League's first season, and had helped the Giants win their first pennant in 1888 and another in 1889. His lifetime average of .310 in nineteen major-league seasons eventually earned him a spot in the Hall of Fame.)

O'Rourke sought out McGraw and pleaded to be put in the New York lineup even "for just a little while." The hard-bitten McGraw was a sentimentalist at heart, and he admired the audacity of the grizzled old veteran, who still wore the long, flowing mustache of his big-league days.

Three great managers: Charlie Grimm of Chicago, John McGraw of the New York Giants, and Joe McCarthy of the Yankees (early 1930s).

But, McGraw said, he just couldn't do it. "I'd like to, Jim, but you're just too old," he said. O'Rourke didn't give up easily. He started enlisting the help of the Giants players, and under their goading, McGraw finally gave in.

Grudgingly, he placed O'Rourke on the active list and told Jim he would let him catch one inning.

O'Rourke performed so well, however, that McGraw left him in for the entire game. O'Rourke made one error but slammed a solid hit in one of his four trips and scored one run!

• • •

That, of course, was the crowning glory of O'Rourke's career. He could have gone back to Bridgeport and rested on his laurels, content with his jobs as owner and manager of his club and secretary of the Connecticut League, which he helped organize in 1897.

He didn't. He played nearly every game for Bridgeport through the 1908 season and caught at least one game—sometimes more—in each of the next six seasons.

O'Rourke, incidentally, was one of baseball's most educated men—and one of its quaintest characters. He was nicknamed "Orator Jim" because of his extensive vocabulary, which at times confused umpires and rival players. Sometimes, however, O'Rourke would direct the vocabulary upon himself after making an error.

One time, after booting the ball, he loudly berated himself: "Mr. O'Rourke, I am pained and astonished at the hopeless incompetency displayed by you in your futile effort to trap that 'daisy-cutter.' If you do not quickly improve the quality of your play, it will be necessary for you to retire from your present position and join a less pretentious organization. I trust I shall not again be compelled to bring this matter to your attention."

IRATE OWNER FIRED MANAGER FROM THE STANDS

Jack Holland, whose son John later served a term as general manager of the Cubs, was one of minor-league baseball's most colorful—and quickly decisive—owners. He bought the Oklahoma City team, and one day from his vantage point in the top row of the grandstand, he quickly concluded that his team was losing because of stupid mistakes by his manager. At midgame, Oklahoma City blew a big chance for a comeback, and suddenly there was a thundering bellow from the back of the stands: "You're fired!"

Holland meant it; he didn't even permit his skipper to finish the game.

● ● ●

In the early days of this century, when Holland was gaining a reputation as a crafty and sometimes feisty man, it was difficult to lure fans to minor-league games. Consequently, Holland cooked up the idea that he and a rival manager would stage a spectacular display of pulled-punches fisticuffs before a game. The idea, Holland reasoned, was that the local newspaper would give the fight big play, and the next day fans would turn out in droves, hoping to see a renewal of the feud.

The plan worked—a huge crowd turned out—but there was one major problem: Holland and his "friendly rival" neglected to tell the players that their feud was a hoax. When the two men approached each other the next day, players poured out from both benches, and the two hoaxers suddenly became victims of some legitimate punches.

BLANCHARD CERTAINLY DIDN'T WANT TO CATCH

Johnny Blanchard did quite a bit of catching for the New York Yankees from 1959 to 1965, but Blanchard originally was determined to keep the Yanks from putting him behind the plate. His protest against catching was so strong, in fact, that a manager once had to hide the lineup card from Blanchard to keep him from tearing it up.

The Yanks originally signed Blanchard in 1950 as a third baseman, but his play at third in the lower minors was far from impressive. Next the Yankees tried Blanchard as an outfielder in Class D—and team officials didn't think much of his prospects there.

So it was decided that they would try Blanchard as a catcher, assigning him to Class C Joplin, Missouri, where Vern Hoscheit was managing. Vern was an experienced catcher, and the Yanks figured he could teach Blanchard the intricacies of working behind the plate.

But Blanchard simply hated catching, "and he got madder about it all of the time," Hoscheit recalled years later. "Finally, one night he was bowled over by a runner at the plate, got up, and threw the ball away, and it cost us an extra-inning game.

"I was in the clubhouse when John stormed in. He had all his gear in his hands, and he threw it right in my face—hard. John says, 'I've caught my last game.'"

Hoscheit said he didn't say anything, but the next night, he posted the lineup in the clubhouse with Blanchard listed as catcher. "John took one look at the card and tore it up," recalled Vern. "I put up another card in the dugout, and he tore that one up, too. I didn't say a word, just sat down and made out a third card. I clutched the card and held it out of reach when John came over and sat down beside me."

Finally, Blanchard pleaded, "Do I *have* to catch?" And after a quiet moment, he got into his gear. Hoscheit said, "I never heard another murmur out of him after that."

2
UNBELIEVABLE HOME RUNS

THE TWENTY-FOUR-INCH HOME RUN

Just about every baseball fan can tell you about that cool April day in 1953 when Mickey Mantle's bat made such violent contact with a pitch from Chuck Stobbs that the ball flew far into the parking lot behind the left-field wall in old Griffith Stadium in Washington, D.C. The ball was airborne an astonishing 565 feet from home plate.

But what about professional baseball's shortest bona fide homer?

In almost every professional park, a ball usually has to travel more than 300 feet to clear a fence in order to provide the hitter a free trip around the bases. And it would take an unusually lucky or extraordinarily speedy player to produce an inside-the-park homer on a ball that didn't travel at least a couple of hundred feet.

That's what makes Andy Oyler's *twenty-four-inch* home run so remarkable. The long-forgotten Oyler achieved his astounding feat while serving as a minor-league shortstop for Minneapolis in the early

1900s. Oyler, a tiny man, was an outstanding fielder but not much of a hitter, even though he made himself a difficult pitching target by maneuvering his minute frame into a pretzel-like crouch at the plate.

The day of Oyler's unusual record, Minneapolis was involved in a tight battle with St. Paul. It had rained the day before, and the grounds were literally a quagmire: baserunners and fielders foundered in the oozing mud as if twenty-pound weights had been strapped to their shoes.

The game was deadlocked when the meager-sized Oyler, whose only claim to major-league fame was twenty-seven games with Baltimore of the American League in 1902, strode to the plate and went into his imitation of a pretzel. The St. Paul pitcher unleashed a blazing brush-back pitch directly toward Andy's head.

Oyler bent his knees slightly and ducked his head. His bat was still on his shoulder, and the ball struck the bat. There wasn't a soul in the park who didn't hear the resounding crack of contact—but *nobody* saw just where the ball went. The St. Paul catcher cast his eyes skyward, presuming that the missile had been popped up. But he didn't see a thing except sky. The first baseman began searching frantically around the bag to see if the ball had landed there.

The pitcher was screaming unintelligibly, and the third baseman was asserting that the umpire was accidentally standing on the ball. But the poor ump was as bewildered as the St. Paul players.

In the meantime, the tiny Oyler was streaking around the bases—or at least running as fast as his stubby legs would carry him. Someone from the stands shouted that Oyler had hidden the ball in his pocket. When the St. Paul second baseman heard that, he gave chase to Oyler, but this prompted Andy to run even faster—fast enough to cross home plate with the winning run just ahead of the outstretched arms of the angry second baseman.

The St. Paul players immediately accused Oyler of pocketing the ball. The Minneapolis player issued a hearty laugh, then pointed downward just in front of home plate.

Sure enough. There was the ball, buried deep in the mud—only two feet in front of home plate.

The hard-pitched ball had bounced off Oyler's bat so quickly that no one but Oyler, whose eyes were on the ground as he ducked from the pitch, saw the ball slam into the mud. The umpire, of course, had to score it as an "official" home run, because the ball had landed in fair territory.

THE ONE-HALF HOME RUN

In the movie *The Natural*, there's a scene in which Robert Redford, playing an aging slugger for a fictitious New York team, smashes the ball with such strength that it literally splits and unravels. Ridiculous, you say. Unbelievable!

Well, there really was a case of an exploding horse-hide in a Missouri semipro game between Cascade and Buckhorn in 1931. Cascade was leading 1–0 with two out in the bottom of the ninth when a Buckhorn batter, whose name has been lost to oblivion, crashed the ball with such force that it indeed split in two as it neared the fence.

Part of the ball cleared the fence, while a fragment of it was caught by Cascade's leftfielder—and that threw the umpire into a dither over just what to do. Buckhorn's players argued that because the ball had cleared the fence, it had to be ruled a homer; Cascade's players said that because the outfielder had caught part of the ball, it was an out.

Beads of sweat broke out on the umpire's forehead as he pondered . . . and pondered his ruling. Suddenly, his eyes lit up; he had a solution—a compromise. He declared that the fielder had caught the third out, but at the same time, because half of the ball had gone over the fence, Buckhorn was entitled to "one-half a home run"—and the final score was one to one-half!

BASEBALL'S FUNNIEST HOME RUN

Once a player was tagged at least five times while circling the bases on an infield hit—and yet he was awarded a home run!

Baseball's funniest and most chaotic home run came about because an umpire neglected to show up for a Federal League game back around 1915. (The Federal League was an abbreviated attempt to launch a third major league in competition with the American and National leagues.)

When ump Bill Brennan's partner failed to show for the series opener between the Chicago Whales and the Brooklyn Feds, Brennan decided he'd handle the game solo. With the bases empty, he'd call the plays from behind the catcher. But when anyone got on, Brennan would judge strikes from behind the pitcher—an old one-umpire method that remained in vogue in some minor leagues through the 1920s.

This tactic called for a lot of running, and Brennan was further handicapped by hot weather and a large supply of baseballs in his pockets that kept shifting uncomfortably when he had to move in a hurry. In the fifth inning, a Brooklyn batter repeatedly fouled off pitches, forcing Brennan to migrate to the sidelines several times for more balls.

Finally, in disgust, Brennan scooped up an extra large supply of balls, dumped them onto the ground in back of the mound, and neatly stacked them into a pyramid. The artistic arrangement brought Brennan physical relief until Brooklyn's Grover Land put a fly—or, rather, a line drive—into the ointment.

Land's sizzling low liner rocketed squarely into the umpire's architectural masterpiece, and baseballs flew in all directions like pool balls ricocheting after a break shot. Every Chicago infielder scooped up a ball—and each infielder tagged Land at least once as he loped around the bases.

But Brennan, surveying the infield that still looked as if it had been pelted with oversized hailstones, ruled that because he had no idea which ball was actually the game ball, he had no choice but to award Land a home run!

THE TEAM THAT "NAILED" A HOMER

Minneapolis once literally nailed a victory against across-Mississippi-River rival St. Paul, according to a favorite story of the late Frank Isbell. Isbell, who later spent a decade in the majors as both a pitcher and an infielder, was pitching for St. Paul in 1898, a time when Sunday baseball was prohibited in the community.

Consequently, he said, the team owners set up a tiny park just outside of the city's corporation limits specifically for Sunday games. "The field was so small and the fences were so high that it was practically impossible to hit for more than two bases," said Isbell.

"One Sunday, I had a two-run lead over Minneapolis in the ninth with two out and two on. The next batter lined one that hit about twelve feet up on the center-field fence. I figured the ball would bounce back, and we'd hold them to one run. It didn't.

"It just stuck there like it was glued. Three runs scored before we could get a ladder and get the ball down. It had hit smack on the sharp end of a nail!"

PLAYER HITS EIGHT HOME RUNS IN ONE GAME

A minor-league player once hit eight home runs in one day—the greatest one-day production by any player in professional baseball. What makes Jay Justin Clarke's achievement even more phenomenal is that it occurred in 1902, the dead-ball era when home runs were a rarity.

But there's a catch. Clarke's homers were all over a left-field fence that was a mere 140 feet—at the most—from home plate.

Clarke, then an eighteen-year-old rookie catcher, did his monumental mauling for Corsicana against Texarkana in a Texas League contest that had been transferred to an Ennis, Texas, park because Sunday games were prohibited in Corsicana.

The Texarkana club had been sold the day before to a man named C. B. DeWitt, according to J. Walter Morris, who played in the game and later served as Fort Worth's business manager.

Morris, the Corsicana shortstop, said a strapping youngster sought out Manager Cy Mulkey of Texarkana before the game. This young man said he was the son of the owner and that he had been sent over to pitch.

Mulkey wasn't pleased with the idea, but orders from an owner were orders, so he decided to let the young DeWitt go the entire horrendous distance. Clarke's eight "pop-fly homers"—he hit four in the first three innings—helped propel Corsicana to a 51–3 victory.

Clarke later spent nine years in the majors with four different teams. During that entire span, he managed a total of only six homers.

WALTER JOHNSON BLEW A HOME RUN

Walter Johnson, the celebrated pitcher of yesteryear, once hit a home run for Washington—only to see the wind blow it back out of the stands. Johnson's shot against the White Sox cleared the fence by a healthy distance, but it came on a day when extraordinarily strong and gusty winds were whipping around the ballpark. One gust caught Johnson's hit before it landed in the stands and, almost miraculously, lifted it into the air back toward the field—and into the hands of centerfielder Johnny Mostil.

THE BALL THAT DRIBBLED OVER THE FENCE

The Brooklyn Dodgers' old Ebbets Field was the site of many unusual plays and players—as well as the site of a couple of major-league baseball's most unusual home runs.

In one game, the Dodgers' George Cutshaw launched a blast that hit the right-field wall, dropped down, and hit a rain gutter on the wall, where it picked up enough reverse English to bounce back to the top of the wall. There the ball bounced straight up and down for what seemed like an eternity before finally dropping over the wall for a homer!

• • •

Then there was the time the umpires became embroiled in a prolonged debate over whether Zack Wheat had hit a homer for the Dodgers. Wheat's solid blast against a Boston pitcher landed in the crease of a flag flying from a staff in the center of the outfield wall. Wheat was circling the bases when the entangled ball dropped loose and onto the field. That set the stage for a lengthy debate.

The Dodgers, of course, argued that it was a homer, while Boston maintained it should be a ground-rule double. The umps finally ruled it a homer, but Boston officially protested to John A. Heydler, then president of the National League. More lengthy discussions followed before Heydler upheld the umpires.

He ruled the flag was flying from a staff in the center of the wall, and therefore the ball would have cleared the wall but for the obstruction.

THE PLAYER WHO CAUGHT HIS OWN HOME RUN

A major-league player once caught his own home run. Obviously there's a catch. Dixie Walker was playing for the Pirates one day in 1949, when he smashed a homer that lodged in the right-center-field screen at old Ebbets Field. When Dixie returned to his outfield position after the top half of the inning was over, he went over and shook the screen, dislodging the ball—and caught it.

A LIGHTNING HOME RUN

Gavvy Cravath, an outfielder for the Philadelphia Phillies back in the teens, is the only major leaguer to hit a home run with the aid of lightning. The Phils and the Giants were locked in a scoreless duel, when a sudden rainstorm furiously erupted. Spectators couldn't see beyond the infield, but the stubborn umpires insisted that the game go on.

Suddenly, there was a burst of lightning and thunder as the pitcher delivered to Gavvy. The sudden streak of light brilliantly lit up the park, and Cravath's bat connected with the ball. Darkness—and silence—followed. Nobody saw where the ball went. Then came the clatter of the ball landing in the wooden seats of the bleachers. It was the only run of the game.

THE FIELDER WISELY JUST STARED AT THE BALL

A Mexia centerfielder had a pretty good reason to stand by and let Eastland beat his team in a West Texas League game in 1922.

The game was tied in the bottom of the twelfth inning, when an Eastland batter cracked a two-out routine bouncing single over second base. Mexia's centerfielder dashed over to scoop up the ball—but stopped dead in his tracks.

Then he walked around the ball, making no effort to go after it. Seeing this, the Eastland batter took off for second. The centerfielder continued to circle the ball, and the runner continued to keep running—all the way around to the plate for an inside-the-park homer and the winning run.

Befuddled fellow players and fans surged to the outfield to see what had produced the centerfielder's mysterious behavior. They found that the ball had rolled on top of a diamondback rattlesnake that had slithered onto the field during the game!

LOST-BALL HOMERS

"Lost-ball" homers have occurred from time to time over the years in even the most meticulously groomed major-league parks. Three of the most unusual ones involved a jacket, a groundskeeper's cupboard, and a shirt pocket.

One lost-ball incident resulted from a simple "nudge" of the ball by Norman McMillan in one of the Chicago Cubs' important pennant victories in 1929. The game with Cincinnati was tied 5–5, and the bases were loaded in the bottom of the eighth, when McMillan rapped a gentle drive that traveled not more than 170 feet. The ball skipped past third in fair territory, then veered into a narrow gutter along the front of the grandstand, headed for the bullpen spot, where pitchers warmed up along the left-field line.

Leftfielder Evar Swanson rushed over to retrieve the ball but suddenly stopped in bewilderment. He peeked into the gutter. He peeked under the steps. He looked around the bullpen area. He even picked up a jacket that Cubs pitcher Ken Penner had dropped on the ground while warming up. He gave the jacket a shake or two, then continued his frantic search for the missing ball.

Swanson's teammates joined the search, and even the umpire came out to inspect the scene. But by that time it was a moot question—McMillan had long before circled the bases and was already resting comfortably in the dugout.

The Cubs quickly retired Cincinnati at the top of the ninth, and Penner casually donned his jacket. He stuck his left arm into the sleeve—and out popped the ball!

• • •

Dode Paskert once recalled that he couldn't remember the name of the opponent who hit it, but he never forgot the time he was involved with a lost ball during his career with the Philadelphia Phillies from 1911 to 1917.

The Phils' groundskeeper had a cupboard at the base of the flagpole in right-center where he kept tools and supplies. One day the door to the cupboard was accidentally left open during a game, and a long fly bounced into it. Paskert, playing center, said he reached in and began throwing out tools—a pick, a crowbar, a shovel, trowels, and a whatnot. But he couldn't find the ball. Finally, the only thing left in the cupboard was a bucket of still-unset mortar.

Paskert plunged his hand into the gooey mess, and the mystery was solved. He gave the mortar-coated ball a mighty heave toward home. It traveled only a short distance before sinking into the turf with a dull thud.

• • •

Shirt pockets were fashionable for baseball uniforms in 1889—but not for the St. Louis Browns after what happened to Cliff Carroll in a game with Cincinnati. Carroll rushed in to field a routine grounder at second, but the ball took a sudden hop and hit Carroll in the chest, then somehow became wedged into his shirt pocket.

Pawing frantically at the bulging pocket, Carroll took out after the runner. He finally overtook the runner before home plate, but he still couldn't pry the ball loose to make the tag. The runner was awarded a home run—and shirt pockets were immediately and forever out of style on St. Louis uniforms.

• • •

A baseball shirt also produced a "disappearing-ball act" in a 1948 American League game. Bill Goodman of the Boston Red Sox lined a fast grounder directly at Eddie Yost, Washington's shortstop. The ball took a hop—and vanished!

Ted Williams, who was rounding third, paused to look in bewilderment. So did Goodman, after passing first. So did every player on the field and the fans in the stands. And so did Yost—until he reached inside his shirt and pulled out the ball, which had hopped right up a sleeve!

PLAYER CIRCLED THE BASES TWICE—BUT WAS CALLED OUT

A minor-league player once socked a fair ball far over the fence. He circled the bases twice. Yet he didn't even get a single from all the strenuous activity. He only got an out.

Elmo Plaskett, playing for Las Vegas of the California League at Fresno, in 1958 circled the bases once on his apparent homer. But a teammate told him he had forgotten to touch first base, so Plaskett set out on another journey around the bases. However, under baseball's rules, he should have retraced his steps to first in reverse order before turning to complete the circuit. On an appeal play, Plaskett was ruled out.

EVERYONE HAD A HOME RUN

No one could ask for a more equitable distribution of home runs than there was for the Douglas Copper Kings one day in 1958. Every man who played for Douglas in that Arizona-Mexico League game had exactly one homer. Douglas triumphed over the Chi-huahua Dorados 22–8 in what is the only time in pro baseball that nine different players on the same team, including the pitcher, have accounted for nine home runs.

HIS HOMER WAS PAINFULLY EMBARRASSING

Perhaps the most painfully embarrassing home run was produced by Steve Teurigliatto of Fort Worth against Amarillo in a minor-league game. After lashing his shot over the fence, Steve started trotting around the bases, got his feet mixed up, and before reaching first base, fell flat on his face and left elbow. He got up and finished circling the bases—after which he was taken to a hospital, where his broken arm was put in a cast.

HOME RUNS ON STRIKEOUTS?

A home run on a strikeout? Technically, it's impossi-ble—but in two instances minor-league players in Des Moines, Iowa, went all the way around to score on strikeouts.

In one case, a player named Josh Clarke was so baffled by a pitch that he swung for what would have been the third strike. But the ball hit the right corner of the plate and caromed high over third base, and Clarke managed to scoot all the way around the bases to score.

Another time, a Des Moines catcher, Homer Ha-worth, missed catching the third strike when the bases were loaded with Omaha players. Haworth's teammates thought that he had caught the ball, and they started walking off the field. None of the Omaha runners advanced. Figuring the umpire had called a third out, Haworth rolled the ball to the mound. But Omaha's manager realized what had happened—and then sent all four of his players around the bases to score.

RUTH'S FIFTY-FOUR HOMERS REALLY WERE AMAZING

Babe Ruth's fifty-four home runs for the New York Yankees in 1920 lose a bit of their gloss when you look at more imposing totals that came in the future—the Babe's fifty-nine and sixty homers, the fifty-eight by Jimmie Foxx and Hank Greenberg, and, of course, the sixty-one by Roger (asterisk) Maris.

But, regarded against the full backdrop of history, that 1920 figure is unbelievable. It came just one year after Ruth set the previous record with a then-phenomenal twenty-nine home runs.

His fifty-hour homers were nearly three times as many as those of his nearest challenger, George Sisler, who finished second with nineteen home runs.

The Ruthian reign was almost as emphatic in 1921, when Babe hit fifty-nine round-trippers to twenty-four for his closest pursuers, Bob Meusel and Ken Williams.

3
HITTING—LUSTY AND LOUSY

WILLIAMS CALLED HIS OWN PITCHES—AND WENT HITLESS

In baseball's early days, one of the rules permitted batters to tell pitchers just where they wanted the ball delivered. The batters could call for a high ball, a medium ball, or a low ball—and the rules forced the pitcher to comply. The rule, of course, eventually faded into baseball antiquity.

What would happen if one of the twentieth century's greatest hitters was allowed to call his pitches? Ted Williams once had that rare opportunity in the heyday of his career—and he didn't get a hit in five trips.

The unusual incident came about when some Detroit players were trying to figure out how to pitch to Williams, who was rapping Tiger hurlers with monotonous regularity. No matter what kind of a pitch was served up, Williams managed to hit it.

It started off as a joke, when one player suggested that since Williams was hitting everything the Tigers called, why not let him simply call the pitches?

The joke became reality when Williams stepped to the plate for the first time, and Birdie Tebbetts, then the Detroit catcher, explained that Detroit planned to let him call his own pitches.

Ted obviously thought it was a gag but called for a fastball. Tebbetts then signaled for a fastball, which swished over the heart of the plate. Williams didn't take a swing.

Again Williams was asked what kind of pitch he wanted, and he asked for another fastball. Another fastball was delivered, but Williams, still positive that he was the victim of a prank, hesitated before swinging and missed the pitch.

The Tigers maintained the unorthodox procedure all day—and Williams didn't even come close to a hit in his five trips. Tebbetts explained years later that Williams was so concerned about whether the Tigers were kidding him that it shattered Williams's amazingly keen concentration on the ball.

WILLIAMS HAD A RIGHT TO BE BRASH

From the first day he stepped on to a major-league field, Ted Williams always displayed a brash, confident determination that nettled opposing players. Rudy York, who later became a teammate of Williams at Boston, liked to recall the time he was catching for Detroit the year Williams made his major-league debut.

The Tigers were ahead by a run, and the pitcher quickly ran up a three-balls-and-no-strikes count on Ted.

"Well, busher," York said sarcastically. "It's three and nothing. I suppose you'll swing on the next pitch."

"You're darned right I will," replied the cocky young Williams. "It will be right down the middle, and I'll never get a better pitch." Whereupon he whaled the next pitch out of the park.

TED OUTFINISHED THE BABE—AND EVEN HIMSELF

Williams didn't break any of the standard home-run records in his 1960 farewell season—but his flourishing finish is unbelievable, in or out of the record books. The Splendid Splinter socked twenty-nine homers in 1960 before he hung up his bat for good at the age of forty-two.

That production outdistanced the two other major home-run producers from baseball's "senility crowd"—Babe Ruth and Hank Aaron. Babe was thirty-nine when he hit twenty-two home runs in 1934, his last season with the Yankees. The next year, he bowed out with six in twenty-eight games—three in one contest—for the old Boston Braves.

At age forty, Aaron hit twenty homers in 1974, his last season with the Atlanta Braves. He had a total of twelve with the Milwaukee Brewers the following season and added ten more in 1976, for his major-league record of 755.

But, what's unbelievable about Williams's final home-run fling is the pace at which he hammered the ball out of the park. He belted one homer for each 10.7 official trips to the plate, an incredible pace even for sluggers in their prime.

And Williams the Ancient even outdid Williams the Kid. Ted's best previous home-run pace was in 1950, when he was thirty-two years old. He averaged a home run for each 11.19 trips that season, a campaign in which his activity was limited by a fractured elbow suffered in the All-Star Game. He finished with twenty-eight homers in eighty-nine games.

MANTLE HIT A 460-FOOT SINGLE

Mickey Mantle once poked baseball's longest single. In 1956, he crashed a 460-foot sizzler that landed on the running track of center field in Yankee Stadium,

Mickey Mantle in his early playing days with the Yankees (early 1950s).

then bounced over the wall. It could only be counted as a single, however, because it scored Billy Martin from third base with the winning run when there were two out in the bottom of the ninth inning.

BROTHERS WERE SIX FOR SIX ON THE SAME DAY

Dick Adams once smacked six hits in six trips while playing for Fresno, California, back in 1941. He was so excited that he dashed off a letter to his brother Bob, who later spent fourteen years in the majors but was then playing for Columbia, South Carolina. A couple of days later, Dick received a letter from Bob (their letters had crossed in the mail), who excitedly informed brother Dick that on the same night, he had been six for six for Columbia.

SIX PITCHERS, SIX HITS FOR ALOU

Jesus (Jay) Alou was six for six in leading San Francisco to a nineteen-hit, 10–3 victory over the Chicago Cubs one afternoon in 1964. That kind of production alone, of course, is a baseball rarity, but what makes Alou's feat even more astonishing was that each hit came off a different pitcher. He singled off starter Dick Ellsworth in the first inning, singled off Lew Burdette in the third, singled off Don Elston in the fourth, homered off Dick Scott in the sixth, singled off Wayne Schurr in the seventh, and singled off Lindy McDaniel in the ninth.

PEPPER MARTIN'S BATTING THONG

Pepper Martin, one of the mischievous ringleaders of the St. Louis Cards' old Gashouse Gang, holds the major-league record for "times bat slipped away from hands while swinging."

One of the most embarrassing accidental flings of a

bat came when "the bat tore loose, and I saw it hit the railing into the box seats," Martin once recalled. "I ran over to get it—and there it was in the lap of Mrs. Sam Breadon." Mr. Breadon was the owner of the Cardinals.

Martin was so upset by the incident that he later was persuaded to try a special thong so that he couldn't throw his bat. One loop fit at the knob of the bat, the other around Martin's wrist. Pepper was supposed to be able to shake his hand loose after he hit.

He gave the thong a try in an exhibition game in Rochester and laid down a beautiful bunt. Martin shook his hand; the bat failed to come loose. He shook it again with the same results. So, he took off for first, dragging the bat along all of the way, repeatedly trying to shake it loose. Pepper was an easy out—and so was the batting thong, as far as Pepper was concerned.

Pepper Martin sliding into third base during a 1940 game with the Cubs. The third baseman for Chicago is Stan Hack.

THE CAKE OF ICE THAT IMPROVED A BATTER'S HITTING

Baseball managers have done many things over the years to inspire hitters to boost batting averages. Casey Stengel once used a cake of ice to get a hitter on track.

It was in the early summer of 1936, when Stengel was managing the Brooklyn Dodgers. One of his players, Stanley (Frenchy) Bordagaray, was miffed because he didn't think Casey was playing him enough. Bordagaray's way of getting even was to keep potting Stengel with throws when the team was warming up along the sidelines: when Casey wasn't looking, Bordagaray would take careful aim and plunk him on the back or on the leg.

Stengel finally figured out that no one could get hit that often by accident and began to quickly squint around from time to time.

One afternoon his timing was perfect; he turned to see Bordagaray taking aim and letting loose with a toss. Stengel ducked out of the way—and then began looking around for a weapon. The clubhouse boy had just brought out a huge chunk of ice and laid it on the bench, preparing to chop it up for the water cooler.

Stengel scooped up the ice and took after Frenchy in a high-speed chase around the Brooklyn park. He finally threw the ice and missed. But Bordagaray didn't stop. He kept right on running—straight into the clubhouse, where he locked the door and refused to let anyone enter. Once the game started, he dressed and sneaked out of the park.

Stengel ranted about the situation for a while, then suddenly burst out laughing. The next day, when Bordagaray got up enough courage to return to the team, Stengel started playing him regularly in the outfield—and his average steadily increased. He finished the season with a .315 mark.

PLAYER SINGLED—INTO A TRIPLE PLAY

Bob Levingston has the distinction of singling into a triple play. It happened in 1962, when Levingston was playing with York, Pennsylvania, of the Eastern League. The bases were loaded when Levingston singled, scoring one run. But two other runners and Levingston were thrown out by Springfield on the same play when the three runners each tried for an extra base.

INVENTOR UPSET FOES WITH HIT-AND-RUN PLAY

During spring training before the 1894 season, manager Ned Hanlon of Baltimore (then of the National League) developed and perfected one of baseball's most exciting plays: the hit-and-run. Hanlon was so contemptuous of the opposition's ability to stop his newly devised strategy that he would have his Orioles demonstrate before games how they worked the maneuver.

And the key word is *worked*. When Baltimore opened the season against the pennant-favored New York Giants, Hanlon successfully used the hit-and-run thirteen times in four games, sweeping the series. Giants' manager John Montgomery Ward was so outraged by this revolutionary play that he seriously considered having Hanlon arraigned before league heads on a charge of not playing baseball, but a new game.

In addition to the hit-and-run play, the innovative Hanlon also originated or developed to its highest efficiency the bunt, the sacrifice, the chop hit, and daring baserunning. He also was one of the first—if not the first—manager to switch batters depending on whether a right-hander or a left-hander was pitching.

His new tactics carried the Orioles to three straight championships (1894–1896). Hanlon then posted two

The Baltimore Orioles of 1894. *Front row, left to right:* Jack Doyle, John McGraw, Willie Keeler, Arlie Pond. *Middle row, left to right:* Steve Brodie, Bill Huffer, Joe Kelley, Ned Hanlon, Wilbert Robinson, Hughie Jennings, Heinie Reitz. *Back row, left to right:* Joe Quinn, Sadie McMahon, Charles Esper, George Hemming, Frank Bowerman, Bill Clark, Jim Donnelly.

consecutive second-place finishes before taking control of the Brooklyn Dodgers, with whom he won two flags in a row.

THE BABE'S "ALL-STAR" HUMILIATION

All-star games—using the term loosely—were limited to fall and winter exhibitions until the midsummer extravaganza of the American's and National's master players was launched in 1933.

Those early "all-star" teams generally consisted of a handful of the game's stars, a number of journeymen big leaguers, and even occasionally a minor leaguer or two. It was in one of those so-called all-star affairs that Babe Ruth suffered perhaps his greatest humiliation.

It happened during a several-game charity affair in Los Angeles in the winter of 1920. While Ruth still had not reached the pinnacle of his home-run glory, he already was the game's most famous slugger—and he was downright proud of his reputation.

The two teams were made up of players wintering in Southern California, and the opposition picked a slow-balling minor leaguer to handle the pitching. Surprisingly, he struck out Ruth five straight times in two games, before the Babe stalked out for vengeance in the final inning of the second game.

As a joke, all three opposing outfielders deserted their posts. Wade Killefer tossed his glove aside, sauntered over to the fence, and sat down. Gavvy Cravath climbed into the bleachers and struck up a conversation with the fans, while Sam Crawford stretched out on the turf and feigned sleep.

Ruth was enraged. Then he literally pleaded with the outfielders to return to their positions. His requests were ignored, so Ruth grudgingly stepped in to face Paul Fittery, a tiny Pacific Coast League pitcher who was hurling his second consecutive game.

Fittery lobbed an easy curve toward the plate, and Ruth, red with rage by this point, dug in and swung as hard as he could. He connected, and observers estimated the ball traveled more than 500 feet—most of it straight up, the rest of it down.

The infielders didn't move and permitted the ball to land unheeded just behind second base, and Ruth puffed in with a double. Although the game was only an exhibition, the incident rankled Ruth for years, and mere mention of it would set off the Babe in a flame of indignation.

● ● ●

Ruth did manage to smash out a measure of revenge in another California all-star appearance four years later. He cracked two gigantic homers off Walter Johnson and also outpitched the old master. Ruth hurled seven scoreless innings.

One of the ironic things about Ruth was that even though he could have eased off during the scores of exhibitions in which he participated, he always gave a full-scale effort.

Of course, when baseball got down to the real business of staging All-Star Games in 1933, Ruth came through in thumping fashion. A fading star, he was slow and out of shape, but he showed up his younger mates with the American League's only homer—the one that sewed up the victory.

RUTH POPPED UP A TRIPLE

Babe Ruth's pitching and home-run-hitting skills have dominated baseball's history and record books for so long that many fans aren't aware that Ruth had another brilliant baseball attribute: the Babe was extraordinarily fleet of foot, particularly during the first decade of his major-league career.

That partly explains Ruth's astonishing achievement of picking up a triple on an infield pop-up. Veteran pitcher Lefty Leifield recalled years later that he was pitching for the old St. Louis Browns against Boston when Ruth was starting to gain more fame as a hitter than as a pitcher.

Ruth stepped to the plate with the bases loaded, swung with all of his might, and undercut Leifield's delivery. A veteran sportswriter said decades later that the swat produced the highest pop-up in baseball history. "The infielders were running around like chickens with their heads cut off, yelling that they couldn't even see the ball," said Leifield.

After what seemed like an eternity, the ball plopped to the ground, bounding high into the air, far away from the nearest infielder. By that time, Ruth had already reached third base—and all three of the other runners had scored and returned to the dugout.

BATTER MISSED THE BALL BY NINETY FEET

You know that old saying about the batter missing the ball by a mile. Juan Plaza didn't miss the ball by a full 5,280 feet—just 90 feet!

It was in a winter league game in Puerto Rico when Cuagas was playing San Juan for the national championship. The game was tied 1–1, when Plaza, Cuagas's pitcher, stepped to the plate with the bases loaded. Plaza wasn't a bad pitcher, but he couldn't hit an elephant with a bat if it was standing next to him. In fact, he was simply terrified every time he had to bat.

San Juan pitcher Eddie Palerm, well aware of this, blazed two quick fastballs past Plaza, who was made even more nervous than usual by the speed of Palerm's pitches. When Palerm started to deliver the next pitch, Juan closed his eyes.

But Palerm suddenly stepped back and threw to first base in a pickoff attempt. Plaza, meanwhile, assuming through clenched eyes that the ball was headed for home, swung with all of his strength. The ump, confused over the whole matter, at first called a strike. He later reversed his call.

TWO CONSECUTIVE TRIPLES FAIL TO PRODUCE A RUN

The Sioux Falls, South Dakota, minor-league team smashed two consecutive triples in a 1937 game—and failed to score a run! Rabbit Padget slammed a zinger to right-center field and streaked around the bases to third, where manager Ralph Brandon waved him home. Unfortunately, the ball arrived before Padget, and he was out.

The next batter, Ralph Cardner, hit the first pitch to the same spot. He raced around to third and was waved home, where he met the same fate as Padget.

KEELER WAS IMMUNE TO STRIKEOUTS

Old-timer Wee Willie Keeler, of "hit 'em where they ain't" fame, was unbelievably difficult to strike out. Keeler went to bat 700 consecutive times without striking out. Playing for Baltimore, then a National League team, he began his streak near the end of the 1895 season, went through the entire 1896 season without a strikeout, then played several games in the spring of 1897 before a third strike was whipped past him. Keeler, who was only 5'4½", didn't let that whiff prevent him from hitting .432 for the '97 season.

He was the best place hitter baseball has ever seen. In practice, Willie could hit a pitched ball into a peach basket placed anywhere in the infield. The opposing team never knew where to play him. If the shortstop moved over toward third base in anticipation of a roller, Keeler would accurately lay one through the spot the shortstop had just vacated. He also achieved a rare batting feat of beating out five hits in one game—all of them fielded by the shortstop! Keeler used the smallest bat he could find and choked up several inches on the handle.

Keeler also was exceptionally speedy for his size. A daring baserunner, he stole sixty-seven bases one year and sixty-four another year.

He spent nineteen years in the majors, with the New York Giants, Brooklyn, Baltimore, and the Yankees, and finished with a .345 lifetime average. After winding up his major-league career with the Giants in 1910, he played a season for Toronto of the International League, served as a coach for Brooklyn's Federal League entry in 1915, and scouted for the Boston Braves for a few years.

In an 1899 interview, Keeler said he always hit the ball hard, but his "long suit is to chop down on the ball and make it bound high. Anytime a ball takes two good bounds on the infield, it means a base hit for me."

Although Wee Willie was one of the game's greatest—he was elected to the Hall of Fame in 1939—his life ended in tragedy. Ill health and poverty—baseball wages were extraordinarily low during most of Keeler's career—forced him to live with his sister for a time in the late teens. Not wishing to be a burden, he soon left. He vanished completely—until early January 1923, when his body was found in an unheated tin-and-paper shack on the edge of Brooklyn. He was only fifty years old.

UNCLE SAM GOT AN ASSIST ON A HIT

Uncle Sam once helped a major-league player get a hit. Detroit was playing an exhibition game with Cincinnati during the World War II years, when by accident the National Anthem suddenly started blaring through the public-address system. It began just as the Tigers' Jim Bloodworth tapped a grounder toward the Reds' second baseman. The infielder, upon hearing the strains of the anthem, immediately straightened up—and the ball rolled between his legs. The official scorer gave Bloodworth a single and, in jest, gave an assist to Uncle Sam.

DOUBLE, TWO SINGLES NEEDED TO SCORE RUNNER FROM SECOND

It once took a double and two singles to score a runner from second base. It happened in a Lone Star League game many years ago, when Lufkin's fleet Bob Marquis was on second base. The next batter, "Cowboy" Jones, smashed a double to left-center field, and Marquis raced for home—but missed third base en route. He scampered back to the bag just in time.

Harry Reed then cracked a liner down the third-base line; it hit the bag and bounced into the air. Because of the way the ball was fielded, Marquis had to hold third base, but the runner beat the throw to first base and was awarded a single. A double and a single, and still no score!

It wasn't until the next batter, Dixie Parsons, lined a single to left that Marquis was finally able to cross home plate.

EQUAL DUTY

In nineteen years in the major leagues, eighteen of them with Brooklyn, Zack Wheat's yearly batting averages ranged from .258 to .375—yet he twice strung together the same marks for two seasons in a row. Wheat hit .312 in both 1916 and 1917. He hit .375 in 1923 and duplicated it in 1924.

SOAKING THE BAT WASN'T SUCH A GREAT IDEA

At one time, most good hitters took as much care of their bats as a master musician does with his fine instrument. The players developed a number of concoctions in which they soaked their favorite bats, claiming that these prevented the bats from breaking. One of the favorite soaking mixtures contained resin and tobacco juice. Some players tried soaking their bats in linseed oil for a short time.

Mike Gazella, who played for the Yankees in the twenties, decided to give the idea a try, and at the end of one season, he gathered up a dozen of his favorite bats, took them home, and stuck them in a huge vat of linseed oil. He forgot about them until spring training—then discovered that they had soaked up so much oil that he could barely lift one of them, let alone swing it!

BATTING PRACTICE IS MEANINGLESS

Frankie Frisch, who spent sixteen years managing the St. Louis Cardinals, Pittsburgh, and the Chicago Cubs, always maintained that pregame batting practice wasn't particularly beneficial. "A .320 hitter steps up and takes a couple of swings—and goes on hitting .320," said Frisch. "A .260 hitter practices and practices—and goes on hitting .260."

4
MOUND MIRACLES AND MISCUES

THE PITCHER WITH THE NO-HIT SEASON

Major-league baseball has recorded many no-hit games over the years, but one player holds the distinction of having the only no-hit *season*.

It was the last day of the National League campaign of 1892 when Charles "Bumpus" Jones wandered into the Cincinnati clubhouse and asked for a tryout. The game didn't mean anything, so manager Charlie Comiskey let Bumpus, a semipro from Xenia, Ohio, be his starting pitcher. Astonishingly, Jones stopped Pittsburgh without a hit.

The Reds, of course, immediately signed Bumpus for the next year but released him after he won only one of his first four games.

PITCHER WINS WITHOUT THROWING A PITCH

A pitcher once won a game without delivering a single pitch! This happened in the Eastern League in 1956, when Jackie Brown of Williamsport was brought in for a relief role. It was the eighth inning with two out; Allentown had two runners on base, and Williamsport trailed 1–0.

Before he had an opportunity to deliver a pitch, Brown picked the runner off second for the third out. Williamsport then rallied with three runs to go ahead, and because Brown was the pitcher of record when his team took the lead, he was awarded the victory.

HURLER'S SLOW RUNNING COSTS HIM THREE NO-HITTERS

Bill Doak three times lost his chance to throw a no-hitter simply because he couldn't run fast enough! The former star of the St. Louis Cardinals first lost his chance at a no-hitter in 1920 against Philadelphia. The Phils' batter tapped a grounder to the first baseman, but Doak couldn't get over to cover first base fast enough, and it went as the only hit of the game.

On May 11, 1922, Dave Bancroft of the New York Giants bunted a Doak pitch. Doak ignored it for a second, thinking the ball was rolling foul. By the time he realized his mistake, he couldn't move fast enough to get to the ball and throw the batter out. There were no other New York hits that day.

Then, on July 13 of the same season, Curt Walker of Philadelphia smacked a grounder off Doak, and the first baseman had to go wide to field it. Doak raced to first to cover the base, but again he was too slow. Walker beat him to the bag for the Phillies' lone hit of the day.

JOHNSON "RESTED" BETWEEN SHUTOUTS BY PITCHING

Back in 1908, Walter Johnson achieved the amazing feat of pitching three shutouts in four days. The Washington Senators' phenomenal hurler shut out New York on Friday and Saturday, then came back on Monday and blanked the old Highlanders, now called the Yankees.

Sunday baseball was prohibited in New York in those days, so what did Johnson do on that one day off? He journeyed up to New Haven, Connecticut, to pick up $100 for pitching five innings in a minor-league game.

POLITE TAP COSTS PITCHER A TWENTY-GAME WINNING SEASON

Dave Wickersham of Detroit missed being a twenty-game winner by one game in 1964, and that was because his polite efforts to get an umpire's attention were misinterpreted.

Detroit was leading when a dispute developed between other Tigers and umpire Bill Valentine. Wickersham made four attempts to ask the umpire to call time because there were runners on base, but Valentine was so engrossed in the argument with the other players that he ignored Wickersham.

Finally, in desperation, Wickersham lightly tapped Valentine on the shoulder to get his attention—and was immediately ejected from the game for laying hands on an umpire.

HE SHOULD HAVE STUCK TO PITCHING TWO GAMES A DAY

Herman Bell was simply amazing on July 19, 1924, when he pitched and won two complete games in one day for the St. Louis Cardinals. In the first game, Bell held Boston hitless until the eighth inning, then permitted the Braves only two hits and won 6–1. In the second game, Boston didn't get a hit in a 2–1 victory.

But what made Bell's performance so amazing was

his proficiency the rest of the season—lousy. He won only one other game all summer, while losing eight. Although he allowed only a total of 2 hits in his one-day eighteen-inning stint, he yielded a total of 118 safeties in the other ninety-five innings he pitched that season.

REMARKABLE RECOVERY PROGRAMS

Talk about a turnabout: Adolfo Luque in one season went from the worst to the best in the National League. Luque lost more games (twenty-three) than any other league pitcher in 1922. Then, in 1923, he won more (twenty-seven) than any other NL hurler.

Victor Gazaway Willis achieved a similar recovery program earlier in the century. In 1905, Willis set a National League record of twenty-nine losses while pitching for the Boston Braves. The year before, he lost twenty-five games. The Braves were delighted when they were able to trade this loser to Pittsburgh before the 1906 season. Jubilation quickly turned to regret, however, when Willis rang up twenty-two victories and lost only thirteen. Then, he followed with successive victory-defeat records of 21–11, 23–11, and 22–11. It goes to show you can't trust first—or second—impressions.

LINKE USED HIS HEAD FOR A DOUBLE PLAY

Washington pitcher Ed Linke used his head the hard way in gaining an assist on a double play against the New York Yankees in 1936. Yank Jesse Hill hit one of Linke's deliveries back faster than it came, and the ball caught Ed right in the middle of the forehead, knocking him cold. When Ed came to a short time later, he learned that the ball had bounced off his noggin straight into the mitt of the catcher, who then doubled up a Yankee runner.

The blow on the head didn't harm Linke's pitching career. After three days in the hospital, he returned to win eight straight games.

HOW TO "FACE" A SLOW PITCH

Today's change-of-pace pitch used to be called a slowball, and an old-timer named Nap Rucker developed the pitch to perfection. He had an uncanny ability to deliver the ball with a fastball motion, only to have the ball float lazily toward the plate.

One afternoon, Cy Williams, a top slugger of the day, went after one of Rucker's slow pitches. Williams swung so early that he pivoted all of the way around just in time for the pitch to arrive—smack in the middle of his face!

TOWN WENT WILD OVER SEVENTEEN-INNING NO-HITTER

Cincinnati's Fred Toney once pitched a ten-inning no-hitter in a 1–0 victory at Chicago in 1917. But that was nothing compared to a no-hitter Toney had authored in the minor leagues eight years earlier.

Toney hurled the full seventeen-inning distance, giving up neither a hit nor a run, while pitching for Winchester against Lexington in a Blue Grass League game on May 10, 1909. Toney allowed only one walk, hit one batsman, and struck out nineteen as his mates utilized a squeeze play for their lone run in the last of the seventeenth.

Baseball interest in Winchester was pretty high that year—or at least during Toney's prolonged performance. The *Reach Guide* of 1910 said that during the long game, business in the city came to a virtual standstill, and bulletin boards posted all over town were "the only thing people thought of. When the victory was announced, all the whistles in town sounded and crowds went wild."

Despite the brilliant performance, Toney remained mired in the Class D league for another two seasons. He finished the 1909 season with a 22–15 record and had a 23–10 mark for Winchester the following year, before the Cubs brought him straight to the majors for a twelve-year career with Chicago, the Reds, the New York Giants, and the St. Louis Cardinals.

LAST BALL POUNDED FOR TWO HOME RUNS

The last ball that Johnny Allen pitched for the Brooklyn Dodgers, on July 30, 1943, was pounded for two home runs!

Working against the Cubs in Chicago, Allen was touched for a long fly to right by Phil Cavarretta. The ball hit the screen above the right-field bleachers at the foul line and was a home run under the ground rules. However, the ball rebounded into the right field of play, and the umpire-in-chief left it in the game.

Allen then served it up to Bill Nicholson, who walloped it clear out of the park. That was Allen's farewell to pitching for Brooklyn; he was traded to the New York Giants and closed out his thirteen-year major-league career after the following season.

ONE-HITTER TURNS INTO A NO-HITTER

Charles Tesreau, a pitcher for the New York Giants, once threw a one-hitter that became a no-hitter—hours after the game!

Tesreau was toiling at Philadelphia on September 6, 1912, when in the middle of the game, a Phillies player smashed an infield single, the first hit of the day off Tesreau. The official scorer recorded the blow as a hit, but as it turned out, it was the only safety off the Giant pitcher.

The players had fled to the clubhouse and the fans had departed for home when two New York sportswriters started pleading with Philadelphia's official scorer, Stoney McLinn, to change the lone hit to an error. History does not record what they said to McLinn, but hours later he made the change.

Most eyewitnesses at the game later said there was virtually no doubt that the hit was a clean single—but the official history books credit Tesreau with a no-hitter!

THE THIRTY-MINUTE BASE ON BALLS

It once took Leon Culberson of Scranton thirty minutes to draw a base on balls in a 1942 Eastern League night game. Springfield's pitcher had a three-and-two count on Culberson, when suddenly an air-raid siren signaled a World War II practice blackout, and the lights were clicked off. It was a good thirty minutes before the drill was over and the park lights were turned on again. Culberson stepped to the plate, and the first pitch was a ball. Talk about waiting out the pitcher!

IF YOU CAN'T BEAT 'EM, JOIN 'EM

Red Ruffing was a perfect example of that old adage, "If you can't beat 'em, join 'em." While pitching for the Boston Red Sox, Ruffing tamed the New York Yankees only once in fifteen decisions—an .067 winning percentage. Ruffing was traded to the Yankees at the start of the 1930 season, and during the next six years, he stopped the Red Sox twenty-nine times in forty-three decisions.

PITCHER HAD 60-12 RECORD IN ONE SEASON

They certainly got their money's worth out of pitchers in the early days of the National League. Pitching for Providence of the National League in 1884, Charles (Old Hoss) Radbourn posted a 60–12 record and 1.38

ERA while appearing in seventy-five games. He struck out 441 and issued only 98 walks. In a postseason "World Series" with the New York Metropolitans of the American Association, Old Hoss pitched three consecutive shutouts.

IF AT FIRST YOU DON'T SUCCEED . . .

If at first you don't succeed, try again. Or, in the case of pitcher Guy Morton, try, try, try, try, try, try. . . .

Morton made his major-league debut with Cleveland on June 24, 1914, and lost. Next time out, he lost again. Then he lost again . . . and again . . . and again—until he ran his losing streak to thirteen games. The season had only a few days remaining when he finally won his first major-league game.

But that solitary victory apparently provided the stimulant he needed to carry on. The next season he had a 15–15 record, then climbed above the .500 mark in 1916 and remained there for several years.

Morton eventually played eleven seasons for the Indians. And, oh yes, he finished his career on the plus side with a lifetime 98–88 record.

THE PITCHER WHO COULD THROW
WITH BOTH HANDS

You couldn't blame batters or baserunners for being bewitched, bothered, and bewildered whenever Tony Mullane was pitching. Tony was ambidextrous—he could throw equally well with either arm. And, because he shunned wearing a baseball glove, neither potential base stealers nor batters had the slightest idea which hand he was going to use until he had launched the ball.

Baserunners were constantly lulled into a feeling of security when Mullane was pitching, figuring that the ball was just resting in his hand, only to have him turn and fire a darter that nabbed them off base.

Ironically, Mullane, who was one of the best and highest-paid pitchers in baseball during the 1880s and 1890s, developed his unusual ability because of an injury suffered in a throwing contest. When he joined Detroit in 1881, Tony was exclusively a right-hander. During that season, the team staged a "field event" in which players participated in a number of activities, ranging from ball throwing to baserunning.

When it came Mullane's turn to throw the ball, he startled teammates and patrons alike with a toss that was measured an astonishing 416'7¾" on the fly. But the effort severely injured Tony's right arm. Undaunted, he started throwing with his left hand and quickly became as proficient a southpaw as he was a right-hander. When his right arm eventually healed, Mullane started throwing with both arms.

His pitching accomplishments were numerous. He won thirty or more games five years in a row in the American Association (then a major league) and had one twenty-four-victory season and a twenty-one-victory year in the National League during his thirteen years in the majors. He threw one no-hitter, and in one season he pitched in sixty-six games.

All told, Mullane appeared in 517 major-league games, winning 295—including 31 shutouts—and losing 213. In a game on July 30, 1892, Mullane, then pitching for Cincinnati, and Addison Gumbert of Chicago each went the distance in a 7–7 tie that was called after twenty innings because of darkness.

In addition to his pitching exploits, Mullane could play every position on the field with skill and generally was used as a hitter when not pitching. He had a lifetime batting average of .316.

He also was regarded as an outstanding skater, on both roller and ice skates, a good boxer, and an extremely talented musician.

PITCHER FANS BATTER HE WAS
SUPPOSED TO WALK

One of Dick Weik's favorite stories was about the pitcher who was so wild that when he was ordered to walk a batter on purpose, he struck out the hitter by mistake!

Weik, a gaunt and gangling right-hander, was generally considered one of the wildest pitchers in baseball during a five-year major-league career with Washington, Cleveland, and Detroit. One season, he averaged nearly ten walks per game for the Senators. But Weik always maintained he was a dead-aim thrower compared with Dick Rozek, who appeared in thirty-three games with Cleveland and the Philadelphia Athletics during the early fifties.

Weik said he and Rozek were teammates on the Great Lakes military baseball team during World War II. During one game, the team's manager ordered Rozek to issue an international pass to the next batter, a dangerous hitter.

Rozek reared back and let the ball fly. The manager nearly jumped out of his shoes, Weik recalled, when the ball zipped right over the heart of the plate. Fortunately, the batter took it for a strike.

The manager raced over to Rozek and said emphatically, "I thought I told you to put him on."

"Yeah, I know," said Rozek, sheepishly admitting that he had been trying to throw a ball and the strike was a pure accident. "But I'll walk him now," he confidently assured the manager—and immediately served up another strike, which the batter missed. You guessed it? When Rozek made a third attempt to toss a ball—the batter struck out!

MR. HARD LUCK

Pitcher Tracy Stallard certainly deserves baseball's wrong-place-at-the-wrong-time honors. Stallard was pitching for Boston when he served up Roger Maris's sixty-first home run. As a St. Louis pitcher, he lost the famous seven-hour-and-twenty-three-minute game to the Giants. He was the loser in St. Louis's last game in Sportsman's Park. As a New York Met, Tracy was the losing pitcher when Jim Bunning hurled his perfect game against the New Yorkers.

PAIGE WARMED UP WHERE IT WAS WARM

Satchel Paige didn't have a difficult time warming up on cold, raw evenings at the start of the baseball season, one of his former managers recalled. Don Osborne was Paige's manager at Miami of the International League in 1956 and 1957. "It was a bitter cold night early in the season in Rochester," said Osborne. "We were in trouble late in the game, and I looked down toward the bullpen to give Satch (who was then in his fifties) the sign to get ready.

"He wasn't down there, so I rechecked the dugout. Not there either. I thought he might have slipped around to get a hot dog, but we couldn't find him at the concession stand. Finally, I told one of the boys to look in the clubhouse. The player came back and said, 'He's there, all right, and he says to tell you he's been throwing in there and he's ready.'

"I said, 'Throwing in the clubhouse? Who's catching him?' The player said, 'Nobody. He's bouncing a ball off the wall—and he says he's ready.'"

● ● ●

Bill Veeck, who originally signed Paige to his first major-league contract at Cleveland, was operating the Miami club in 1956, and one night scheduled a game against Columbus in the Orange Bowl in an effort to set a minor-league attendance record.

Osborne said he and Veeck wanted Paige to pitch, but under the agreement they had with him, they couldn't start Satch without his express permission.

"I put it up to Satch a few days in advance, and he

Satchel Paige (1948).

wouldn't give me an answer," said Osborne. "Next day, he said, 'Tell you what, Manager'—I don't think he ever knew my name—'I got a little bill up in Mobile. If the club pays that, I'll pitch.' I asked him how much the little bill was, and he said, 'Just $500.'

"We gave him the extra money, and the night of the game, Veeck had all kinds of entertainment in the Orange Bowl, including a big-name band—Louis Armstrong's, I think. Satch was a camera bug, and he was all over the place taking pictures. Suddenly, I realized it's only ten minutes to game time, and Satch hasn't picked up a baseball yet."

Osborne said he yelled at Paige to start warming up, but Paige grinned back and yelled for him "not to worry, I'll be ready." It was only three minutes to game time, Osborne recalled, before Paige put away the camera and picked up a baseball. "Then he threw maybe six pitches, just flicking them with his wrist, and started the game.

"It was only a little over 200 feet down the right-field line, and Columbus had a lot of left-handed power hitters. They figured to murder a right-hander like Satch. But they just hit one ball into right field off Satch all night. He just kept nipping the outside corner of the plate against the left-handers and made them hit to left field.

"Satch finally got a little tired in the ninth inning, and I got him some help for the last two outs—but it was one of the greatest pitching exhibitions I ever saw."

ONE PITCH, THREE OUTS

It took just one pitch for a hurler to get out of a bases-loaded, no-outs jam! Bruce Haroldson came in as a relief pitcher for Lewiston in a 1961 Northwest League game with Tri-Cities. The bases were loaded, and there were no outs. Haroldson's first delivery to Tri-Cities' Ron Youngdahl was grounded to third baseman Dick Green, who stepped on third and fired to Ossie Chavarria for out number two. Chavarria fired a bullet to first baseman Ed Olsen to nab Youngdahl for the triple play.

ALEXANDER THE GREAT

During Ronald Reagan's terms as president, local television stations around the country got into the habit of pulling from their files an old movie of Reagan starring in the life story of Grover Cleveland Alexander. But the syrupy movie version of Alexander's feats during the 1926 World Series pales in comparison to what actually happened.

Alexander created such a stirring climax to that Series that history has virtually neglected his other glittering achievements in the 1926 postseason classic. Alex always will be remembered by baseball aficionados for striking out New York's Tony Lazzeri with the bases full in the seventh inning, then going on to protect the St. Louis Cardinals' decisive victory. (Ironically, he didn't get credit for the victory; Jesse Haines claimed that.)

Earlier in the Series, Alexander's performance was even more remarkable. In the second game, he yielded two runs off three hits in the second inning. Then, after Earle Combs opened the third with a single, Alex retired twenty-one men in order—and only one ball was hit out of the infield.

In the sixth game, Alexander pitched again, with the Cards needing a victory to stay in contention. He retired the first three Yankees, before Bob Meusel led off for the Yanks in the second with a high pop up to shallow left. Shortstop Tommy Thevenow ran around in circles and misjudged the ball as it fell, and Meusel got a fluke double. Except for that, Alexander would have retired twenty-seven Yankees in succession. As it was, he posted a 10–2 success to go with his previous 6–2 victory.

Not a bad performance for a man who was then thirty-nine years old and who had been traded away by the Cubs during the summer because team officials considered him washed up!

● ● ●

Alexander had such an admirable major-league career—373 victories and 208 defeats in twenty seasons—that few realize he also ranks as one of the greatest minor-league pitchers since the turn of the century.

He launched his pro career with last-place Galesburg of the Illinois-Missouri League in 1909 and finished the season with a winning record. In two successive games that year, July 22 and July 25, he didn't permit a run. He pitched a 2–0 no-hitter in the first game and an eighteen-inning 1–0 victory in the second, striking out nineteen. The next year, when he played for Syracuse, he strung together fifty-four successive scoreless innings!

Alexander, incidentally, wouldn't put up with much rankling from the opposition. Clark Griffith, who was managing Cincinnati in 1911 when Alexander broke in with the Phillies, discovered that the hard way.

Alexander had been mastering the Reds, until they suddenly filled the bases with no outs. Griffith figured this would be a dandy time for a few well-chosen words of scorn to hasten the rookie's downfall. He took over the third-base coaching box, cupped his hands into a megaphone, and let loose with a stream of verbal abuse directed at the young pitcher.

Alex's ears turned red, then his face flushed in anger. He turned to Griffith and shouted, "Just for that, I'm going to show you some pitching."

He struck out the next three batters on ten pitches!

YOUNG DIDN'T BELIEVE IN WARMING UP

The great Cy Young, who won 511 games during his twenty-two-year big-league career, always contended pitchers spent too much time warming up. Said Cy, "When I'd go to spring training, I'd never touch a ball the first three weeks—just do a lot of running and walking. I figured the old arm had just so many throws in it, and there wasn't any use wasting them.

"I never warmed up ten or fifteen minutes before a game like most pitchers. I'd loosen up for maybe four or five minutes. When I relieved, I generally went straight from the bench to the box and took only a few warm-up pitches."

THEY WERE ORIGINALLY "NORTHPAWS"

When baseball's first diamonds were laid out in the 1860s and 1870s, the rules called for the field to "have the outfield so situated that the fielders would not be obliged to face the sun." It solved the "sun-field" problem, but it forced the batters to operate with the sun smack dab in their eyes. The complaints of batters forced the rules to be changed so that the direction of the fields was reversed. Because of this, when a left-handed pitcher stands on the mound, his pitching arm is toward the south—hence the name *southpaw*.

FAST FIZZLE

Charles "Lady" Baldwin was an unfortunate victim of one of the most meteoric climbs—and then descents—in baseball history. After a season and a half with Milwaukee, he won eleven games and lost eight for the Detroit Nationals in the latter part of the 1885 season. Not bad for a rookie, but it was only a modest preview of his first full season in the majors in 1886: He pitched in fifty-six games, all but one of them complete, and rang up forty-two victories! He pitched a total of 487 innings and struck out 323.

He was hailed as one of the greatest pitching prospects ever. Then, suddenly, Baldwin's pitching arm developed an ache, and in 1887 his record skidded to 13-10, then to 3-3 the next season. By 1889, Baldwin was out of baseball. He made a comeback attempt with Brooklyn and Buffalo in 1890, but won only three of eight decisions. Few pitchers have faded faster.

5
FIELDING FEATS AND FIASCOES

FIELDER NABS RUNNERS AT THREE DIFFERENT BASES

Jack Strum undoubtedly is the only player in pro baseball who ever made all three putouts in a triple play—with each out being made at a different base. Strum was playing first base for Joplin's minor-league team in 1936. Muskogee had runners on second and third, when a Muskogee hitter bounced a hot one to the shortstop, who fired the ball to first, where Strum retired the batter. While trying to regain third, the Muskogee runner got caught in a run-down and was eventually tagged by Strum, who was covering the plate. When that happened, the runner on second took off—but Strum beat him to third and tagged him out for the triple play!

PLAYER RIDES TO OUTFIELD IN STYLE

At one time, it was a custom in many major-league parks to deliver relief pitchers from the bullpen in an automobile. But in one game, an outfielder was delivered to and from his position by a car.

It was in the 1962 championship game of the Kickapoo Valley Amateur League in Illinois. One of the teams, Carver Centre, had only nine players on its roster, and in the opening inning, Haso Mayo, Carver's rightfielder, suffered a severely sprained right ankle.

The rules stipulated that each team must field nine players at all times or face a forfeit. Gazing sadly at Mayo's swelling ankle, the Carver players were ready to give up—until someone came up with the idea of transporting Mayo by automobile to and from his right-field position.

Once in the field, Mayo made no attempt to field the ball: the team depended upon the centerfielder to cover right field. When it was time for Mayo to bat, his teammates carried him to the plate, where he was called out on strikes four times.

Incidentally, Carver won the title 22–5.

CATCHER WORKS BOTH ENDS OF DOUBLEHEADER FOR BOTH TEAMS

It's rare today to see a catcher work both ends of a doubleheader—but there was one backstop in 1912 who not only caught both games, but did it for *both* clubs. The Columbus, Mississippi, catcher was injured in the second inning of a doubleheader opener against Yazoo City in the Cotton State League.

Columbus didn't have a substitute, so catcher Robert Taylor of Yazoo City volunteered to keep the competition going by doing the receiving for both clubs. (Each club used an eight-man batting order.) Taylor caught the equivalent of more than thirty innings in one sitting, so to speak.

FOUR ERRORS IN ONE PLAY

It certainly wasn't Mike Grady's day one afternoon in 1899, when a ground ball came rolling toward the New York Giants' third baseman. First, Grady fumbled the ball, permitting the batter to reach first. Then he made a wild throw to first, allowing the runner to go to second and head for third base. The first baseman recovered the ball and threw it to Grady at third. Grady fumbled the throw, and the runner headed for home. Grady recovered the ball and fired it toward home, but it sailed over the catcher's head, and the runner scored on Grady's fourth error on one play.

TEAM KICKS ITS WAY TO A PENNANT

Seattle literally kicked its way to the 1909 Pacific Coast League pennant. In a deciding game against Spokane, Seattle's shortstop overran the ball on a crucial play. But, by accident, he kicked the ball—directly into the hands of the second baseman for a force-out that preserved Seattle's victory.

ONLY THE METS WEREN'T BUTTERFINGERED

The New York Mets once played a baseball game without an error. What's so amazing about that day of perfection on June 13, 1885 (yes, they were called the Mets then—short for Metropolitans), was that every other team was contributing to an astonishing day of errors. The Mets were in the American Association, then a major league, and the thirteen other big-league clubs in action that afternoon committed an average of 9.2 errors each. Louisville of the American Association committed 20 errors, and the Detroit team of the National League had 19 miscues.

EVEN THE STARS COMMITTED
BONEHEAD PLAYS

Sometimes even the best of baseball's players have been involved in bonehead plays. One of the funniest involved Rogers Hornsby and Charlie Grimm, when

Rogers Hornsby and Grover Cleveland Alexander at an
old-timers game (early 1940s).

they were playing in the infield for the Chicago Cubs
in the late 1920s. The Giants' Andy Cohen was on first
and suddenly started running to second, and Hornsby
and Grimm went into a dither trying to nab him in a
run-down. The ball changed hands a dozen times
between Grimm and Hornsby as they vainly—and
soon angrily—sought to nab the elusive Cohen, who
made the infielders even madder as he laughed with
glee while miraculously avoiding their tags.

Finally, the umpire broke up the fun. He quietly
informed Grimm and Hornsby that the man at the

plate had received a walk and therefore Cohen had been entitled to free passage to second base all along.

SECOND BASEMAN NEEDED CATCHER'S EQUIPMENT

A couple of times, major-league players have borrowed the catcher's protective equipment while working out at a new position in the infield to avoid serious injury while adjusting to the new spot. But one infielder actually played part of a game fully armored in catcher's gear. It was back in 1928, when Pueblo was admitted to the Western League on such short notice that there wasn't enough time to get the playing field in shape. Consequently, the games were played on a rock-hard dirt diamond on which hard-hit ground balls took wicked hops.

The Pueblo players eventually grew accustomed to the erratic skips and bounces of the grounders, but it was a different story for visiting players used to performing on well-manicured fields. On Wichita's first visit to Pueblo, second baseman Glenn McNally had a bad hopper slam into his chin in the first inning. An inning later, the ball took a weird skip and plunked McNally hard in the chest.

When McNally took his position in the third inning, he was ready for anything: he wore a catcher's mask, chest protector, and shin guards. The Pueblo players and home fans howled in protest, and McNally eventually shed the mask and chest protector—but he stubbornly refused to remove the shin guards!

"BUT I DIDN'T KNOW HIS NAME . . ."

Nemo Leibold was managing Syracuse of the International League when his team allowed an easy pop fly to fall safely in short right field. Leibold jumped all over his veteran rightfielder, Vince Barton, because he didn't call for the rookie second baseman to make the catch. "You know, I thought of that, Nemo," explained Barton, "but I couldn't think of the guy's name."

FOUR OUTFIELDERS COULDN'T STOP PEPITONE

New York's Joe Pepitone once experienced a prolonged streak of batting success against the old Kansas City Athletics that particularly bothered A's manager Al Dark. In desperation, Dark came up with a unique defense. When Pepitone came to the plate in a tight situation, Dark sent shortstop Campy Campaneris into left-center field, thus giving the A's four outfielders!

The idea worked—but only partially. Pepitone cracked a hard shot to the outfield, but Campaneris was able to snap it up in time to hold Pepitone to a single and to allow a runner on first to advance only to second base.

TEAM PULLS OFF TRIPLE PLAY WITHOUT TOUCHING BALL

Just about anything can happen in amateur baseball, including a game where a team executed a triple play without a single fielder touching the ball. Oklahoma Military Academy was playing an Indian team one afternoon in the late thirties, when the opposition put runners on first and second with none out in the fourth inning.

The batter popped up to the second baseman and was called out on the infield-fly rule. However, the second sacker misjudged the ball, and the runner on first, attempting to advance, ran into the descending ball and was called out for interference. The infuriated runner on second picked up the baseball and tossed it out of the park. He too was called out for interference, thus completing the triple play.

6
DISCIPLES OF DECEPTION

HUGGINS "ICED" THE OPPOSITION

Years before Miller Huggins became the manager of
the New York Yankees, he was a minor-league second baseman with St. Paul, and one afternoon he
produced an astonishing nineteen putouts and as-
sists. It was years before Huggins finally admitted
that his outstanding performance was all part of a bit
of deceit perpetrated by St. Paul's manager. The manager had put the game balls on ice for twenty-four
hours before the game—and second base was as far
as anyone could hit the frozen ammunition.

IMMEDIATE SUBSTITUTION

In the early days of baseball, the rules makers neglected to put in a rule barring a substitution while a
play was in progress. The quick thinking of Michael
(King) Kelly caused this to be changed.

Kelly was manager of the Cincinnati Reds when,
one afternoon in 1891, an opposing batter hit a foul
ball toward the Reds' bench. It was obvious that the

Cincinnati catcher couldn't get to it, so Kelly jumped up and shouted, "Jones out, Kelly in!" Then he caught the fly in his bare hands. Because of the rules of the time, the umpire had no choice but to call the batter out.

A DECEPTIVE SEARCH FOR A MISSING BALL

The Chicago Cubs' bullpen is located in foul territory just outside the left-field line. Cubs relief pitchers had a lot to do with an inside-the-park home run hit by teammate Tony Taylor against San Francisco in 1958.

Taylor's grounder bounced into the bullpen and disappeared from sight. The Cubs' pitchers began looking under the bullpen bench, thus decoying left-fielder Leon Wagner into searching there too. Actually, the ball had rolled fifty feet beyond the bullpen into a rain gutter. By the time Wagner realized that he had been duped, Taylor was across the plate.

DON'T ALWAYS TRUST YOUR ELDERS

In the Old-Hidden-Ball-Trick-Still Works Department, top honors go to Frank Thomas, a player with the Mets in 1963. Jim Wynn, a rookie with Houston, had just singled. Thomas, playing first that day, asked him if he would step off the base so he could "kick the dust out." Wynn politely complied—and was tagged out by Thomas who had had the ball all the time.

STENGEL'S TRICK PLAY WORKED TOO WELL

Casey Stengel once came up with a trick play that worked all too well. Stengel was in charge of the lowly Boston Braves in the late 1930s, when he developed what he thought was a foolproof plan to pick a runner off third. Casey told the pitcher to throw directly at the batter's head and loudly yell a warning at the same time. Stengel reasoned that the runner would freeze,

Joe DiMaggio, Ralph Houk, Casey Stengel, and Mickey Mantle at an old-timers game in 1971.

and a quick throw by the catcher would nail him off base.

The idea sounded good—on paper. But when it was executed, Stengel's third baseman also froze when the pitcher yelled. The catcher's throw went sailing into left field, permitting the runner to score.

GOING THROUGH THE MOTIONS DECEIVED PLAYER

Jimmy Sheckard of the 1910 Chicago Cubs was a victim of one of the most outlandish bits of deception pulled off in a World Series game. Sheckard was on first base when teammate Wildfire Frank Schulte knocked an easy fly to Danny Murphy, rightfielder of the Philadelphia Athletics.

Sheckard lost the flight of the ball, and shortstop Jack Barry and second baseman Eddie Collins of the Athletics quickly caught on. So they went through maneuvers suggesting that the ball had gone safe and that they were awaiting a throw-in from the out-field. Sheckard was suckered in and dashed to second.

He was dusting himself off after his "safe" slide when the umpire presented him with the distressing information that he had been doubled off first.

THE TRICK THIRD STRIKE

Chattanooga's minor-league team came up with a "trick third strike" that was surprisingly effective during the 1950s. Whenever an enemy batter got two strikes, the pitcher would begin to walk the batter intentionally. But, after the third ball, the pitcher would fire his delivery directly over the middle of the plate. It was amazing how many players were caught napping and fell victim to a called third strike.

"HERE'S MY HAND—AND IT'S DRY"

Cincinnati pitcher John Ogden was taming St. Louis one day in the early thirties, when Cardinals out-fielder Rube Bressler complained to the ump that Ogden was tossing a spitter. Bressler requested that the ump check Ogden's fingers.

As the umpire walked toward the mound on a warm, sunny day, Ogden held up his hand. "It looked as though I was cooperating when I showed my fingers so willingly," Ogden recalled years later. "Actually, I was holding my fingers up so that the sun would dry them before the ump got there. It did."

FRISKY FOOTWORK CHANGED THE RULES

Baseball players seem to have a certain knack for developing ways to get around the game's rules. In the 1880s, the rules permitted pitchers to run up as far as a chalked restraining line at the front of the pitching box when they delivered the ball. Pitchers soon started deliberately fudging on stopping before the line, and it was virtually impossible for umpires to detect the cheating.

So the rules makers passed a regulation requiring that a smooth piece of marble be placed in the ground and on the surface, just in front of the forward line of the box. The idea was that any pitcher overstepping his bounds would tread on the marble with his spikes and was sure to slip. It worked at first—until pitchers evaded the purpose of the marble slab by wearing spikeless rubber-soled shoes.

The rules makers eventually came up with the rule still in effect today: the pitcher must keep one foot in contact with a strip of rubber at the top of the pitching mound.

RUNNER OBEYED WHAT HE HEARD

One of the game's funniest—and most effective—bits of deception took place a number of years ago in a Dominican Winter League game in which a number of major leaguers were playing.

There was a runner on third, and Byron Browne, then a Chicago Cubs outfielder, was on second. There were two outs, and the count against the batter was three balls and two strikes. Tito Fuentes, then a member of the San Francisco Giants, was playing shortstop for the opposing club. Just as the pitcher delivered, Tito yelled out to the second baseman, "Go to first with the ball, because everybody will be running with the count three and two."

Browne fell for the deception and took off with the pitch. The batter walked, and Browne suddenly discovered that he was sharing third base with a fellow runner. Browne was nabbed, of course, in a rundown for the final out.

THE HIDDEN-CALL TRICK

Bobby Bragan was managing Milwaukee one day, when rain held up a game with Philadelphia. Bragan was waiting it out in the dugout when the phone next to him rang, and someone asked for Bobby. "This is Bragan," he said, assuming that the call was from some writer in the press box. He was confronted with a series of questions about the game.

Then the caller asked, "What is your opinion of Dick Stuart?" Bragan had managed Stuart, a horrible fielder, one year with Pittsburgh during spring training. Bragan hemmed and hawed, seeking a diplomatic way to answer the question. "There seems to be divided opinion on his fielding ability, but . . ." Then Bragan glanced at the Phils' dugout and spotted Stuart on the phone—doubled over with laughter.

TRENCHING THE BALL FOUL

One time when Joe Sewell was playing third for the New York Yankees in the early 1930s, a Chicago batter laid down a perfect bunt along the third-base line. Sewell quickly realized that neither he nor anyone else had a chance of getting the ball in time—so he dragged his front spike across the foul line before third base, creating a miniature crevice. The slow-rolling ball hit Sewell's man-made canyon and rolled foul. That winter, the rules makers added a rule prohibiting such action.

THE "HIDDEN BUSH" ATTACK

The hidden-ball trick is virtually as old as baseball itself, but for years one team practiced a hidden-*bush* trick. In the late 1940s and 1950s, the field for the Asheville, North Carolina, team was a city park. And to preserve its landscaped beauty, city fathers prohibited the team from putting up a fence around the outfield. Instead, thick bushes marked the outfield boundaries.

The ground rules of the park said that if the ball went cleanly over the bushes, it was a home run. If the ball landed in the bushes, it was still in play.

On the quiet, a couple of the Asheville outfielders hid a number of balls at different spots in the bushes, so that they could "find" them in a hurry. The outfielders got away with the deception until one night a batter lofted a shot into the bushes in right-center. Two Asheville players arrived on the scene at the same time—and to the astonishment of everyone in the park, two baseballs suddenly came flying in from the outfield!

Dizzy Dean in a typical pose: arguing with umpires (1937).

7
THE MEN IN BLUE: BRIGHT AND BRUTISH

THE UMPIRE WHO MADE THE TWO MOST UNUSUAL DECISIONS

Television's instant replay has quietly proved the fallibility of today's major-league umpires—but no one needed a TV camera to prove that veteran ump Billy Summers made two of his profession's strangest decisions. One call involved the reversal of a decision after the victorious players had left the field for the clubhouse, forcing them to return to the field—where triumph turned to defeat. The other decision involved calling off a game because of rain—when there was not a drop of rain around.

Summers's first weird decision came while he was working behind the plate during a 1943 doubleheader between the St. Louis Browns and the New York Yankees.

St. Louis, the home team, was behind by one run in the bottom of the ninth. A Browns runner had reached first with no one out, then the next batter smashed a hard single to center. The Browns runner on first took off for third, while Yanks centerfielder Johnny Lindell scooped up the ball and threw a hard shot to third.

Lindell's throw bounced past third and rolled into the Browns' dugout. That, of course, enabled the tying run to score. In the meantime, the batter who had crashed the single continued around the bases and crossed home plate. Everyone assumed that it was the winning run. The crowd let out a roar of delight, and the Browns and Yanks departed for the clubhouse.

But the Yanks' manager, Joe McCarthy, angrily argued with Summers that the Browns' runner was only entitled to free passage to third base because of the so-called one-and-one rule—which said that on a ball that went into the dugout, a player was permitted only two bases: the base he was attempting to reach and one additional base. McCarthy contended that the Browns' runner had not reached second by the time the ball rolled into the dugout.

The problem was that only one other ump was working the game with Summers. That umpire, Hal Weafer, was concentrating on the possible play at third base. Summers was concerned with a play at the plate. Because neither umpire had seen whether the Browns' runner had reached second in time, in a rare change of heart, Summers was finally convinced that McCarthy was right.

Summers called the players in the clubhouse back to the field, and the game resumed with the Browns' runner on third. The Yankees then retired the side and ultimately went on to win the game in extra innings.

Summers's second unusual ruling came exactly ten years later, again in St. Louis and again involving a game between the Browns and the Yankees.

This was the Browns' last year in St. Louis, and it was already a foregone conclusion that the team would flee the city at season's end. The crowds were sparse that year, even when the powerful Yankees visited for a series late in the campaign.

One night, the two teams plunged into a brawl, a good old-fashioned donnybrook in which punches were exchanged with reckless abandon. The next afternoon, members of the two teams obviously were still seething as they warmed up, and it appeared likely that the preceding night's fight would resume.

When Umpire Summers assumed control of the game, a few dainty sprinkles dotted the field. Summers immediately called time. Thirty minutes later, Summers appeared. There was nary a raindrop to be seen, and the field was as dry and dusty as the Sahara. But Summers immediately called the game—on account of rain!

THE FASTEST EJECTION IN BASEBALL

Stan Williams has the record for the quickest ejection from a baseball game: he was tossed out even before he had a chance to formally launch his pro career.

Stan, who later pitched fourteen years in the majors, broke into pro ball at Shawnee, Oklahoma. He arrived late for his first game, quickly donned his uniform, and walked into the dugout. The first thing he confronted was an angry umpire yelling at him that he was being kicked out of the game. It turned out that a veteran had yelled something at the ump, and the arbiter mistakenly identified Williams as the culprit—and Stan spent his first game in the clubhouse!

THE WIT GAME

Before finger poking, dirt throwing, bumping, and other childish behavior came into vogue in disputes between umpires and players and managers, there was a better way of solving most baseball disputes: with whimsy and wit. The baseball combatants of days past were well aware of something that their modern counterparts apparently have forgotten. A well-timed repartee can be more disarming than dirt flung on an umpire's shoes; a flash of rapier wit can pack more force than a poke in the eye.

The verbal exchanges between umpires, managers, coaches, and players have produced some of baseball's best humor. Take the case of "Uncle" Charlie Moran, who was nearing the end of a long and commendable umpiring career in the National League when he became embroiled in a heated dispute with several Chicago Cubs over a decision. Charlie Grimm, the Cubs' manager, silenced the argument with one sentence: "I'll fine the first guy who dares lay a hand on this poor, blind old man!"

Here's a collection of some of the best examples of baseball's war of the words.

● ● ●

Jack Wilkinson was umpiring in the Western Association during the 1920s when he came up with the perfect squelch to silence hecklers. Wilkinson was behind the plate in Hutchinson, Kansas, when the local fans were loudly challenging every one of his decisions. The catcalls and riding grew more boisterous as the game progressed.

Finally, Wilkinson turned to the crowd and said, "If you can see the pitches better from up there than I can, then I'm obviously in the wrong place." Whereupon he jumped into the grandstand and started to call the game from there!

● ● ●

Bill Byron, a National League arbiter many years ago, was known as "The Singing Umpire" because he would sing out his decisions, sometimes making up a ditty to suit a particular occasion. Once a batter bitterly protested a called third strike, and Byron responded with this song:

Let me tell you something, son,
　　Before you get much older—

You cannot hit the ball, my friend,
   With the bat upon your shoulder.

• • •

Tommy Connolly had a calm manner of silencing batting critics while serving as an American League umpire. Once a young rookie loudly protested that Connolly was calling strikes on pitches that were high and low and outside. Connolly listened patiently, then replied, "They may be high, or they may be low, or they may be inside or out, my boy—but they are all official."

• • •

Manager Frankie Frisch was one of the more flamboyant of umpire baiters. Once Frisch had argued for several minutes with a plate ump over a close call and, seeing that he was getting nowhere, gave up and walked away, muttering to himself. "What did you say?" yelled the rabbit-eared umpire. Frisch turned and replied, "Just what I suspected. You can't hear—either."

• • •

Tim Hurst was undoubtedly the most colorful major-league umpire around the turn of the century. One day, George Moriarty, who later became an ump, was playing third for Detroit, and Hurst was behind the plate.

Hurst first called a ball on Moriarty, then a strike. "Why, that strike was worse than the one you just called a ball," protested George.

"It really was worse than the other pitch?" Hurst asked in mock innocence. "Then I made a mistake, my boy. The first one should have been a strike too. Strike two!"

When Moriarty turned to argue the point further, the pitcher whipped in another delivery—and Hurst called George out.

It was Hurst's integrity that ruined the finale of a stage play starring Cap Anson, a celebrated player of the last century who once gave acting a try. The climax of the production came when Anson sprinted in from the wings and slid into the plate with the winning run. As the umpire yelled, "You're safe!" the curtain came down.

Anson figured that the colorful Hurst would add a touch of realism to the play and asked him to take the role of the ump. The curtain was beginning to descend when Anson slid home and an actor-catcher made a swipe at Anson. Forgetting the script, Hurst bellowed, "You're out!"

•   •   •

Another famous Hurst story involves the time he called a player out in a tight play, and the player said, in effect, that Tim was a crook.

"Do you really think I'm a crook?" asked Hurst. When the player responded in the affirmative, Hurst told him to leave the game, adding, "You're too nice a boy to be associating with the likes of me."

•   •   •

Dom Dallessandro, a 5'6" bundle of hustle who played for the Chicago Cubs for seven seasons during the 1940s, once was called out on strikes by umpire George Magerkurth. Dallessandro immediately went into a rage over Magerkurth's abilities as an umpire.

Magerkurth, a big, broad-shouldered man, at first listened calmly and patiently to Dallessandro's diatribe. But when the little outfielder showed no signs of stopping, Magerkurth drew himself up to his full height, looked down at the diminutive player, and said, "That's enough out of you, Dallessandro. If you don't stop squawking, I'll bite off your head."

"If you do," retorted Dallessandro, "there'll be more brains in your guts than in your skull."

•   •   •

Umpire Bill McGowan one day made some close calls against the old Washington Senators. Later in the game, a ball was fouled into the stands, and McGowan noticed a woman being carried out. "Did the ball hit that woman?" he asked third-base coach Nick Altrock.

"No," replied Altrock in a loud voice. "You called one right, and she fainted!"

• • •

Umpires generally ignore hecklers, but Joe Rue couldn't resist the temptation to reply one afternoon. A loud-mouthed customer in a box seat at an American League game needled Rue on every decision. One team made a number of changes at the start of an inning, and Joe walked back to the screen to yell the information up to the press box. After he told who was now playing where, the heckler yelled out, "Who's the umpire?"

Rue froze him with a stare, then said, "You are—but I'm getting paid for it."

• • •

Bill Klem, who umpired in the National League from 1905 through 1941 and later was named to the Hall of Fame, is credited with many of umpiring's most notable retorts. Once in 1930, Klem called slugger Hack Wilson out on strikes. "You sure missed that one," said Wilson.

Klem nodded, then snapped, "Maybe—but I wouldn't have if I had a bat in my hands."

• • •

When Leo Durocher was a young shortstop for the St. Louis Cardinals, a player on the opposing bench was heckling Klem while Leo was at the plate. "Take a pitch," Klem told Durocher, "and see if you can spot the guy who's yelling at me." Klem called a ball, and Durocher started to point with his bat toward the offending voice.

The umpire immediately dropped his pretense of

aloofness and bellowed at Durocher, "Don't point, you dumb busher! . . . And that was a strike."

• • •

Klem took baseball very seriously—so seriously that he once failed to see the slightest bit of humor in a stunt pulled by Rip Collins in an exhibition game. Collins was playing with the St. Louis Cards and was sent in as a pinch hitter late in the exhibition. Before leaving the dugout, he stuck a ball under his left arm, concealing it so that no one could see it.

On the first pitch, Collins laid a drag bunt and at the same time let loose the ball under his arm. The pitcher ran in to scoop up the ball Collins had batted, while the catcher picked up the ball Collins had dropped. They were both so startled that neither threw the ball, and most of the players got a good laugh out of the joke.

Not Klem, who tossed Collins out of the game, adding this stern admonition: "There will be none of that, young man. This is serious business, even in an exhibition game!"

• • •

Pitcher Burleigh Grimes and Klem became embroiled in a dispute over a Grimes pitch that Klem had called a ball. Finally, Burleigh turned to his catcher, Johnny Gooch, and asked, "Where was it? Where was it?"

"Answer the question, and you're out of the game," Klem warned Gooch.

But Grimes persisted: "Where was the pitch?"

"Right over the plate," said Gooch, and that prompted Klem to toss Grimes and Gooch out of the game. "Why me?" asked Gooch. "All I did was answer a question."

Responded Klem, "For being such a lousy umpire!"

• • •

Klem later became supervisor of National League umpires, and he was once badgered by a persistent young man who wanted to be an umpire in some league—any league. The youth said he had twenty-twenty vision and that he could read a car's license plate blocks away.

Klem said the young man undoubtedly would have to gain experience in the minor leagues, but because of the low pay, it probably wouldn't be worth it for him. "If your eyesight is as good as you say it is," Klem explained, "you ought to be able to find that much money just walking around the streets."

• • •

Leo Durocher was rarely at a loss for words in a tete-a-tete with an umpire. Yet, there was a time when an umpire left Durocher utterly speechless. Leo was managing Brooklyn then, and umpire Babe Pinelli called a Dodger out at first when he obviously was safe. Durocher bolted from the dugout and bellowed to Pinelli, "What's the matter with you? He was safe by two yards!"

Pinelli whispered back, "Yeah, Leo, wasn't that an awful decision?" Durocher said he was so flabbergasted by the admission that he simply couldn't think of a thing to say, so he turned on his heels and returned to the dugout.

• • •

Durocher was once kicked out of a game before the first pitch was tossed. When Leo was managing the New York Giants, he was exiled one day after a debate with umpire Larry Goetz. The next day, Durocher went up to the plate to present the lineup cards to the umpires, turned to Goetz, and asked, "Do you remember what I said yesterday?" Goetz said he did.

"Well," responded Durocher, "it still goes." And Leo was gone.

• • •

Before he moved up to the majors with the Cardinals, Pepper Martin got into a heated argument with a Texas League umpire and used a word that never got into print in those days. The dispute cost him no more than banishment from the ball game—but it also caused Pepper more mental anguish than he could endure.

That night, Martin called on the umpire in his hotel room. "I didn't come to argue over the decision," Martin said. "It's all over, and you can't change your decision now even if you wanted to. But I want to tell you that I never called any man what I called you today and meant it. I couldn't sleep without coming here and telling you how sorry I am."

• • •

Minor leaguer Buzz Artlett of Oakland was expelled from a game many years ago when he used the opposing catcher to relay a message to the umpire. After the ump called a strike on a close one, Artlett turned to the catcher and said, "Turn around and see the world's worst umpire." In a few minutes, Artlett was taking a shower.

• • •

John J. McCloskey, who managed the Cardinals in the early days of this century, once recalled an incident in his managing days in the minors when a California League ump "punched out" some pretty extreme punishment. The team was in such terrible financial condition that the players had to work a couple of weeks without pay. Their salvation, however, was a benevolent local restaurant owner who provided each player and the manager with a free meal ticket each day.

McCloskey admitted that one day he went a little overboard in sassing umpire Jim McDonald. McCloskey said he knew the ump couldn't do much, because the ump knew "as well as I that he couldn't fine me, because there was no money coming in."

The next day, McCloskey said, he started screaming at the ump about a close play. McDonald didn't say a word. He reached into McCloskey's shirt pocket and pulled out his meal ticket, then produced a punch from his pants pocket, "and knocked thirty cents' worth of beefsteak and onions out of my ticket."

"It pains me very much to do this," said McDonald, "but duty is duty. Don't think that poverty cuts any ice in baseball. Pop off again," he warned, "and you'll lose a few pieces of pie!"

• • •

"Pongo" Joe Cantillon was an umpire for several years before he became manager of the Washington Senators early in the century. One afternoon, Cantillon had a run-in with ump Jack Sheridan, who said he thought Cantillon's insults were a bit unseemly for a former umpire. "By the way, Joe," Sheridan added later in the debate, "why did you quit umpiring?"

"I was a good umpire," Cantillon retorted, "but when I got as blind as you are, I got another job."

• • •

Umpire Bill Valentine had a great sense of humor. The American League arbiter also doubled as a basketball official, and it was during one of those winter games that Bill had a head-on collision with one of the players. A photographer caught it at the moment of impact. The picture appeared in the local paper the next day with, in jest, this caption: "Valentine hit from the blind spot—right between the eyes."

Bill loved it. In fact, he bought up dozens of extra copies of the paper to send to his friends.

• • •

Charlie Moran became a big-league umpire after a successful career with the Centre College football team, whose nickname was the Praying Colonels. Once, in an argument with Moran, Fresco Thompson sneered, "With you as coach, no wonder they prayed."

Without a pause, Moran replied, "Young man, since you've turned this conversation into religious channels, suppose you go to the clubhouse and baptize yourself with an early shower."

•   •   •

Bill Guthrie maintained iron discipline on the field when he was calling balls and strikes in the American League. One day, while the Red Sox were in the field, Boston's bench started riding Guthrie. He took it for no more than five minutes before clearing the bench with an angry wave of his arm.

A bit later, he noticed the Red Sox third-base coach standing in his box, and Guthrie yelled that he too had been tossed from the game.

"What for? I didn't say anything," protested the coach.

"Maybe you didn't, but you were thinking," replied Guthrie.

"How do you know I was thinking?" the coach demanded.

"I'm giving you credit for it—now get out," barked Guthrie.

•   •   •

Early in his career, Guthrie was calling balls and strikes in a minor-league game in the South. Larry Gilbert, who was managing one of the teams, rushed up to protest that he thought Guthrie was calling a lot of low balls as strikes. Guthrie removed his mask, fixed Gilbert with a hard stare, and jerked a thumb, signaling him out of the game. "You're taking on too big a job," said Guthrie. "You can't umpire and manage at the same time!"

•   •   •

When Bob Engel made his debut as a National League umpire, he was having trouble with low pitches. After Engel called two low pitches as strikes, the batter complained bitterly, then started to walk away. "Hey," said Engel, "you only have two strikes."

"I know," said the batter, "but I now know the game we're playing, so I'm going back for a wedge."

•   •   •

Years before Kid Gleason became a big-league skipper with the Chicago White Sox, he was an infielder for the Philadelphia Phillies—and in eleven straight games he was tossed out by umpire Cy Rigler. Gleason and Rigler went their separate ways after that, but eventually Rigler turned up to work a Philadelphia series in Chicago.

The moment Rigler walked onto the field, Gleason spotted him and ran over. "I wouldn't stay on the same field with you," he said, and he turned and walked to the clubhouse, where he remained throughout the game.

• • •

Bill Friel, who later became a baseball executive, loved to recall the time he was cut to the quick by a young pitcher when Friel was umpiring a minor-league game in Kansas City.

Before the start of the game, the Kansas City pitcher, Mike Regan, emphatically told the ump that he had "just two things I wish to say to you, Mr. Friel. When a ball is pitched between a batter's knees and his shoulders and over the plate, it is a strike, and should be so called. Whenever a ball is above the batter's shoulder or below his knees and not over the plate, it is a ball and should be so called. I trust you will remember that."

The pitcher then walked out to the mound, and the game began. With two out in the first inning, Regan delivered a pitch that he was confident was a strike. Friel called it a ball.

Regan raced up to the plate and shouted, "You dumb boob! You can't remember for an inning what I told you."

• • •

Fresco Thompson regularly had run-ins with umpires during his nine-year major-league career with Pittsburgh, Brooklyn, the New York Giants, and the Philadelphia Phillies. One afternoon, Fresco challenged a rule, and the umpire whipped an official rule book out of his pocket to show Thompson.

"That book won't do me any good," said Thompson. "I don't read Braille."

• • •

Dee Williams, a former Chicago Cubs catcher, was once involved in a long—but as usual, losing—argument with umpire Charlie Berry. Finally, Williams asked, "Tell me one thing, Charlie: how do you get your square head in that round mask?"

• • •

The Giants' John McGraw once asked an umpire, "What would happen to me if I called you a blind bat and a robber?"

The umpire told McGraw he would be fined and suspended.

"Well, then," said McGraw, "what if I only thought it?"

The ump pondered briefly, then replied, "Why, I guess nothing could be done about it."

Retorted McGraw, "OK, let it go at that."

• • •

Umpires and ballplayers are not always combative. Tommy Bridges, who was the ace on Detroit's pitching mound during much of his sixteen-year career with the Tigers, always credited an umpire for some valuable help when Bridges made his major-league debut. Bill McGowan was behind the plate, and Bridges was having a miserable time on the mound. He was so nervous and so wild that he quickly walked three batters.

McGowan called time and walked to the mound, Bridges recalled: "He said, 'Listen, kid, take your time and take it easy. Don't let them hurry you. You've got all afternoon—it's just another ball game.'

"I think this was the biggest lift I ever got in my career," said Bridges, who posted a 194–138 lifetime record with the Tigers and also won four of five World Series decisions.

• • •

There was once a pro game in California between Alturas and Cedarville—a pair of bitter rivals—but not once during the game did a player question an umpire's call, even some questionable ones. That was because, prior to the game, the umpire called the players together and said there would be absolutely no arguing about any of his calls. Then he pointed to the gun that he had tucked into his belt—and reminded the players that in addition to being an ump, he was also the county sheriff.

WORDLESS WITTICISMS

In some of their exchanges, players and umpires have been able to make their point without uttering a word.

For example, umpire Bob Emslie used an unorthodox procedure to respond to criticism of his eyesight from New York Giants' manager John McGraw. The next day, he turned up at the Giants' morning practice with a rifle in the crook of his arm. He strode directly to second base, split a wooden match, stuck a dime in the slit, and then pushed the match into the earth. Calmly he stepped back to home plate, lifted the rifle, and fired. The dime went spinning into the outfield. He walked off the field without a word—and McGraw and the Giants never questioned his eyesight again.

• • •

Harry (Steamboat) Johnson, a veteran Southern Association umpire, had a more subtle way of fending off managers' and players' advice that he see an eye doctor. Johnson always carried a card, signed by an optometrist and stamped by a notary public, certifying that his vision was twenty-twenty in each eye. He got a new card each year and repeatedly showed it to managers and players, with or without provocation.

• • •

One umpire of the early baseball days, John P. Keefe, used his running skills to show up pitcher Guy Hecker, who had ignited Keefe's wrath during an argument. When Hecker was at bat and tapped a ground ball, Keefe took off from his position behind the catcher and beat Hecker to first base, where he called him out with an exaggerated flourish.

• • •

Hugh Rorty, an old-time minor-league umpire, had the perfect answer for a manager who insisted that a game be called because of fog. The manager, Bill Luby, also was the rightfielder, and he claimed the fog made visibility impossible.

Rorty asked for Luby's glove, went out to right field, and ordered Luby to hit him some fungoes. Luby responded with three towering flies. The umpire galloped back and forth and caught all three.

Then he came back in and handed the glove to Luby. Without a word being said, the manager and the rest of his team returned to the field.

THE UMPIRE WHO SHOT HIS INQUISITORS

Of course, words and wit were not the only weapons in battles between umpires and players. Physical violence between players, fans, and umps also flared several times—and some of those arguments were downright deadly.

In Lowdesborough, Alabama, in 1899, umpire Sam White endured an afternoon of abuse from one player until he reached the breaking point. He shoved the player to the ground, whereupon the player slowly climbed to his feet and swung his bat at the umpire's head. The blow fractured White's skull, and he died on the spot.

Umpire Ora Jensen reportedly was killed in a similar incident in 1901 in Farmersburg, Indiana.

Then there was a man named "Flo" Israel who was

pressed into serving as a volunteer umpire when Los Angeles' minor-league team had a spring-training game many years ago. Lack of experience led Israel to make a number of horrendous calls, which drew sharp inquiries from the players.

That evening, an angered Israel turned up at a gathering of his critics, pulled a gun, and fired five or six shots into the group of players. Fortunately, Flo was as bad a shot as he was an ump. Despite the barrage of bullets, the only casualties were pitcher William Tozer, who was wounded in the left arm and shoulder, and Lou Guernsey, a sportswriter who suffered a wound in the foot.

Research turns up at least two other incidents of gun pulling by umpires in the days before newspapers carried first names. One ump named Williams used two revolvers to hold off a hostile crowd at Birmingham, Alabama, in 1886. Another umpire named Raphun of the Ohio-Pennsylvania League pulled a revolver and threatened to shoot a spectator who had slapped him before a game June 29, 1910, at Lancaster, Pennsylvania.

Umpire Billy Evans was nearly killed when he was struck by a bottle tossed at a St. Louis park early in the century. White Sox owner Charles Comiskey came up with a simple way to prevent such an occurrence at his field. The prices of all seats within throwing range of the umpires were doubled from twenty-five cents to fifty cents. Comiskey figured that a fan who could afford fifty cents for a seat would be much more dignified and refined than the cheaper-paying customers, and thus less likely to hurl bottles at the umps.

The idea worked.

ARGUMENTS THAT FAILED

When Frankie Frisch was managing Pittsburgh, he felt the umpires were making a mistake in halting a game because of darkness. Frisch bolted from the dugout to grab the arm of one of the umps to argue that there was still enough light to continue play. Frisch's argument came to an abrupt halt when he discovered he was holding the arm of his first baseman!

• • •

Casey Stengel suffered similar embarrassment when he was managing Oakland's minor-league team. When the umpires started to halt the game because of fading light, Stengel grabbed a couple of baseballs and rushed to the middle of the diamond.

"Look!" he yelled at the umpires, "I'm sixty years old, and I can still see the ball." Stengel then flung a ball up into the gathering gloom, reached up to catch it—and was smacked square in the face.

THE UMPIRE WHO FOUGHT FOR HIS HONOR

The late Cal Hubbard, a long-time supervisor of umpires in the American League, literally chose to fight for his umpiring honor—in the ring against a professional boxer. Hubbard was umpiring a game in Macon, Georgia, when he made a call that greatly displeased the local patrons. Several of the aroused fans went so far as to dare Hubbard to "meet a representative of the fans" in a Labor Day boxing show at Macon.

The representative was Spike Webb, a pro. Nonetheless, Hubbard climbed into the ring. He was out of condition for boxing and had to give up after two rounds, but he drew lusty cheers from the fans for his courage and aggressiveness.

"NO BALL GAME IS WORTH AN UMP'S JOB"

Frankie Frisch never hesitated when he had a chance to argue with an umpire, and he waged a long and bitter feud with hulking George Magerkurth. Nobody, with the possible exception of the fiery Leo Durocher, rivaled Frisch for providing Magerkurth with trouble during his twenty years in the National League.

Yet Magerkurth once revealed that he strongly admired Frisch because of the gutsy stand the man once took to preserve the job of an umpire.

"There was a ball-up on a decision once, and it went against the Pirates when Frisch was managing them," Magerkurth explained. "It was so bad that [National League president] Ford Frick called a hearing at league headquarters. I wasn't involved. Thank God for that, because it looked bad for the ones who were.

"Anyway, Frisch was a little late, and as he started to go into Frick's office, he heard Frick say, 'This is a serious situation, and I wouldn't be surprised if at least one umpire doesn't lose his job because of it.'

"Then Frankie walked in and said, 'Mr. Frick, did I understand you to say that you might fire an umpire over this affair?'

"Frick nodded his head, and Frankie said, 'No ball game in the world is worth an umpire's job. Good day, gentlemen.' He spun on his heels and walked out.

"Bill Benswanger was president of the Pirates then, and Frick asked him, 'Are you ready to proceed with your protest, Mr. Benswanger?'

"Benswanger just shrugged his shoulders. 'You heard what my manager said.' And he got up and left, too. All of the umpires got dressed down pretty good—but they all kept their jobs."

HOT ARGUMENT BURST INTO FLAMES

There have been some hot arguments between players and umpires. But none was so hot that it burst into flames, except for one in a minor-league game in the 1940s.

Catcher Dave Dennis was playing for Miami, Oklahoma, of the Kansas-Oklahoma-Missouri League, when he got into a heated argument with the plate umpire. Suddenly sparks began to fly from the catcher's chest protector, and smoke curled out. The protector burst into flames when Dennis hastily threw it off.

A cigarette had been carelessly tossed from the stands and had landed in the chest protector between innings.

WHEN UMPS REFUSED TO EJECT ABUSIVE PLAYERS

In the latter part of the nineteenth century, it wasn't uncommon for players to lash umpires verbally in an effort to be tossed out of a game.

In those days, major-league teams had a limited number of players on their rosters. Managers were loath to send in replacements for a pitcher who was being badly battered by enemy hitters, replace a hitter who was in a slump, or even bench a player who complained that he needed some rest.

So players began circumventing their managers by provoking arguments with umpires, who would then banish them from the game. It didn't take long, however, for the umps to catch on. Then they retaliated against abusive players by refusing to eject them from the game!

UMP HIT A SINGLE

Umpires call balls and strikes and outs, and batters produce hits. Not always. An umpire in the Pioneer League once was credited with a single! Of course, there's a catch.

Ogden, Utah, was playing Great Falls, Montana, on June 17, 1945, when one of the umpires scheduled to work the game failed to arrive. Consequently, one player from each team was designated to handle the calls on the bases.

Late in the game, Great Falls' designated umpire, Jim Keating, was pulled from his umpiring post and replaced by another Great Falls player. Keating was sent to the plate as a pinch hitter, where he lashed the single that helped carry his team to an 11-10 triumph.

8
THE LADY WAS A GENTLEMAN, AND OTHER OFF-BEAT TALES

THE LADY WAS A GENTLEMAN

There were Tilly, Fern, Mandy, Sadie, Gracie, Kitty, Lady, and Little Eva. And don't forget Daisy, Bridget, Peaches, Baby Doll, Liz, Kittie, Nellie, and Minnie.

Since this is a baseball book, you would naturally assume these persons have something to do with our national pastime. Wives or girlfriends of our masculine heros? Hardly. Members of an all-woman baseball team? Wrong again. These were all nicknames of hard-muscled, hairy-chested, probably tobacco-chewing major-league players.

For some strange reason, the supposedly macho sport of baseball has been liberally laced with players carrying nicknames of a definitely feminine nature. A Mother, Grandmother, and Grandma all played in the majors, and there have been a Beauty, a Candy, a Queenie, a Toots or two, a Rachel, a Camille, an Opal, and a Wilma.

Probably the best of the males with a female tag was Charles B. Baldwin, who was a most proper gentleman—that's why he was tabbed "Lady." Baldwin was a nice, mild-mannered young man whose base-ball talents, unfortunately, matured during the 1880s, when most pro players were an exceedingly rough and rowdy lot. Because Baldwin didn't chew, drink, or cuss, his teammates called him Lady—and the moniker stuck with Baldwin until his dying day in 1937. Even most modern record books still list him as "Lady Baldwin."

Others who achieved fame because of—or despite—their nicknames included William (Little Eva) Lange, a hard-hitting outfielder in the 1890s; William (Baby Doll) Jacobson, an outfielder who hit with vigor; Dave (Beauty) Bancroft; Max (Tilly) Bishop; John (Sadie) McMahon; John (Biddy) McPhee; Tully Frederick (Topsy) Hartsel; William (Kitty) Bransfield; Arthur (Tillie) Shafer; Johnny (Grandma) Murphy; Jacob Nelson (Nellie) Fox, and Saturnino Orestes (Minnie) Minoso.

We also had Vivian Lindaman, Lynn King, Peaches Graham, Cuddles Marshall, Candy Cummings (usually credited with being the first to throw a curveball), Candy Nelson, Blondie Purcell, Rosy Ryan, Toots Shultz, Bubbles Hargrave, Goldie Rapp, Kitten Prentiss, and Kitten Haddix.

Even a couple of managers got in on the funny-name game: There was Birdie Tebbetts, who managed Cincinnati, Milwaukee, and Cleveland during eleven years in the majors, and Russell Blackburne, who piloted the White Sox in 1928 and 1929. Everyone called Blackburne by his nickname of Lena.

The old Kansas City A's once had a promising young player named Rachel Slider, who was christened that way by his parents. The stories behind the feminine nicknames of many of the other players have been lost in antiquity, but a few explanations have survived.

Looks had nothing to do with Beauty Bancroft's nickname. It was what he said—and that was "beauty"—every time a pitcher would whip a called strike past him.

Lefty Gomez, who shared pitching duties with Murphy for the Yankees, hung the label "Grandma" on his teammate because, according to Gomez, Murphy was "as prim and fussy as an old woman about ordering meals and things like that."

Phillip Powers, who caught in the majors from 1878 through 1885, was called Grandmother, while Walter Watson was called Mother by virtually everyone during a brief 1887 pitching stint with Cincinnati of the American Association. Just why they acquired those matronly nicknames still baffles researchers.

Ironically, the parents of a number of players gave them names generally associated with females. Danny Bell, a Pirates outfielder in the late thirties, originally was named Fern. Dee Wilma Sanders pitched for the St. Louis Browns in 1945, and Lloyd Opal Russell contributed a couple of pinch hits for Cleveland in the thirties.

Camille Van Brabant pitched a couple of seasons with the Athletics in the midfifties. He strongly preferred to be called Ozzie. Fay Thomas, who oscillated between the majors and minors from the midtwenties to the midthirties, also showed disdain for his given name. For some unknown reason, he was better known as "Scow."

In many cases, the feminine names were a corruption or abbreviation of a masculine name, such as Nelson (Nellie) Fox, or Gracie (Grayson) Pearce, a player of the 1880s.

A pitcher for the Cards, Giants, and Tigers in the teens was quickly nicknamed Pol. His last name was Perritt.

It was a combination of first and last names that caused snickers when the 1927 Senators tried out a second baseman for two games. His name was Buddy Dear.

BOSTON'S ATTEMPT TO SIGN
BOB FELLER BACKFIRED

Imagine what the Boston Red Sox would have been like with both Ted Williams and flame-throwing Bob Feller on the payroll during the late thirties, forties, and early fifties. Oh, what a dynamic duo they would have made!

Baseball's hardest-throwing pitcher of that era might have wound up in Boston rather than in Cleveland—if the Red Sox hadn't made such a lucrative offer to land Feller!

The strange tale dates back to late 1936, when the sleepy little midwestern community of Des Moines, Iowa, was invaded en masse by baseball scouts and executives.

The eighteen-year-old Feller's contract with Cleveland had been challenged by the local Des Moines team, which claimed Feller had been signed illegally under a special agreement between the majors and minors. The matter was in the hands of Commissioner Kenesaw Mountain Landis, who had previously infuriated many big-league executives by declaring scores of players to be free agents. Consequently, although the crusty old commissioner seemed to be taking an extra long time to rule on the Feller matter, the betting was heavy that Landis would uphold the Des Moines club's complaint and declare Feller a free agent.

And, by late 1936, there wasn't a major-league executive who wasn't well aware that the young Iowa farm boy had the potential—and the steaming fastball—to become one of baseball's greats. They were aware that by the age of eleven, Feller pitched against adult amateurs and semipros and repeatedly gunned them down with blazing pitches. They had seen scorebooks of games that Feller had pitched as he matured as an amateur—scorebooks that

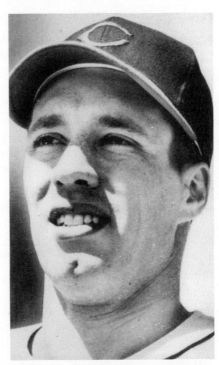

Bob Feller (1950).

showed virtually nothing but *K*s for opposition batters. And they knew that during a brief test in the majors in 1936, the young athlete had struck out more men in one game than any other American League pitcher in history.

The complication that had aroused such interest in Feller was that the teenager originally had signed a contract in 1935 with Fargo-Moorhead of the Northern League, which transferred the contract to New Orleans, then a Cleveland affiliate. New Orleans then transferred Feller to Cleveland in July 1936.

Feller went directly to the Indians, where his awesome talents quickly became apparent. The first time he pitched in an Indian uniform, he struck out eight of the nine men he faced in an exhibition. Later, in a regulation game, he struck out seventeen Philadelphia Athletics, at the time a league record.

The Des Moines club argued, however, that Feller had been signed illegally, because Cleveland had clearly violated a clause in a special major–minor-league agreement prohibiting big-league clubs from dealing directly with sandlot players.

While the baseball world waited for Landis to rule, baseball executives and scouts were valiantly trying to reach the Feller family with enormous offers if Landis should declare Feller a free agent. The problem was that Bill Feller and his son, Bob, who lived in the little community of Van Meter, just a few miles outside of Des Moines, refused to see anyone or discuss any offers from other teams.

That's when Billy Evans, then general manager of the Red Sox, came up with the idea of using Garner (Sec) Taylor, a veteran and highly popular sports editor of the *Des Moines Register,* as a secret emissary between the Red Sox and the Fellers. He dispatched Bibb Falk, a scout who later became a University of Texas coach, to meet with the sports editor, Taylor recalled years later, and the first thing Falk did was pull out $1,000 in bills!

The scout said the Sox were willing to pay as much as $120,000 for Feller to sign with them, or they would match any other offer made by a major-league team. It was known that the Yankees also dearly wanted young Feller, and insiders said club officials were considering offers above the $150,000 range.

The scout said that if the commissioner did rule in favor of Cleveland, the $1,000 he handed to Taylor was for the Fellers to keep, no strings attached. Taylor said he agreed to meet with Feller's father, who after a long discussion told Taylor that he would allow Boston an opportunity to meet any other club's offer.

Taylor met with his private attorney to draw up an agreement, but several days later Bill Feller called to say he was hesitant about signing an agreement at that time, giving Taylor the impression that he wanted

Sec Taylor, sports editor
of the *Des Moines Register*,
acted as a secret go-
between for Boston and the
Feller family in the 1930s.

to mull over the proposal a bit longer. That hesitation
may have been an expensive decision for the Fellers,
Taylor said.

Taylor said Bill Feller apparently called Cleveland
to tell club officials about the proposal, and Taylor
said he suspected someone from the Indians then
tipped off Landis about the huge offer, apparently
prompting Landis to issue a quick decision: he reluctantly validated Feller's contract with Cleveland but
at the same time ordered the Indians to pay $7,500
damages to the Des Moines club.

There was no doubt that Cleveland officials had
used subterfuge and had signed Feller illegally, said
Taylor. He noted Landis did offer a lengthy and detailed report of his interpretation of the matter and
soundly criticized Cleveland officials. But, Taylor
noted, he and many other veteran sportswriters felt
that the real reason behind the cantankerous Landis's
ruling was that the commissioner believed it would

be unfair for the Fellers to make such an enormous profit on the controversy, especially when the nation was mired in the Great Depression.

● ● ●

Feller, incidentally, posted a 266–162 record and struck out 2,581 in eighteen seasons with the Indians. He pitched three no-hitters and twelve one-hitters, and finished with a 3.25 ERA. He led the league in victories five times and tied one other time.

Williams was the last batter to hit over .400 (.406 in 1941). In his nineteen seasons, he averaged .344.

THE MOVIE THAT BROKE BABE RUTH'S HEART

Babe Ruth was slowly dying of cancer in 1948, when his spirits were buoyed after a Hollywood studio hired him to serve as technical adviser on the movie *The Babe Ruth Story*.

Ruth's role as an adviser turned out to be a terrible ruse, and the movie itself was one of the worst sports movies ever produced, as well as one of Hollywood's all-time stinkers, period.

Ruth had envisioned a film comparable in quality to *The Pride of the Yankees*, the warm and superb biography of Lou Gehrig. Babe dieted some forty to fifty pounds off his portly frame to portray himself in the Gehrig film, and he wasn't bad. The movie drew critical acclaim when it was released in 1942, but Babe was dissatisfied, because he felt some of the baseball scenes were portrayed less accurately than they should have been.

Things would be different with his own life story, he happily told friends. As technical adviser, the Babe was giddy with excitement over the responsibility of assuring the authenticity of diamond activities.

Paul Douglas, then a young actor with a build similar to Ruth's during his playing days, actively sought the role. He wouldn't have been a bad choice; Douglas was an athlete in his younger days and could have provided a realistic portrayal of Ruth.

Instead, the role went to William Bendix, then known chiefly for a popular radio role in which he played a bumbling aircraft construction worker. Bendix was a ludicrous selection. He looked as much like a baseball player as Grandma Moses, one observer at the time noted. He threw like a girl, and his efforts to imitate Ruth's batting style were laughable. At one point in the movie, Bendix, then obviously in his forties, played Ruth as a teenager—and, despite thick coatings of makeup, still looked like a man well into his forties.

Meanwhile, when Ruth arrived in Hollywood, he was billeted in the plush Beverly Hills Hotel. The studio purposely kept him away from the shooting, denying his requests to see any of the already-shot footage. Instead, Ruth's monthlong stay was devoted to scores of interviews set up by studio publicists.

The Babe finally did get a chance to meet Bendix and gave him a brief lesson on the basics of holding a baseball bat. But Ruth gave up in disgust and frustration when his repeated efforts to teach Bendix the proper way to swing went for naught.

Studio personnel, meanwhile, were worried about Babe's drawn appearance and rushed the film through the final stages so that it could be released before the Babe died. Studio executives apparently felt that a story about a live hero would be a better draw than one about a dead hero.

There isn't one kind word that can be said of the film biography of the man who probably contributed more to baseball than any other individual. The movie, dripping with sentimentality and overloaded with brash distortions, was poorly written, poorly acted, and poorly edited. One critic summed up the film in four words: *An insult to Ruth.*

Babe attended the New York premier. He left before

the picture was half over, his heart broken, his vision blurred with tears. He died less than three months later.

FIELDERS WOULD HAVE BEEN FORCED TO DODGE CARS

In the late 1950s, when the Chicago White Sox were first becoming potential pennant winners, Chicago mayor Richard J. Daley came up with what he thought was a brilliant idea: the Windy City end of the World Series would be played in Soldier Field, which could accommodate thousands more customers than the Sox' own Comiskey Park.

On paper, it sounded like a grand idea—until park officials started checking the cost of converting the football field to baseball standards. First, they discovered that one wall of the stadium would have to be knocked down at a cost of more than $100,000 to make room for the left and right outfielders. Even then, the leftfielder would end up stationed in the southbound lanes of heavily traveled Lake Shore Drive! The rightfielder would be in the northbound lanes!

Needless to say, the White Sox opened the 1959 World Series against the Los Angeles Dodgers at Comiskey Park.

TOUCH THAT BOY'S HAND, AND OFF COMES YOURS

If a doctor's advice had been followed when Hollis (Sloppy) Thurston was a child, he never would have pitched nine seasons in the major leagues. Thurston was a youngster when he nearly severed his right hand with a knife. When a doctor told family members he would have to amputate, Thurston's uncle picked up a hammer and growled at the physician, "If the boy's hand comes off then yours comes off too."

The doctor decided that he could stitch up the

wound after all, and Thurston eventually used the hand to deliver baseballs for four major-league teams. He was a twenty-game winner one season with the Chicago White Sox.

MUSIAL HAD NO REGRETS QUITTING WHEN HE DID

In 1963, Stan Musial had appeared in more major-league games than any other man except Ty Cobb. When Musial retired just a few weeks before his forty-

Stan Musial (1946).

third birthday, he had played in 3,026 games—only 8 short of breaking Cobb's record.

Musial was asked years later if he had any regrets about quitting before claiming the mark. "I retired at just the right time," replied Musial. "If I hadn't quit when I did, the club would not have gone after Lou Brock," obtained from the Chicago Cubs. Brock, of course, reached superstar status in his sixteen years with the Cards.

FAN INFORMS PLAYER HE HAS BEEN TRADED

Dale Long, who spent ten years in the majors with a half-dozen different teams, is probably the only big leaguer to learn from a fan that he was traded to another team. Long was a utility first baseman for San Francisco in 1960, but he seldom got into a game. His main duty was to help warm up pitchers in the bullpen. One day, Long was lounging on the bullpen bench when a fan with a portable radio leaned over the railing and shouted, "Long, you lucky bum, you've just been sold to the Yankees!"

CATCHER DISCOVERED WHY HE SHOULDN'T HAVE NEEDLED COBB

Catcher Hank Severeid made an embarrassing discovery when he needled Ty Cobb about his baserunning—when Ty was approaching his fortieth birthday. Severeid was behind the plate for the St. Louis Browns when he taunted Cobb that old age was catching up with him, then added there wasn't a remote chance that the veteran could even come close to stealing a base against him.

Cobb got on base twice that day—and each time, he stole both second and third against Severeid. To make it worse for Hank, before each steal, Cobb loudly yelled to the crowd, "I'm going to steal on the next pitch!"

HERMAN WAS A HERO, NOT A GOAT

Babe Herman earned a reputation as baseball's prize blockhead because he once doubled into a double play while performing for the old Brooklyn Dodgers. One of baseball's most colorful legends concerns the time that Herman, running with his head down, passed second and arrived at third base to discover that two of his teammates were already there. The opposing Boston Braves quickly turned this weird situation into a double play, thus ending the inning.

But what has been forgotten in the telling and retelling of this story over the years was that the bases were loaded when Herman got his hit—and his drive scored the winning run!

WHAT AN INSULT!

Babe Ruth's popularity and status as a hero were so solid that during World War II, when Japanese soldiers in Pacific jungles wanted to draw position-revealing night fire from American soldiers, they would shout, "Babe Ruth eats mud," or similar uncomplimentary remarks about the Babe.

They were the greatest insults the Japanese could think of.

THE EFFEMINATE GIANTS

Ethel Levey, a popular musical comedy star in the early days of the century, once was scheduled to sing a baseball song during an appearance in New York. Hoping to add a little pizzazz to the number, Levey asked Giants manager John McGraw if he would allow nine or ten of his biggest players to stand behind her in uniform while she belted out the song. McGraw agreed.

The next day, a New York reviewer told his readers, "It is painful to report that Miss Levey dared to use a group of obviously effeminate chorus men to masquerade in the uniforms of the New York Giants"!

LITTLE LEAGUES CAUSE POOR BATTING PERFORMANCE

Jim Fregosi, who spent eighteen seasons in the major leagues, once proposed an intriguing theory as to why the batting averages of today's major-league hitters are lower than those of their counterparts of days gone by.

Fregosi put the blame on Little League baseball. The Little Leagues tend to use the better players as pitchers, according to Fregosi's theory. Consequently, by the time a child reaches the age of twelve, he has developed solid confidence in his pitching and isn't afraid to challenge the hitter. Augment that confidence with experience in Babe Ruth, American Legion, or high school play, and the pitcher is already a polished performer by the time he's ready for pro ball, Fregosi said.

PITCHER FAKED SPITBALL

Today's pitchers do everything they can to mask throwing an illegal spitball. But a pitcher once deliberately faked a spitter by making a production of spitting on the ball.

It was back in the days when the spitball was still a legal pitch, and one of the top Yankees (then Highlanders) pitchers in 1910 and 1911 was Russ Ford. Russ couldn't master a spitter. Instead, he illegally sewed a small bit of emery paper into his glove. He'd then rough up one side of the ball, which, because of the air resistance, would break in such a baffling manner that it was virtually unhittable.

To get away with his ploy, Ford would go through the motions of spitting on the ball before throwing it, and for years everyone assumed that the crazy meanderings of the ball were caused by spit. Ford was 26–6 in 1910 and 22–11 the next season.

COACH RETIRED HIS OWN PLAYER

A major-league coach once caught a pop-up—and retired one of his own players! Burt Shotton was coaching third base for the Indians in 1945 when a Cleveland batter hit a flimsy pop-up that was headed toward the third-base coaching box. Acting on reflex, Shotton reached up and caught the ball. The hitter was promptly called out because of interference.

CLARKE'S PRO START WAS A PURE ACCIDENT

Fred Clarke, who spent twenty-one years in the majors as a player and player-manager, got his professional start because a good friend suddenly backed out of a tryout. In 1892, the Hastings, Nebraska, club had a serious eye on Byron McKibbon, a Des Moines, Iowa, semipro star. The team begged him to report to Hastings for a tryout, and sent along a railroad ticket.

But, at the last minute, McKibbon got cold feet and offered the ticket to his friend Clarke, also a dandy semipro player in Des Moines. Officials of the Hastings club were upset when Clarke showed up instead of McKibbon—but the disappointment was quickly erased. Clarke had a great season, and two years later he was in the National League, headed for a .315 lifetime average, a flock of fielding records, and four pennants as Pittsburgh's manager. He was elected to the Baseball Hall of Fame in 1945.

CLARKE LITERALLY STOLE HOME ON A STROLL

It was Fred Clarke who once stole home in the majors—without realizing it! Clarke was the player-manager for the Pirates in a 1906 game with Chicago and

Fred Clarke shows his batting grip (1959).

managed to reach third base with other runners on first and second in a tight game. The count on the batter was three balls and one strike. Clarke thought the next pitch was high; the umpire didn't make a sound, so he assumed it was ball four, thus forcing in a run. Clarke casually strolled to the plate. The batter also assumed the pitch was a ball and started slowly trotting to first. The Chicago catcher reached the same conclusion.

As Clarke stepped on home, the umpire croaked, "Strike two!" Embarrassed, he explained that he had had a frog in his throat and for a few seconds couldn't utter a sound. But the damage was already done. Clarke was officially credited with a steal of home!

PLAYERS SOLD THEIR SEATS TO SPECTATORS

The pay of early baseball players was meager at best, but members of New York's team once came up with an ingenious way of augmenting their incomes. An overflow crowd was funneled onto part of the playing field at New York's park for a game with Boston on May 3, 1883. All of the New York players and their manager, Jim Mutrie, sold their chairs—which then served as the players' bench or dugout—to spectators for fifty cents each!

IT DIDN'T PAY TO WIN

Boston's Red Sox trimmed Pittsburgh five games to three in baseball's first genuine World Series in 1903. Ironically, the losing players received more money than the winners. Each member of the winning Red Sox received $1,182, while each member of the Pirates drew $1,316.

The reason for this strange dispersal was that the Pirates' owner, Barney Dreyfuss, threw the team's share of the profits into the players' pool. Henry Killilea, owner of the Red Sox, kept his share of the team's profits—$6,700.

THERE'S A REASON FOR "ALIBI IKES"

When a baseball player commits a blunder on the field, it's common to explain it away with an alibi—any kind of an alibi. Christy Mathewson, one of the game's greatest pitchers, once explained why he felt our national pastime has so many "Alibi Ikes": "The alibi often helps a player with an inferiority complex to keep part of his self-respect and part of his confidence," said Mathewson. "He may be kidding himself, but there are certain types that need this support, or they would break down completely."

Famed writer Grantland Rice agreed in a broader sense. "If all alibis were suppressed," he once wrote, "and we all had to admit that every failure was our own fault, what a dejected race we would be! After all, an alibi rarely does any harm—because no one believes it!"

WHO CARES WHAT IT COSTS?

In the early days of the American League–National League hostilities, obtaining tickets to a World Series game was as hard as it is today. The first World Series played under a board of commission authorized by both leagues was in 1905, and one of the major worries was that the crowds would be too large.

"So great was the demand for seats . . . that the Board of Commission wisely" increased the price of admission in an effort to encourage fans to stay at home, reported the 1906 *Spalding Guide*. The idea didn't work. "Despite their efforts in this direction," the guide reported, "the attendance was such as to crowd the fields to repletion, both at New York and Philadelphia; all previous attendance records being placed in the background."

And what were the upped prices to discourage the fans? The five games drew 91,723 paying customers, and total receipts were $68,435. That figures out to an average admission price of seventy-five cents!

THE TEAM WITH THE ROLLING FENCE

After World War II, a number of major-league clubs moved their fences in a bit closer in a blatant effort to hike their team's home-run production. In retaliation,

Clark Griffith, who owned the Washington Senators, half-jokingly threatened to put the fence at Griffith Stadium on rollers and move it in or out, depending on the opposition's power hitters.

The idea wasn't as farfetched as it sounds. Griffith got the idea from a commanding officer at the Norfolk, Virginia, naval base, who ordered the facility's baseball team to win—or else. Consequently, the

Mickey Mantle at the height of his batting career.

team's backers quietly erected a portable outfield fence, and it was moved either forward or backward during the night by Seabees in an apparently successful effort to stop opposition hitters.

• • •

By the way, at the start of the 1948 season, Griffith briefly joined the parade and moved the left-field wall of Griffith Stadium closer to the plate and put in some temporary seats. In the season's opening game, Yankee pitcher Allie Reynolds and teammate Tommy Henrich crashed home runs into the temporary seats.

During the night, the temporary seats were removed, and the 400-foot distance was restored. The next day, Joe DiMaggio cracked two tremendous flies that were snagged just in front of the wall. "I swung too late," DiMaggio laughingly observed, "twenty-four hours too late."

THE REASON MANTLE BECAME A SWITCH HITTER

Mickey Mantle once explained the real reason he became one of baseball's greatest switch hitters. Mantle said his grandfather was a right-hander and his father was a left-hander. They each started teaching him how to bat when Mickey was only five years old, and Mickey would switch from the right to the left side of the plate, according to whether Dad or Grandpa was throwing.

WOULD THE YANKEES HAVE VOTED TO KEEP BILLY MARTIN?

Baseball's most hallowed trait is tradition. Virtually all of the changes in the game have been made slowly and grudgingly during the last 100 years or so.

It's too bad that the game's mossbacked conservatives weren't around to preserve one of baseball's original rules for selecting players. It certainly would have added an interesting wrinkle to today's games.

In 1868, when baseball first gained status as our national pastime, the Model Constitution for a Base Ball Club called for the players to be selected this way:

Early in the spring, the club's board of directors would meet and select five players, who, in turn, would pick four other players "to constitute a 'first nine,'" according to the rules. These nine players then would elect their captain (or manager), as well as "five substitutes, from whom the captain shall fill any vacancies by absence of members of the 'nine.'" The five subs would pick four other players for the "second nine," along with a captain for the reserves.

Then the rules added another interesting twist. Suppose one of the players on the first team suddenly develops a batting slump or it turns out that he's not performing as well as expected. It would seem logical that the captain could bench him and call on one of the reserves. Nope.

"It shall require," said the Model Constitution, "the vote of six of the 'nine' (at a meeting of which each member thereof shall be notified twenty-four hours previously) to pass a vote to retire one of its members." Then the players were required to cast "a majority of votes of those still present" to select a replacement from the reserve team.

The Model Constitution also granted the two captains strong authority. They "shall have absolute direction of the game, appoint a scorer, designate the positions each player shall have in the field, giving preference in each position to members, which position cannot be changed with out the captains' consent."

To top it off, the captains also selected the umpire. The rules said the ump "shall settle all disputes and differences relative to the game, and direct the scorer to note in the score book, under the head of 'Remarks,' all violations of the rules of the game or by-laws of the club. From the decision of the umpire there can be no appeal."

The rules for selecting the players had a relatively short life. Perhaps it's a pity. Just imagine what it would be like if they were in effect today. Imagine the apoplexy they would cause George Steinbrenner!

A CAREER TRAVELER

The juggling of major-league franchises from one city to another in the 1950s and 1960s had an unusual effect on the career of veteran infielder Eddie Mathews.

Mathews played with Atlanta in the minor leagues in the early 1950s and with Atlanta in the majors in the 1960s. He also played with Milwaukee in the minors in 1951 and with Milwaukee in the majors during the middle and late fifties. And, of course, Mathews also played with the Braves in three different cities—Boston, Milwaukee, and Atlanta.

THE GAME THAT TOOK MONTHS TO DECIDE

It once took thirty-seven innings and nearly four months to decide an American Association game between Minneapolis and Indianapolis in 1913. The two teams first met on April 25, and the score was tied 1–1 when rain halted play at the end of six innings. A playoff was scheduled for June 15, and this time darkness ended a 6–6 deadlock after nine frames. On August 7, another playoff was knotted 2–2 when play was stopped because of darkness after the thirteenth inning. Another playoff was scheduled for the next day—and this time, Minneapolis won 11–1 in nine innings.

AN EMBARRASSING REPLACEMENT

As an eighteen-year-old rookie, Freddie Lindstrom suffered one of the greatest embarrassments that a batter can face: he had a pitcher pinch hit for him in his first World Series game in 1924. Lindstrom had gone zero for five when he was replaced by pitcher John Bentley, who then drew a walk in the twelfth inning.

After the fourth and fifth games of the Series, however, there was no chance that a pitcher—or anyone else—would pinch hit for the New York Giants' teenager: Lindstrom totaled seven hits in those two contests.

RUTH GOT REVENGE FOR COBB'S NEEDLING

Ty Cobb and Babe Ruth became embroiled in a feud in 1921, and Cobb—an accomplished needler—repeatedly got the best of the Babe in their vocal exchanges. But Ruth found a way to get revenge. Although he hadn't pitched in three years, Ruth persuaded Yankee manager Miller Huggins to let him pitch against Cobb. Babe walked Cobb on his first trip to the plate. The next time up, Ruth whisked three strikes past Cobb, whereupon he signaled for a relief pitcher and trotted back to right field!

LIGHTNING SETTLED OUTCOME OF A GAME

Lightning once helped settle a semipro game. The two teams were scoreless in the thirteenth inning of the game in Cincinnati on August 15, 1909, and the rightfielder was poised to scoop up a grounder and hold the hitter to two bases, when lightning suddenly struck near the ball. The fielder raced off, and the ball rolled away, permitting the decisive run to score.

Half-burned, the ball fell to pieces when it eventually was retrieved.

A RALLY THAT REALLY WAS A RALLY

One of the joys of baseball is that one can never tell just what may happen in a few short minutes. A key example is a National League game in 1894 between Boston and Baltimore. The lead repeatedly changed hands during the first nine innings, with neither team able to build more than a one-run advantage. Then, wham, in the top of the ninth, Boston scored sixteen runs to win 25–9.

RUTH'S DEBUT WAS VIRTUALLY IGNORED

Babe Ruth was baseball's biggest drawing card, attracting millions to major-league parks—yet his debut as a pro drew one of the smallest crowds on record. Ruth was a pitcher when he broke in with a victory for Baltimore of the International League in 1914. Baltimore also had a club in the Federal League, which made a short-lived attempt to operate as a third major league, and it cut into attendance for the International League club. The paying customers for Ruth's first pro performance numbered exactly seventeen!

HE STOLE THIRD WITH BASES FULL—AND GOT AWAY WITH IT

Stealing third base with the bases full sounds like one of the most stupid things that a player can do—but one runner actually got away with it. Ray McGee of San Francisco did it in a Pacific Coast League game with Salt Lake City on June 21, 1917. McGee was safe, and the runner on third scored when the umpire called a balk on the pitcher.

POPULAR PLAYS WERE IMPROMPTU INNOVATIONS

Three of baseball's most popular plays—the bunt, the steal, and the double play—were all impromptu innovations. And when the three plays were executed for the first time, each was greeted with consternation.

The bunt was used for the first time in 1866, when a team called the Brooklyn Atlantics was unable to solve the opposition pitcher's speedy delivery. Dickey Pearce then stepped to the plate, and when the pitcher delivered a fast one, Pearce quickly slipped his right hand up the stalk of the old-fashioned bat and deliberately let ball strike bat. The opposition was so stunned by the maneuver that no one reacted—until Pearce had reached first. Word of Pearce's strange way of hitting spread quickly, and within weeks most of the teams in existence had adopted the bunt.

The first steal was tried in 1865, when Eddie Culthbert of the Philadelphia Keystones was on second base in a game with the Atlantics. Culthbert, who was familiar with the rules, suddenly was inspired to light out for third base. It set off a howl of protest from the opposition; the game was stopped. "Show me something in the rules which says I cannot steal a base," Culthbert demanded, thus coining the word still used today.

Someone hauled out a rule book, and sure enough, the rules made no mention that players couldn't swipe a base. Within weeks, everyone was attempting steals. The next year, Bob Addy of the Rockfords of Illinois came up with the idea that it would be a heck of a lot harder to catch a player trying to steal a base if the player slid into the base. Again, the idea caught on—and before season's end, the sliding steal was part of every team's repertoire.

The double play didn't arrive until June 14, 1870,

and the Atlantics were involved again, this time in a game with the Cincinnati Red Stockings. In the tenth inning of a tied game with runners on first and second, a Brooklyn batter popped up to George Wright at second base. Instead of catching the ball, Wright trapped it, then threw the ball to third to nab one runner. The third baseman whipped the ball back to second base to get the second out.

Brooklyn's players screamed in anger that the play was illegal, but when the rule book was trotted out again, it displayed no prohibition against retiring two runners on one play. Again, the play quickly became a routine part of the game, although the infield-fly rule was later established to prevent infielders from purposely trapping a ball.

RIGNEY WALKED NEARLY NINE MILES TO THE MOUND

One of the charms of baseball is that there is a statistic for just about every conceivable activity in the game. In the 1962 season, one person actually kept track of the number of visits Los Angeles Angels manager Billy Rigney made from the dugout to the pitching mound, then calculated that Rigney walked 46,470 feet—nearly nine miles—during those trips.

DIMAGGIO WASTED LITTLE TIME STARTING NEW HITTING STRING

Virtually every baseball fan knows that Joe DiMaggio had a fifty-six-game hitting streak in 1941. But few realize that after his string was halted by Cleveland on July 17, DiMaggio started a new streak that lasted until August 3. All told, DiMaggio hit safely in seventy-two out of seventy-three games.

Joe DiMaggio (1941).

SPEAKER WAS TRADED
FOR BOSTON'S EXPENSES

When Boston completed spring training at Little Rock, Arkansas, in 1908, Red Sox officials suddenly discovered that they didn't have enough money to pay the Little Rock minor-league team for use of its park and other incidental costs of the training season.

To satisfy the claim, the Red Sox turned over a young rookie named Tris Speaker to the local team. Fortunately, the Red Sox left him with the stipulation that he could be reclaimed for $500—and the Red Sox were more than delighted to shell out that amount to regain Speaker after he quickly ran up a league-leading .350 batting average for Little Rock.

Speaker, of course, went on to become one of baseball's all-time greats, posting a lifetime batting average of .344 during his twenty-two-year tenure in the American League.

PLAYER BELONGED TO THREE TEAMS
IN TWO DAYS

Gail Henley holds the dubious distinction of once belonging to three major-league teams during a forty-four-hour period—and he never got to play for any of them the next season. The New York Giants recalled Henley from Tulsa, Oklahoma, on October 13, 1952, and immediately traded him to Cincinnati for pitcher Frank Hiller. The next day, the Reds swapped Henley, an outfielder, to Pittsburgh, along with catcher Joe Rossi and outfielder Cal Abrams, for outfielder Gus Bell.

The Pirates shipped Henley to their New Orleans farm team before the start of the next season. It wasn't until two years later that Henley got his first—and last—chance in the majors. He hit .300 in fourteen games for Pittsburgh but nonetheless was shunted back to the minors, never to return.

BASEBALL'S MOST EVENLY MATCHED GAME

There couldn't have been a more evenly matched game than the one in which Pittsburgh took on Brooklyn on August 13, 1910, in a game called after nine innings because of darkness. The two teams came out dead even in virtually every statistic. Look at the totals:

	AB	R	H	PO	A	E
Pittsburgh	38	8	13	27	12	2
Brooklyn	38	8	13	27	12	2

And that's not all. Each team had ten players in the lineup, including two pitchers. The opposing pitchers struck out the same number of batsmen (five), allowed the same number of walks (three), and hit the same number of batters (one).

Each of the catchers had a passed ball. Each of the

second basemen, John Miller of Pittsburgh and John Hummel of Brooklyn, had two hits and two runs. Each of the shortstops, Honus Wagner of the Pirates and Pryor McElveen of the Dodgers, collected two singles and scored no runs.

THE FOUR-SIDED BAT

Major-league baseball once experimented with the idea of using a four-sided bat. In 1881, the innovation was hailed as a great boon to the pastime, according to the *Baseball Guide* of that year.

"The change from the round to the four-sided bat is to enable the batsman to 'place' the ball better," explained the editor of the *Guide*. "With skilled handling of a four-sided bat the batsman ought to be able to 'place' the ball with ease—that is, send it to any particular direction he chooses. The use of the new bat certainly promises a larger percentage of base hits."

The extra base hits, however, failed to materialize, and baseball quickly returned to using the rounded bat.

THERE WAS A REASON FOR THE LONG GAME

In the early 1940s, officials of the Cotton State League decided that baseball games were dragging on too long and ordered all umpires to report to the league president the precise reason when any game lasted more than two hours. When Hot Springs, Arkansas, and Pine Bluff, Arkansas, engaged in a game that took nearly three hours in May of 1940, the two umpires wired the league president the following one-phrase explanation of why the game took so long: "Twenty-four hits, twenty-one runs, seventeen bases on balls, nine errors, twenty-three left on base, six pitchers."

• • •

Baseball officials have been concerned for years about ways to speed up games.

In a special experiment to determine the minimum time for playing a regulation baseball game, Atlanta and Mobile of the Southern Association once completed a full nine innings in thirty-two minutes! Under the rules for the September 17, 1910, game at Atlanta, players were required to run to and from their positions. They were forbidden such time-killing practices as pounding dirt from spikes, arguing with umpires, gathering around the mound for conferences, or doing virtually anything that would slow the game. For the record, Mobile scored a run in the ninth inning to win 2–1.

• • •

In the formative years of the American League, loop president Ban Johnson, perturbed about long games, sent a form letter to all umpires, asking how, in their opinion, playing times could be shortened. Umpire Tim Hurst answered, "I think the most practical way to shorten games would be to cut them down to seven innings."

HOW TO TENDERIZE A STEAK

The first large catcher's mitts weren't permitted in baseball until 1891. Before that time, catchers, like their teammates, were required to wear "finger gloves," which provided scant protection from a hard-thrown ball.

But one big-league catcher, Frank (Silver) Flint of the Chicago White Stockings, came up with a way to protect his hands. Before the game, he'd stuff a large piece of raw beefsteak between the glove and his palm to ease the sting of fast pitches. It must have worked—the idea was quickly picked up by many other catchers in an era when beefsteak cost only a few cents per pound.

SPAHN SPURNED $100,000 FOR SECURITY

Warren Spahn had a miserable season for the 1952 Boston Braves, winning only fourteen of thirty-three decisions. At season's end, Spahn's contract called for a salary cut, but Spahn rejected that idea. In an effort to break his holdout, the Braves offered him a special deal: he would receive ten cents for every admission over 800,000 during the 1953 season. Spahn turned down that offer, figuring there was no way that 800,000 fans would turn out in Boston that season, so he settled on a pact calling for only a modest cut.

Spahn was right about Boston's 1953 attendance. No one showed up for a Braves game there, because during the winter the team suddenly moved to Milwaukee, where it attracted 1,800,000 customers. If Spahn had accepted the dime-per-customer offer, he would have received an extra $100,000.

SUNDAY BASEBALL

Sunday baseball games are taken so much for granted today that it's hard to believe that both the National and American leagues were well into their mature years when Sabbath contests were still outlawed in some of their top-drawing cities.

The Sunday prohibitions forced many a baseball executive, in both the majors and the minors, to come up with some devilish chicanery to field their athletes on what is normally the sport's largest-drawing day.

It wasn't until 1934 that Pennsylvania repealed its blue laws, thus permitting its three big-league clubs—Pittsburgh, the Philadelphia Athletics, and the Phillies—to schedule home games on Sunday. As late as 1928, the Boston Braves and Red Sox were invariable Sunday visitors because of Massachusetts law.

At the time, in addition to Pennsylvania, at least fifteen other states banned Sunday baseball—although baseball executives quickly found ways of evading the laws through legal loopholes.

Most of the statutes prohibited only the Sunday competition at which admission was charged; others prohibited all forms of labor on Sunday, except those involving charity or necessity. Consequently, the scorecard plan of admission was used in many cities, with the cards selling for the then highly inflated price of fifty cents or more. Some clubs threw open the gates but bluntly made it clear that "free-will" contributions were expected.

In a number of instances, Sunday ball was banned only within city limits. Detroit and Minneapolis were among the clubs that built or leased parks outside the limits for use only on Sundays. The New York Giants escaped the New York law by playing Sunday games at Weehawken, New Jersey.

The Sunday games were marked by one distinguishing characteristic: fans were requested to maintain serene dignity, because there was always the fear that anti-Sunday activists would have players and spectators arrested for disturbing the peace.

In fact, one Sunday exhibition game between the New York Highlanders (later the Yankees) and Jersey City of the Eastern League in 1909 was played before a large crowd in virtual silence. Before the game, club officials issued cards to the patrons, pleading with them to refrain from cheering or making any loud noise. The crowd obeyed the request. Observers said it was a strange sensation to see players making spectacular plays or hits, followed by nothing but deathly quiet.

The Yankees' crosstown rivals, the Giants, ran into problems when they played their first game at the Polo Grounds in 1918, contending it was a military benefit for the war effort. Managers John McGraw of the Giants and Christy Mathewson of Cincinnati were arrested. The charges were dropped, but it wasn't until 1919 that Sunday baseball was officially allowed in New York State.

The National League refused to schedule any Sunday games during its first sixteen years, although its strongest rival, the American Association, formed as a major league in 1882, decided to flout the Sunday law.

In 1892, the National came around to Sunday competition, but the decision wasn't unanimous: Pittsburgh and New York didn't agree to play on Sundays—except on the road—until 1898, and Boston and Philadelphia declined Sunday games until 1903. As late as 1918, only three National League cities—Chicago, Cincinnati, and St. Louis—played Sunday games at home.

Even when Sunday ball began, a number of players, for personal reasons, refused to perform on the Sabbath. Mathewson never touched a ball on Sunday in nineteen pro seasons, seventeen of them with the Giants.

Branch Rickey refused to have anything to do with baseball on a Sunday during nearly forty years as a player, manager, and club official. When he was a manager—for the St. Louis Browns during 1913–1915, then for the Cardinals during 1919–1925—Rickey turned the boss-man duties over to someone else on Sunday. The only exception that Rickey ever made was when he attended a war-bond drive held in connection with a Sunday game in 1943.

• • •

Cy Young had the same compunction, but he once found justification in the Bible to make an exception and pitch on a Sunday. Young was hurling for Cleveland when the club traveled to St. Louis for a Sunday game.

Manager Pat Tebeau was in a quandary. His pitching staff was crippled with injuries, and the only hurler he had available was an untried rookie. Yet

Tebeau had such respect for Cy's religious convictions that he didn't even dream of asking Young to make an exception for what was a vital showdown.

But when Tebeau arrived at the park, he discovered that Young already was warming up and said he planned to pitch. After notching a victory, Young explained his motivation. "I found justification in the Scriptures," he said solemnly. "I was reading the Good Book last night, and what did I find but this: 'If thy neighbor's ox or ass shall fall into a pit on Sunday, thou shalt help him out.'

"That gave me the justification and inspiration. I don't know any bigger jackass than Tebeau, and he was in an awful hole. So I just thought it was up to me to help him out."

● ● ●

Many minor-league teams challenged the Sunday baseball ban in the courts, generally without success. One team, Logansport, Indiana, of the Northern Indiana League, did score a court victory—albeit an embarrassing one.

Manager Charles Sellers was hauled before a Judge Gifford after a local minister complained that a Sunday game between Logansport and Huntington had been played nearer to his church than the Indiana law permitted.

The judge listened to testimony from three witnesses, who also mentioned how poorly the game had been played. Judge Gifford pondered for a few minutes, then announced, "The evidence shows that the exhibition was so bad it could not be considered a ball game." And with that, he tossed the case out of court.

AIKEN WAS A RECORD TABLE TURNER

Roy Aiken is undoubtedly the only professional player who hit into an unassisted triple play and also personally executed a solo triple play. Aiken was a third baseman for Los Angeles of the Pacific Coast League in 1911 when he came to bat against Vernon with runners on first and second. He cracked a low liner, which was caught by centerfielder Walter Carlisle. Carlisle had time to race to second, then to first to retire both runners, who had taken off at what appeared to be a sure hit.

The next year, Aiken was traded to Waco of the Texas League, and it was in a game there that he got even. He caught a line drive, touched third to double off one runner, then chased down another runner to complete the unaided triple play.

PHILLIES HAD TWO MANAGERS FOR ONE GAME

The 1945 Philadelphia Phillies started one game under one manager and finished it under another manager! Fat Freddie Fitzsimmons was managing the Phils on June 3 when they had built an 11–9 lead over Pittsburgh in a game that was suspended after six innings. Fitzsimmons was later fired and replaced by Ben Chapman, who was managing when the suspended game was finished on July 13.

NEW YORK BLEW A CHANCE TO GET THE GREATEST PLAYER

The New York Yankees were able to land the services of Babe Ruth because of some financial problems of the Boston Red Sox owner in 1920. But, fifteen years before that, the New Yorkers completely blew what would have been one of the greatest trades in baseball history.

In 1905, New York and Detroit were working on a one-for-one trade on a couple of players whose names have been lost to baseball oblivion. The New York management, however, decided that the deal wasn't sweet enough, so Detroit offered to toss in a young outfielder.

Ty Cobb (1928).

But the New York management wasn't particularly impressed by the young fielder. He was only nineteen years old and had managed a mere .240 average in his first season with Detroit. Thanks but no thanks, said the New York bosses—and they called off negotiations. That young fielder was Ty Cobb.

BASEBALL'S FIRST WORLD SERIES

How about a World Series in which the two league champions tied in the first game of the postseason classic, continued to three victories apiece—then called the whole thing off and split the gate receipts fifty-fifty?

Or what about a World Series in which the two major-league winners agreed to a battle for the championship on a winner-take-all basis?

As ridiculous as it sounds, two World Series were played under such circumstances. No, you won't find the evidence if you look only in the records from 1903, when the American-National hostilities began, through the present.

Actually, World Series competition was begun in 1882 (although it didn't gain genuine recognition until 1885), and some of those inaugural interleague affairs were dillies.

Chicago's National League champions and Cincinnati, winner of the pennant in the American Association (then considered a major league), engaged in the first interleague championship showdown in 1882.

After splitting the first two games, Cincinnati's players were bluntly notified by the Association president that they would be expelled from the league if they persisted in playing a club from the rival league. They called off the whole thing.

But under the prodding of fans and sportswriters, another postseason showdown was given a try in 1884, although it was officially labeled an "informal exhibition series." It was supposed to be a best-two-out-of-three-games series, and the New York Metropolitans—champions of the American Association—lost all three games to Providence of the National League. It may seem a bit strange that they played that unneeded third game, since the winner of two contests was to be proclaimed champion. But in those early World Series days, the rivals played out the scheduled games regardless of the standings.

In 1885 Chicago and St. Louis were scheduled for seven games. Each won three and tied one. But they didn't play it off—they were scheduled for exactly seven games, and by golly, that's all they'd play! The $1,000 purse was divided evenly, instead of what was supposed to have been a sixty-forty split.

In 1887 Detroit and St. Louis agreed to a fifteen-game series. Detroit won eight of the first eleven games, but the teams played four more games, as meaningless as they were. Contributing to this prolonged competition was the surge of popularity of the World Series. It was decided that the Series wouldn't be confined to the home fields of the two combatants. The title clashes were played in St. Louis, Detroit, Pittsburgh, Brooklyn, New York, Philadelphia, Boston, Washington, and Baltimore.

In 1886, St. Louis and Chicago agreed that the winner of their six-game classic would take all of the gate receipts. St. Louis lost two of the first three games but then roared back with three straight victories.

The original World Series continued until 1891, when the National League absorbed the then-troubled American Association. The National League won four Series, the Association only one, and three—including the brief 1882 melee—were deadlocked.

The Temple Cup Series, baseball's climax from 1894 through 1897, was not an interleague competition. It involved the first- and second-place clubs of the National circuit, which had swelled to twelve teams because of the addition of several teams from the old American Association.

Strangely, the second-place teams won three of the four series. The first three years, Baltimore won the pennants and lost two playoffs. Then, in 1897, Baltimore finished second—and won the Temple Series from flag-winning Boston. The cup was donated by William Chase Temple of Pittsburgh as the prize in these best-four-out-of-seven-games series.

The substitute for a World Series in 1892 was the championship playoff after the National League's only split season. Boston won the first half with a 52–22 record; Cleveland took the final portion with a 53–23 mark.

The first game of the best-of-nine playoff at Cleveland was called because of darkness, with the score 0-0 in the eleventh inning. Then Boston won the next five 4-3, 3-2, 4-0, 12-7, and 8-3.

The 1884 series was the only one of the ancient classics to be swept in successive games. Providence won 6-0, 3-1, and 12-2.

Spalding's *Baseball Guide and Official League Book of 1886* wound up its summary of the rout with, "These games were too one-sided to be interesting." The guide neglected to mention the pitching record of Charles (Old Hoss) Radbourn, who on successive days hurled every victory and yielded not one base on balls.

● ● ●

Those early World Series of the eighties and nineties certainly weren't devoid of altercations. The sharpest flare-up occurred in the 1885 Series. All was placid and pleasant when Chicago of the National League and St. Louis of the Association opened their showdown. The players even indulged in a friendly field test of baserunning and ballteasing before the debut game.

The game itself ended in a 5-5 tie, and everyone was happy. The clubs moved from Chicago to St. Louis for game number two, appearing before an estimated crowd of 4,000 inestimably partisan souls. Hugh S. Fullerton, a veteran sportswriter of the era, said there were eight near-riots up to the end of the fifth inning, when Chicago had built a 4-2 lead.

The umpire was a target of unmerciful criticism from players and the vocal home team fans. Several times the Browns held up the game to hotly protest his decisions. But the ump was a brave man; he stood his ground before the hostile crowd and escaped unharmed . . . until the eighth inning.

Then, Fullerton reported, the White Stockings "got a runner on second base with one out. The batter hit a ball on the end of his bat. The ball, striking foul ground, was rolling and twisting while shouts of 'Foul!' sounded through the grounds.

"The St. Louis fielders who were running to field the ball stopped. The ball, twisting and squirming, took English on the grass, curved, and rolled into the diamond before it reached first base. The batter had crossed first place [base], the runner from second had raced across the plate."

Fullerton said the bewildered umpire hesitated. "Whether he made a decision or not has never been clear. He stated afterward that it was a fair ball and that the run scored."

The Browns rushed at the now-frightened umpire, who insisted that he had not called it a foul ball, "that it was Cap Anson [the Chicago manager and first baseman] who lifted his voice and yelled 'Foul!'" while the ball was still rolling.

"The angry Browns swarmed around the umpire, even Billy Sunday [who later gained fame as a popular evangelist] joining the rush. The crowd commenced to pour onto the field," but the umpire managed to escape from the park in all the commotion.

St. Louis manager Charlie Comiskey took his men to the clubhouse, "and the White Stockings were left in possession of the field," timidly claiming victory.

Both teams remained bewildered, however, because there was no higher authority to which the teams could appeal, and the umpire was hiding out in his hotel room.

At nine o'clock that night, the ump, from the sanctity of his hotel room, issued a ruling that the Browns had lost the game 9–0 on forfeit.

● ● ●

Boston, of the "upstart" American League formed in 1901, won the first modern World Series from Pittsburgh in 1903. Boston again won the American League title in 1904, but the National League champion New York Giants stoutly refused to take part in the postseason affair.

"I do not wish to endanger the standing of my team by sending it against a minor-league club," said John McGraw, manager of the Giants, although the real reason was probably retaliation and anger over the American League's decision to move its Baltimore franchise to New York. The team eventually became the Yankees.

But tempers cooled at the ensuing winter meeting. The two leagues reached a truce and an agreement to the annual postseason series, directed by a National Commission and under a code devised by John T. Brush, one of the Giants' officials, whose refusal to let his team play in the 1904 series touched off a storm of protests from fans and sportswriters.

In 1905, McGraw's Giants defeated Philadelphia four games to one, and the modern World Series was on the way to becoming an American tradition.

BASEBALL WAS NOT A SPORT FOR WOMEN!

In its infancy, baseball was strictly a man's sport, both for players and for observers. It was considered most improper for a woman even to show up as a witness at a professional ball game.

So it caused quite a stir in genteel New Orleans when a group of women there formed the Freeman's Female Baseball Club in the 1870s. The league got off to a near riotous start. The first game had just begun when a young man dashed out of the crowd, grabbed the shortstop, and tried to drag her off the field.

When she loudly and violently objected to this treatment, dozens of patrons leaped to the aid of the young woman and soundly beat the young man—until he had a chance to explain that he was the girl's brother and was trying to take her "home to ma" for making a public disgrace of herself!

PICKING SITES FOR WORLD SERIES WAS HAPHAZARD

It's almost amazing that the players and fans knew which park to attend during the first quarter-century of baseball's World Series. Until 1925, the site of the first game of the fall classic—and sometimes the last game—generally was determined by the flip of a coin. To complicate things even more, a variety of complex, sometimes unexplainable, patterns were used to decide where and how many of the "middle games" of the World Series were to be played—and the total number of games needed to decide the championship.

The first of the modern World Series, between the Boston Red Sox and Pittsburgh in 1903, was a best-of-nine affair that began with three games in Boston. The next four games were at Pittsburgh, before Pittsburgh wrapped it up in the eighth game at Boston.

It wasn't a bad system. But, after the Giants refused to play in the 1904 World Series, officials of both leagues got together to forge the rules for a permanent season-ending series to decide the champion of the world.

The problem was that the rules for the interleague classic left it up to the competing clubs to work out where they would play. The clubs responded by coming up with new ideas each year until 1914–1915, when the same pattern was used for two consecutive years.

In 1905, the Series opened on the Athletics' turf in Philadelphia for one game, switched to the New York Giants' home ground for one game, back to Philadelphia for one, then to New York for two more, in which the Giants won the title. Alternating game by game was no problem in 1906, when Chicago had its first and only monopoly on the series.

But the following year, the Cubs played the first three games in Chicago (one ended in a tie), then went to Detroit to complete their championship. The pairing was the same in 1908, but this time the opening game was in Detroit, then there were two games in Chicago before the fourth and the finishing fifth game in Detroit.

In 1909, when the Tigers lost their third straight Series, the first and second games were in Pittsburgh. The teams moved to Detroit for games three and four, back to Pittsburgh for game five, then to Detroit for the sixth and seventh games.

The Athletics played their first two games in Philadelphia in 1910, then completed their five-game triumph in Chicago. The A's and the New York Giants were the combatants in both the 1911 and 1912 World Series, and both Series were alternative game-by-game affairs.

The 1912 Series between the Giants and the Red Sox resumed the crazy-quilt pattern of play. First there was a game in New York, then two in Boston (the first a 6–6 tie), one more in New York, one in Boston, one in New York, and the last two in the home of the winning Red Sox.

Finally, in 1914 a consistent pattern began to emerge, when two games were played in one city, and two in the other city. That's as far as it went; the Braves swept all four games from the Athletics. In 1915 and 1916, the fifth game was played in the city where the first two games were played, because that's as long as either of those Series endured.

In 1917, it was back to the same old confusion. The first two games were played in Chicago, and the next two in New York. But then it was back to Chicago for one game, then back to New York for the sixth game, where the White Sox claimed the championship.

The 1918 fall classic was a one-trip affair because of World War I travel restrictions: the first three games were in Chicago, then Boston won the championship with three games on its own field.

The best-of-nine format was resurrected for baseball's most infamous World Series in 1919: games one and two were in Cincinnati; three, four, and five in Chicago; six and seven in Cincinnati; and the eighth and last in the "Black Sox" park.

The 1920 Series was another best-of-nine showdown, but only one trip was needed before the Indians won in seven games: three in Brooklyn and four in Cleveland. The 1921 Series, the last of the best-of-nine confrontations, and the 1922 and 1923 Series were all New York monopolies. Both clubs shared the Polo Grounds in 1921 and 1922, and the Giants served as the home team for each of the first games. The two teams then alternated as home teams. In 1923 the Yankees served as the home team in the World Series debut of their new stadium, followed by daily switches between the Polo Grounds and Yankee Stadium.

In 1924 the two-three-two pattern was used when Washington defeated the Giants four games to three, and, for the last time, a coin flip was used to decide the site of the opening game.

The National's champs were the coin-flipping champs—they won the first-game home rights in nine of the twelve World Series from 1911 through 1922. Despite that advantage, they weren't so fortunate on the field. The National League won only three of those home-start games, and one of them was the tainted 1919 World Series.

In 1925, officials of both leagues settled on the two-three-two system used today and decided that the opening games would alternate between leagues each year. But there were two interruptions in that sequence.

Chicago was slated to be the home team against

the Tigers in 1935, but Cubs officials asked that the opener be switched to Detroit in order to give the Cubs extra time to complete construction of some temporary bleachers. An adjustment also was made in 1936, when the Giants were permitted to start as hosts to the Yankees. Ever since, the National League champs have had the even-year opener, while the American League titlists have the odd-year opener.

The only other change since 1925 was dictated by World War II travel restrictions. In 1945, Detroit played at home for the first three games, then traveled to Chicago for four games and the title.

WHY GEHRIG WATCHED HIS LANGUAGE WHEN NEAR AN UMP

In public Lou Gehrig always modestly brushed off his consecutive-game record, which reached an astonishing total of 2,130. But privately, Gehrig's friends said, he was virtually obsessed with his achievement and insisted on playing with ailments and injuries that would ordinarily keep a player out of a lineup. Once he played three straight games with a high fever (his batting was superlative during that spell), and another time he played after he was knocked unconscious the day before.

But the streak also made Gehrig a Mr. Nice Guy around the umpires. Even when he felt he had a legitimate beef, he always took care to avoid conflict and carefully watched the language he used with the men in blue—for fear of being tossed out of a game and then being suspended!

Gehrig privately had a goal of playing in 2,500 straight games. But when he realized that the illness that was eventually to take his life was slowing him down and hurting the Yankees, he immediately pulled himself out of the lineup, goal or no goal.

Lou Gehrig, Christy Walsh, and Babe Ruth during
barnstorming days of the early 1930s.

A SIMPLE SOLUTION FOR HIGHER BATTING AVERAGES

A group of sportswriters once asked a major-league
manager what he thought could be done to increase
sluggish batting averages in the big leagues.

"I do not believe there is any great demand on the
part of the general public for an increase in hitting,"

the manager replied. "The fans have become accustomed to small scores and close games and have learned to like them.

"However, I think that, if it were desirable, the most simple course to increase batting would be to cut down pitching staffs. It stands to reason that a small staff of pitchers, each man working often and forced to go through with practically every game started by him because of an absence of reserve pitchers, would yield more hits than one who was not worked so hard."

The statement was made in 1917 by Miller Huggins, who only a few years later managed the New York Yankees, who had the greatest array of sluggers in one set of uniforms.

SIXTY-FIVE RUNS TO WIN

Amherst and Williams played a college baseball game on July 1, 1895, and the two teams came up with a rather unusual method to determine the winner: the first team to score sixty-five runs! It took Amherst twenty-six innings to achieve that total in winning 66–32.

TWENTY-FIVE CITIES HAD MAJOR-LEAGUE TEAMS A CENTURY AGO

There were more major-league baseball teams in 1884 than there are today, even after the expansion binge the majors conducted during the 1960s and 1970s. Thirty-four big-league teams represented twenty-five cities, a record total, in 1884.

New York, St. Louis, Cincinnati, Pittsburgh, Baltimore, Boston, Chicago, and Washington each had two teams in the three major leagues in existence that season. The Union Association gave a whirl at being a major league in 1884, but the experiment lasted through only one campaign.

At various times, the fledgling circuit had thirteen members, but only five of them played complete schedules—pennant-winning St. Louis, Cincinnati, Baltimore, Boston, and Washington. St. Paul was in for only eight games, Milwaukee and Pittsburgh eleven each, Wilmington for seventeen, and Altoona, Pennsylvania, for twenty-five. Other members were Philadelphia, Chicago, and Kansas City.

The National League played through the season with Providence, Boston, Buffalo, Chicago, New York, Philadelphia, Cleveland, and Detroit, finishing in that order. Washington was the only club that did not complete the season in the third major league, the American Association. It was replaced for the last forty-two games by a club labeled as Virginia. In order of finish, the teams were New York, Columbus, Louisville, St. Louis, Cincinnati, Baltimore, Philadelphia, Toledo, Brooklyn, Pittsburgh, Indianapolis, and Washington (Virginia).

MARIS WAS TOO SMALL

A scout for the Chicago Cubs was roaming the Dakota frontier one day in the 1950s, when he chanced to see a young player slam a couple of line drives in an amateur game in Fargo. He was so impressed with the kid that he sent the youngster into Chicago to display his talents before the Cubs' top brass at Wrigley Field. Observers in Chicago said the kid was OK, but he was much too small to be considered a major-league prospect—so he was sent back to the Dakotas.

The young man eventually did sign with Cleveland and was traded to Kansas City, then to New York, where in 1961 he accomplished what no other major leaguer has ever achieved: he hit sixty-one home runs in one season. His name was Roger Maris.

Roger Maris in 1961, the year he hit sixty-one home runs.

STAN, PUT YOURSELF IN THE LINEUP

When Stan Musial became general manager of St. Louis after his fabulous playing career, he was the only GM in baseball assigned a uniform. It was to please his mother, who lived in Pennsylvania. He had

Stan Musial (1943).

called his mother to tell her that he had been named general manager, and the first thing she asked was whether that made him the boss over the manager too. His mother was delighted when she was told that was the case—and she ordered Stan to put himself back on the active list and start playing again!

SENATOR HELPED SIGN KILLEBREW

Former U.S. Senator Herman Walker of Idaho played a key role in Harmon Killebrew's major-league career. Walker was impressed when he saw Harmon play a game in Idaho and later contacted Washington Senators officials, who signed the young prospect. Killebrew hit more than 500 homers in his career.

AWRY BOOK LISTING

A few years ago a major Los Angeles bookstore issued a catalog listing "fiction—all sports." One entry, among the baseball books, was *Catcher in the Rye* by J. D. Salinger.

HANDSHAKE SAVED KOUFAX FOR DODGERS

Los Angeles Dodgers great Sandy Koufax could have been a Milwaukee Brave, if Sandy's father hadn't believed in the sincerity of a handshake. The Dodgers dealt with Koufax's dad, an attorney, because the hard-throwing pitcher was a minor. On the basis of a handshake, the Dodgers and the elder Koufax agreed upon a $14,000 bonus for Sandy.

Before the actual contract-signing, however, the Braves offered Koufax $35,000 to sign with them. Legally, Koufax's father could have accepted the Braves' bonus for Sandy—but because he had shaken hands on the agreement, he kept his word with the Dodgers.

PLAYER INFLATION

In this age of millionaire baseball players, it's hard to believe that in 1958 the payroll for all players in the eight-team American League totaled $3.7 million!

BASEBALL GAVE HIM A HEADACHE

Hal Trosky left little doubt that he had a glowing future in baseball when he broke in as a first baseman with the Cleveland Indians in 1934. He hit thirty-five home runs, a record for rookies then, and knocked in a rookie-record 142 runs. Trosky continued to produce headaches for opposing pitchers through 1941.

The trouble was, baseball also was causing head-

Hal Trosky of Cleveland.
Baseball gave him
a headache.

aches for Hal. Simply playing the game brought on
such terrible migraines that in 1942 he was forced to
quit baseball. Trosky made a couple of comeback
attempts with the White Sox in 1944 and 1946, but
both tries ended in failure. Trosky said that once he
left baseball, the migraines vanished.

9
SURPRISING ANSWERS TO OFT-ASKED QUESTIONS

HOW DID THE BABE RUTH "POINTED HOMER" MYTH GET STARTED?

There is no legend in baseball more enduring nor more beloved than the story that Babe Ruth "called" his famous home run against the Chicago Cubs in the 1932 World Series. In historic defiance to the terrible taunting he was receiving from the Cubs, so the story goes, the mighty Babe majestically pointed to the center-field stands of Wrigley Field—and on the next pitch smashed a towering home run to the exact spot!

It's a magnificent story. But it's also a fairy tale. The Babe *never* called his homer—and in all likelihood, the home run itself was a *fluke*. Ruth was undoubtedly trying to slice a sizzling liner directly into the Chicago dugout—and the homer was as much a surprise to the Babe as it was to everyone else in the park.

Yes, you've probably read about the famous homer in hundreds of baseball books and articles during the last half-century. Yes, you've seen dozens of paintings of the legendary point, including, perhaps, the famous one hanging in baseball's Hall of Fame. Yes, Ruth himself talked about his historic homer many times during the late 1930s and early 1940s. Yes, you've seen the famous incident in movie and television biographies of the Babe or in an opening segment of NBC's coverage of the World Series. And yes, the *Village Voice* did publish pictures in 1988 taken from a home movie showing the Babe appearing to point.

That all sounds like pretty convincing evidence that the story is true.

Nonetheless, the "called homer" has as much validity as the story of Goldilocks and the Three Bears! The gesturing, bat pointing, and hand motions the Babe performed during that fifth inning of the third game of the fall classic had nothing to do with a potential home run.

The Babe's only pointing that day pertaining to a home run was *after* Ruth took his left-field position in the second inning following his first-inning home run. In response to vociferous booing from the bleachers, Ruth defiantly pointed to the right-center-field area where his homer had landed.

To put things in proper perspective, the '32 Series, swept by the Yankees in four games, was a bitter rivalry. Ruth was a particular target of the catcalls: while Cubs fans repeatedly razzed and booed Babe, the Chicago bench directed a steady stream of vulgar and uncomplimentary remarks toward Ruth.

Now let's dissect the legend step by step.

First, there's Charlie Root, the Cub pitcher who served the home-run ball. Root conceded that the Babe made antagonistic gestures toward the Cub dugout and that Ruth held up one finger after the first strike and two fingers after the second—both called. Root said Babe even swung out his bat with one hand—but noted it was a habit he performed before each pitch.

Root said that if the Babe had had the audacity to point or call his homer, Root would have wasted a

Charlie Root (1950).
Root said Babe Ruth
did not call his famous
World Series homer.

pitch "as hard as I could throw" directly at the Babe. "He would have been sitting on the ground—if he could have gotten out of the way of the pitch in time, said Root, "and anybody who knew me then knows that I would have done it." (Mention of the Ruthian homer always brought out a torrent of rage from Root, who angrily turned down some pretty hefty cash in 1948 to play himself in the movie *The Babe Ruth Story*, which, of course, featured the called homer.)

Root said he never talked to Babe about the homer. In fact, Root said, he didn't even hear about the legend until long after the Series was over.

Then there was the huge cadre of veteran sportswriters covering the game. One of them was the late Herbert Simons, who later became the publisher-editor of *Baseball Digest*. Simons, covering the series for the Chicago *American*, witnessed the game from the center section of the press box, hung from the second deck directly behind home plate.

He said he was less than 150 feet from Ruth, and "he did not call his shot." After the legend surfaced, Simons tried to track down just how it started. He said he talked with scores of veteran sportswriters who had witnessed the game. None said they actually had seen the Babe call his shot.

Simons also noted that Daymon Runyon, who was sometimes inclined to add a bit of dramatic flair to his stories, made no mention of the called homer in his two-and-a-half column story in the next morning's New York *American*. Nor was there any mention of the incident by scores of other veteran sportswriters, who had a variety of vantage points of the Babe from the press box.

There were several exceptions. John Drebinger's story in the next day's *New York Times* said that when Ruth came up in the fifth "in no mistaken motions the Babe notified the crowd that the nature of his retaliation would be a wallop" out of the park. However, there was no mention of an actual "called shot." Thirty years later, Drebinger formally retracted his 1932 story.

In a feature story written by another *New York Times* writer, William E. Brandt, who interviewed the Babe after the game, there was nary a mention of a called homer. Noting that both he and Lou Gehrig had each hit two homers, Ruth shrugged it off with, "The wind was with us, that's all. Anytime they let us hit into the air, zowie—the wind did the rest."

A West Coast reporter is said to have written that the Babe called his homer. But veteran sportswriters noted that Drebinger and the West Coast writer were basing their statements on pure speculation, because they had to file stories as quickly as possible after the game to meet first-edition deadlines for the next day's Sunday papers.

The Sporting News, considered baseball's bible, devoted a huge proportion of its October 6, 1932, issue to the four World Series games. It provided detailed and lengthy coverage of each game, plus feature stories and gossip on each game.

In its story on the third game, *The Sporting News* said this about the fifth inning: "Ruth quickly broke the tie with one of the longest homers at the park. After Sewell had grounded to Jurges, the Babe sent a line drive over the bleacher screen in center field and as he circled the bases, he taunted the Cubs, who had been wise-cracking about his inability to bend."

In its detailed, inning-by-inning report of the game, *The Sporting News* said simply, "Ruth hit a home run which cleared the wire fence in center. Gehrig then hit a home run which hit the flag pole in right field."

Ruth's and Gehrig's superlative Series hitting was mentioned numerous times in various stories and columns, and there was a brief mention of Babe's second-inning "pointing" incident after his first-inning homer. But nowhere in the massive coverage was there even the slightest hint that Ruth pointed or called his homer.

Remember, the men covering that Series earned their living by dint of watching big-league games. They were constantly on the lookout for the strange, the different, the unusual to enhance their game stories. So it seems simply incredible that the Babe could point to the outfield and call his homer with virtually every sportswriter missing it.

But what about those photos of the Babe pointing? Ralph J. Knudsen, who was sitting with Jess Halstead, secretary of the Chicago Stock Exchange (now the Midwest Stock Exchange), in a front-row box seat on the first-base side of the diamond, has an answer for that. Knudsen said that, from his vantage point, he quickly grasped that Ruth was motioning to call attention to a temporary wooden railing atop the outfield wall. One end of one of the railing's boards had come loose and was swinging like a pendulum.

Babe Ruth, Jimmie Foxx, and Lou Gehrig, three of baseball's all-time great hitters (1930).

Knudsen said Ruth pointed toward the board in an effort to alert park personnel that it might fall onto the playing field.

History and some sportswriters may have misinterpreted Ruth's gestures, but Cubs park employees did not. They immediately rushed to the fence and nailed back the swinging board.

It wasn't until after the Series was over that the

legend gained momentum. The New York *World-Tele-gram*'s Joe Williams contended that Ruth had called his shot and "pointed to center field" before his homer. A couple of days later, Bill Corum of the New York *Journal* wrote of Babe's called-shot homer—although Corum had neglected to mention the feat in his coverage of the game for the October 2 edition of the paper. Tom Meany of the *World-Telegram* also wrote a post-Series story crediting the Babe with calling his shot.

Then, in late October, Ruth appeared on a radio show and for the first time claimed credit for the called homer. Later that winter, at a New York Athletic Club dinner, he said it was the most thrilling experience of his life.

Ruth repeated the story many times during the late thirties and early forties, but each telling was slightly different from the one before. By the midforties, Babe's story was that he had just waved his hand at the outfield. In an interview with a reporter just months before his death, the Babe repeatedly brushed aside questions about the called homer, mumbling something to the effect that it had been overplayed.

One can only speculate, but Ruth probably latched onto the story simply because it was a humdinger. The Cubs players and fans had treated the Babe unmercifully, and the tale of a called home run added to the wound of the Yankees' four-game sweep. More important, it also dramatically lifted the Babe back into the spotlight at a time when his worn-out body was facing the fading days of his playing career.

In all probability, the Babe actually was attempting to silence his Cubs critics with a deliberate searing foul directly into the Chicago dugout. Lou Gehrig once told a friend that that's what he thought Ruth attempted, noting that the Babe had executed the practice many times in his earlier playing days.

Even Ruth is reported to have admitted years later that he intended to smash a shot down "the throat of Charlie Grimm," the Cubs' manager. But Root's third pitch fooled Ruth. Root had picked up the first two called strikes with belt-high, down-the-middle fastballs. The home-run pitch, Root said, was a change-up curve intended to throw Ruth off stride.

The pitch was only about a foot off the ground and was a good four inches outside the plate, said Root. Apparently, the surprise pitch, coupled with Ruth's aging reflexes, didn't permit the Babe to get his heavy bat around in time. Instead of hooking a shot into the dugout, Ruth hit the ball squarely and sent it high into the heavy wind currents that were blowing toward center field!

Now, about those shots of Babe pointing that you saw on TV. NBC-TV used an actor's hand to "re-create" the famous pointing incident, and this was included in a collage of famous baseball scenes once used to open the network's coverage of the World Series.

The Arts and Entertainment cable network went even further in deception when it presented a biography of Ruth in the fall of 1988. It used two sequences from a different game to show Babe swinging and missing two strikes. Then an actor's hand and arm were dramatically displayed, with the sky as the background, pointing the called shot that never happened. The next shot showed Ruth trotting around the bases in a scene swiped from still another game.

WHY IS ABNER DOUBLEDAY CREDITED WITH INVENTING BASEBALL?

On a warm spring day in 1839, a young man named Abner Doubleday and a group of his friends gathered on a grassy open field in the little New York village of Cooperstown, and Abner taught his friends an exciting new game he had just invented—which he called baseball.

It was a catchy name and a catchy game, and it soon caught on all around America. One hundred years later, baseball's most hallowed shrine, the Hall of Fame, was erected just down the street from where Abner invented America's national pastime. Each year, two major-league teams are given the privilege of playing an exhibition game smack dab on the same field where Abner and his friends frolicked. And each year, millions of tourists traipse to Cooperstown to gawk at the greatest collection of baseball memorabilia ever assembled, then take a walk or drive over to Doubleday Field to gaze lovingly at the very spot where this great game was born.

Young Abner had no idea what he had wrought. Of course, the reason is that Doubleday and Cooperstown had absolutely nothing to do with the invention of baseball.

The Doubleday legend is the outgrowth of a dispute between baseball's first sportswriter and its first major sporting goods magnate—and the ingenious efforts of a millionaire to capitalize on an obscure report to convert his hometown into a tourist mecca.

The whole controversy was launched during the latter part of the nineteenth century and the first decade of this century. Apparently, there wasn't much else exciting to argue about then, because one of the burning debates of the era was whether baseball was truly an American innovation or was derived from the British game of rounders, a sport that can trace its lineage as far back as Elizabethan times—and possibly as far back as ancient Egypt.

This wasn't just a friendly, casual disagreement. In some cases, it was a fighting matter—or at least a friendship-splitting argument. The matter was debated hotly in the papers and magazines of the time.

Finally, the battle settled down to a confrontation

between Henry Chadwick and Albert G. Spalding. Chadwick is considered baseball's first sportswriter. He originated the box score and the idea of keeping player records, in addition to serving on the game's rules committee for years.

Chadwick also was a native of Great Britain, and in the 1903 *Baseball Guide*—which was published by Spalding—Chadwick wrote a lengthy article noting that he had played rounders as a schoolboy and that it formed the basis of "town ball" (later baseball) in the United States in the early 1830s.

Spalding was a former pitcher and captain (manager) of the Chicago White Stockings and a millionaire from the sporting goods firm he had launched. He also was a fanatic about anyone even suggesting that baseball wasn't as American as Mom's apple pie. In 1905, he wrote an article for the *Baseball Guide* denouncing Chadwick's views.

In 1906, in an effort to resolve the dispute, a special six-man committee was formed. Nationwide interest in the committee was so great that thousands of elderly men wrote recalling how they felt the game was invented. In addition, Chadwick and Spalding gave the committee lengthy reports upholding their views on the subject.

It's often been charged that Spalding stacked the committee, but in reality he forcefully and convincingly argued in support of the American birth of baseball in Cooperstown. The catch was that the report was tainted with errors, and the committee never made an effort to verify any of Spalding's statements.

Part of Spalding's report quoted a letter from seventy-three-year-old Abner Graves, who said he was a boyhood playmate of Doubleday's. Spalding reported that Graves said he was present in 1839 when Doubleday "first outlined with a stick in the dirt the present diamond-shaped Base Ball field, indicating the position of the players in the field, and afterwards saw him make a memorandum of the rules for his game, which he named 'Base Ball.'"

Spalding also noted, "It certainly appeals to an American's pride to have had the great national game of Baseball created and named by a major general in the United States Army."

The major flaws in Spalding's report were that Graves—who later died in an insane asylum—was only five years old in 1839, the same year the twenty-year-old Doubleday was a cadet at West Point, New York. There's no record that he was granted leave to visit home in 1839—and even if he had been, he wouldn't have gone to Cooperstown; his parents moved from the village in 1837.

Doubleday, who later became a general and a Civil War hero, kept diaries virtually all of his life—a total of nearly seventy separate volumes—and not one of them contains the word *baseball*. He died in 1893, thirteen years before Spalding credited him with inventing baseball. His obituary in the *New York Times* failed to mention the word *baseball*, and one of Doubleday's lifelong friends said after Abner's death that his friend really never cared for outdoor sports.

Nonetheless, on December 30, 1907, the special committee issued a formal statement crediting Doubleday with inventing baseball at Cooperstown. The State of New York immediately placed road markers designating the Cooperstown Field as the birthplace of baseball. The Cooperstown Chamber of Commerce staged a fund drive and in 1919 purchased the field, which first was used as a public playground and in 1920 was converted into Doubleday Field.

Meanwhile, the report of the special commission was quietly tucked away and forgotten. The village of Cooperstown reverted to being more noted as the home of writer James Fenimore Cooper than as the birthplace of baseball.

That was until 1935, when Stephen Clark, a Cooperstown millionaire, conspired with baseball's top executives to pull off one of the great con jobs ever inflicted upon the American public. Harking back to the commission report—which by then most baseball historians had quietly disproved—Clark came up with the idea of a baseball museum in Cooperstown, a museum that would lure millions of tourists to a community that is hundreds of miles from anything that can even be loosely described as a metropolis.

Baseball's leaders, deeply concerned over the Depression's effect on baseball attendance, decided not only to build the Hall of Fame in Cooperstown, but also to celebrate the entire 1939 season as baseball's centennial year. Nearly everyone made big bucks out of the promotion. Magazines issued special centennial collector's issues, souvenir producers went wild, and every major-league team had some kind of crowd-drawing centennial celebration.

The shame was that, by 1939, baseball's leaders, historians, and writers knew full well that the Doubleday story was a hoax. One young sportswriter had an article about the real inventor of baseball rejected by a major sports magazine in 1939. A simple note accompanied the story: "I know it's true, but to publish your story this year would be sacrilegious!"

Bruce Cartwright, whose grandfather, Alexander Cartwright, is now credited with being the father of baseball, wrote a letter to Commissioner Kenesaw Mountain Landis asking that baseball honor Cartwright rather than Doubleday. Landis knew the Doubleday story was a phony but ignored the letter.

Baseball didn't want the truth to stand in the way of a good promotion—and big money. The centennial celebration attracted more than twenty-five million customers to minor- and major-league games that year—then an all-time high—and Cooperstown prospered mightily under an influx of thousands of tourists anxious to see baseball's new shrine.

• • •

Although residents of the continental United States were fooled by the Doubleday hoax, citizens of the territory of Hawaii weren't. On June 11, 1939, Hawaii staged a special Cartwright Day to honor "The Father of Organized Baseball."

Cartwright, who had moved to the islands during the 1870s, was honored with a special memorial, wreaths were placed on his grave, and the various islands were host to scores of all-day activities honoring the Father of Baseball. One of the most moving ceremonies involved thousands of fans joining hands at Honolulu Stadium in a tribute to Cartwright.

WHAT WAS MAJOR-LEAGUE BASEBALL'S BEST RELIEF PERFORMANCE?

There are a lot of candidates for the best relief performance in baseball, but few would top what Lefty Grove of the Philadelphia Athletics did in 1931. Connie Mack called him in as a relief pitcher with the bases full of Yankees—and no outs. Grove promptly struck out Babe Ruth, Lou Gehrig, and Red Ruffing on nine pitches!

HAS A WOMAN EVER PLAYED PROFESSIONAL BASEBALL?

Surprisingly, the answer is yes. Lizzie Stroud—whose nom de diamond was Lizzie Arlington—once pitched in a recognized professional men's league.

Her accomplishment dates all the way back to 1898, though with such a lack of fame that baseball's history and record books have ignored her unprecedented step into a "man's world."

But Ed Barrow, the baseball executive who built the New York Yankee dynasty in the 1920s, once recalled baseball's brief brush with the female touch. Barrow was president of the Atlantic League then, and he permitted the circuit's Paterson, New Jersey, club to sign Stroud to a professional contract. Lizzie "packed speed, control, and nicely distributed weight," said Barrow, but it was the need of a novelty—not her baseball talent—that brought Lizzie into pro ball.

The Spanish-American War was in full swing then, said Barrow, and minor-league teams were plagued with declining crowds. "We used circus tricks now and then to coax in customers," said Barrow, "and I hired big-name fighters—John L. Sullivan, Jim Jeffries, and Jim Corbett—as added attractions."

And then along came Lizzie. Barrow couldn't remember how many games she won—if, indeed, she won any—but extra customers did turn up at Paterson, Newark, Wilmington, and other cities in the league, at least until the novelty wore off.

"The fans eventually lost interest in Lizzie," said Barrow, adding that a year later, "they lost interest in the whole league, and we disbanded at the end of the '99 season."

• • •

At least one other woman was signed to a legitimate pro contract, but she never got into a game. In 1952, Harrisburg of the Interstate League signed twenty-four-year-old Eleanor Engle to play shortstop. She worked out with the team for a while—until the fuddy-duddies in the league office voided her contract.

• • •

Kitty Burke is the only woman to get a "hit" in a regulation major-league game—but there's a catch to the story. It was on July 31, 1935, when the novelty of night baseball lured an overflow crowd to Cincinnati's park. The standing-room-only customers were herded onto the field. In the eighth inning, Burke grabbed a bat and ran to the plate, and the boisterous fans yelled for pitcher Paul Dean to let her hit. He tossed a soft pitch toward the plate, and Kitty hit it. Dean fielded her tap and tagged her out. The out, of course, wasn't charged against the Reds.

• • •

Several other women have appeared in exhibition games against all-male teams. In 1932 Chattanooga, Tennessee, of the Southern Association signed Jackie Mitchell for exhibition play only. One of her pitching accomplishments was striking out Babe Ruth and Lou Gehrig, but the feat was due more to the gallantry of Ruth and Gehrig than to Mitchell's hurling abilities.

Lizzie Murphy handled the first-base duties when a group of American League All-Stars played the Boston Red Sox in an exhibition in 1922.

In the 1960s, Eleanor (Chicky) Kruglinski, a twenty-five-year-old reporter for a Miami newspaper, got an exhibition hit off Steve Barber—after nearly wearing out the hard-throwing pitcher's arm.

Kruglinski wanted to do a story about what it's like to face a major-league pitcher, and she persuaded Barber to throw his hardest. Barber complied for a long time, but Kruglinski missed every pitch. Finally, Barber stepped off the mound and threw an easy toss to the reporter. She hit it—and her drive carried all of the way to the fringes of the outfield grass.

• • •

Babe Didrikson Zaharias, undoubtedly this century's all-around greatest female athlete, once gave a pitching demonstration at the St. Louis Cardinals' spring-training camp, and observers said her performance was "creditable."

Babe also pitched for a time for the old touring House of David team. (In her case, the team waived its ironclad rule requiring each member of the team to grow a beard.)

• • •

Zaharias's pitching for an otherwise strictly male team was a direct reversal of a procedure that was common when several "Bloomer Girl" teams toured the country during the last century and the early part of the 1900s. The Bloomer Girls played mostly small-town men's teams, and they usually won. One reason was that the pitchers, third basemen, and shortstops for the girls' teams were often close-shaven young men or beardless youths who wore wigs and "falsies."

WHY DOES *K* MEAN A STRIKEOUT?

Anyone who has kept score during a baseball game knows that the letter *K* is used to designate a strikeout. (Some purists use a backward *K* to designate a batter called out on strikes.)

But why has the eleventh letter of the alphabet become the symbol for strikeout—a word that begins with the letter *S*?

For the explanation, we'll have to hark all the way back to *DeWitt's Base-Ball Guide for 1868*, Volume 1, Number 1, which hit the newsstands at the time when baseball was just emerging from infancy to the toddler stage.

The guide was the primary source of information for some 220 newly formed amateur teams—legitimate pro ball was still a year away—about the new game that had suddenly become the rage during the Civil War years.

Because of the complexities of the game, the guide pointed out, "for the purposes of scoring more fully . . . a system of abbreviations will be found necessary." These were: P—pitcher; C—catcher; A—first base; B—second base; D—third base; H—home base; S—shortstop; L—left field; M—center (or middle) field; R—right field; K—struck out.

These abbreviations will be quite simple, the ancient guide explained:

> For the words pitcher and catcher, the first letter in each is used; to designate first and second bases, the first and second letters of the alphabet

are used; but for the third base the last letter of the word 'third'—D—is used, to avoid the possibility of confounding it with the catcher, which would unavoidably occur if the third letter of the alphabet were used.

'Home' base is designated by the first letter of its name—H—and in the same way are derived the abbreviations for the positions in the field, short, left, middle, and right.

These abbreviations are used only to show where and by whom the work was done, but to record how it was done, further abbreviations are used, viz: E, fair ball on the fly; F, foul ball on the fly; G, ground ball on the bounce. [In those days, the batter was out on a foul ball caught on the first bounce.]

These are derived this way: F, being the first letter in the word foul, will be more readily remembered in connection with 'foul' balls, while E is F with an addition, and is appropriately used to denote a fair ball, which is more than a foul ball [got that?]; and G, coming immediately after F, can easily be remembered in connection with a foul bounce.

The scorekeeper of that early era literally had to know his ABCs.

And now, the esoteric folderol about the *K* for strikeout:

When a player is out on three strikes, the letter K is used to denote the feat. This letter is used because it is the last letter in the word 'struck'; and if S were used, it might be confounded [sic] with short-stop.

Logical or not, that's how the letter *K* was shoved into the baseball vocabulary—and it's survived unchanged to today.

WHAT DOES INDIAN FIGHTING HAVE TO DO WITH THE WORD *BULLPEN?*

Most history books offer a simple explanation of how the word *bullpen* landed in baseball's vocabulary: Huge Bull Durham tobacco signs were prevalent at many ballparks before and after the turn of the century. Pitchers for the Brooklyn Dodgers warmed up under one of those signs, and the editor of the local paper took to dubbing the area the "bullpen."

The story may contain as much bull as the sign it exploits, because it appears that *bullpen* was part of baseball's terminology before the Bull Durham signs were ever erected.

Probably the word came from a much earlier derivation: In America's Indian-fighting days, a bullpen was a square enclosure of logs, frequently used in early times as a place of confinement. The word was carried over into colloquial speech to mean a place of confinement, and it most likely was associated with early relief pitchers, who were "confined" to their warm-up space until needed.

HOW COME THEY CALL IT A DIAMOND, WHEN IT'S A SQUARE?

Baseball has performed a geometric impossibility for the past 125 years or so—it's transformed a square into a diamond. A baseball infield has four right angles with all four sides of equal length, which any geometry book or dictionary will define as a square.

Technically, to be a diamond, the field would have to have two acute and two obtuse angles. Simply translated, that means the distance from home plate to first base and from home to third would have to be longer than from first to second and from second to third, or vice versa. It certainly would add a new dimension to the game.

But fortunately baseball's diamond had more to do

with colloquial speech than dimensions. When baseball was in its infancy, most towns were built around a town square. In the East, where baseball first gained its popularity, most folks didn't call it a square; they called it a diamond, and the phrase carried over to the new sport—and stuck.

Presumably if the game had first gained popularity in the Midwest, we'd be calling the diamond its correct name—a square!

HOW DID SPRING TRAINING GET STARTED?

History doesn't record what Manager Cap Anson said when, late in the winter of 1886, he checked out the condition of his Chicago White Stockings, who had won the National League pennant the year before. It's a safe bet, however, that Anson's language was liberally laced with profanity, accompanied by angry hand waving.

Virtually all of his champions were supporting newly acquired bulges in the area of their midriffs. And, there was little doubt that their prime winter conditioning exercises consisted of pushing open swinging saloon doors.

Anson knew something had to be done—and fast. So he packed up the entire team and headed for Hot Springs, Arkansas, "to boil out the blubber" in the community's therapeutic baths—and to exercise his charges back in shape for the new season.

It wasn't the first time a team had headed south before the start of the season, but it was the first trip specifically designed to get baseball players in shape for the coming season.

The "spring training" tag didn't come along until many years later, but the White Stockings reaped so much publicity from the Hot Springs jaunt that they made it an annual custom. Other big-league clubs swiftly followed suit.

• • •

Strangely, the idea of traveling south for six weeks of spring training each year drew sharp criticism from some players and baseball officials well into this century. The anti-spring-trainists would point to such examples as Joe DiMaggio, who hardly ever attended spring training because of holdout sieges or injuries; Ty Cobb, who bluntly refused to don a uniform or work out until a few days before the regular season; or Al Simmons, who was a holdout until opening day—when he slammed a homer. Simmons finished with one of his best seasons ever.

Even Joe McCarthy, the skipper of the New York Yankees, questioned the need for the annual pilgrimage to the South. He always contended a team could benefit as much by training in an indoor gymnasium. McCarthy spoke from experience. In 1915 McCarthy was playing for the Buffalo Bison, and the club owner didn't have enough money to send his talent south for training.

So the team worked out in the Brockton, Massachusetts, gym, then played only six exhibitions before the season started. The Bison won the pennant.

Cobb complained that spring training hurt a team more than it helped. His theory was that weeks of conditioning and exhibition games made his players lose their endurance by August and September—just the time when they should be at their best in the stretch drive for the pennant.

WHO WAS THE SMARTEST MAN IN BASEBALL?

There's a saying in baseball that the catcher is usually the dumbest player on the team. Part of that is a result of the lunkhead statements attributed to former Yankee catcher Yogi Berra. Part of it has to do with the feeling that a player has to be an outright numskull to choose a position that requires him to (1) toil for two or three hours each day in an uncomfortable squatting position, (2) repeatedly face bombardment with baseballs that travel faster than ninety miles per hour, and (3) be subjected to exceedingly painful foul tips.

Surprisingly, the position has been manned by more eggheads than any other playing spot. And, although baseball boasts a large number of intellectuals over the years, the smartest of the lot undoubtedly was catcher Moe Berg.

Berg, who spent fifteen years in the majors, was undeniably brilliant. He could discuss virtually any conceivable subject knowledgeably. He studied classical and Romance languages at Princeton and at the prestigious Sorbonne in France. And he could speak a dozen languages—fluently. He also earned a law degree.

Berg wasn't bad as a catcher either. He played for Brooklyn, the White Sox, Cleveland, Washington, and the Red Sox and posted a .243 lifetime batting average.

WHAT HAPPENED TO THE HITTERS IN 1930?

What happened to the 1930 hitters is that they went wild. There has never been a season in modern times to match the unrelenting bombardment produced by those batters. The unbelievable hitting extended throughout professional baseball, from the lowliest of the minor leagues to the big show itself.

A .294 batting average would be considered a fairly good mark by today's hitters. But in 1930 the average for *all* of professional baseball was .294. That included pitchers, utility men, and defensive wizards who kept their jobs because of their glove work. It also included a number of incompetents who were released outright before the season was over.

In the National League alone, anyone batting

below .303 that season was below average. The American League wasn't quite the hitters' haven; the average in the AL was .288. All told, seventy-eight major leaguers in 1930 hit .300 or better, led by Bill Terry's .401 mark.

The massive hitting resulted in scoring sprees that sounded more like football scores. Philadelphia Phillies fans, for example, saw their heroes score a total of thirty runs in two consecutive games—and lose both contests!

Within one short period, the Phils lost at home to New York 18–5; to Chicago 17–4; and, on consecutive days, to St. Louis 15–7 and 19–16. But the Phils also won by gigantic scores, beating Brooklyn 16–15; Pittsburgh 18–14 and 15–14; and Chicago 12–11. Fresco Thompson was the lowest hitter on the team; his season average was .286, quite respectable by today's standards. Despite the hitting, the Phils finished dead last, winning only 52 games while losing 102.

And what was happening to lowly Philadelphia also was happening to every other pro team in baseball. In the minors, batters produced some horrendous challenges for the pitchers. Consider the Central League pitchers who had to work against Fort Wayne, Indiana. When the pitcher was finished with—or by— a .419 hitter named Wright, he still had to contend with a .406 batter named Jones, then a bundle of hitters in the high .300s.

Fort Wayne's team batting average for the season was .337, and its victories included such calamities as 32–8 over Canton, 31–13 over Erie, and 27–15 over Richmond. A tremendous ball club? Even with that kind of production, Fort Wayne could finish no higher than third in each half of a split season.

Although Fort Wayne's team average was the best in pro baseball, Cedartown of the Georgia-Florida League was only a point behind, and league-rival Lindale set a collective .331 pace.

Other minor leagues that also had league averages above .300 included the Central (.308), American Association (.307), Southern Association (.304), New York-Pennsylvania League (.303), and Pacific Coast League (.302). Not one of the 160 pro clubs that operated in 1930 batted below .258; only six were below .265.

No one has come up with an adequate explanation of just why the hitters went wild. There was talk of a livelier ball, but a hyped-up ball just travels faster and farther; you've got to hit it in the first place.

After the 1930 batting spree, the general pro average skidded sixteen points to .278 in 1931, and a downward trend continued from that point.

• • •

Considering the 1930 hitting, the late Dazzy Vance's 2.61 earned-run average for that season is remarkable. A lot of pitchers, of course, have posted better ERAs, including Vance himself (2.16 in 1924).

But in 1930, the second-best ERA in the National League was registered by Carl Hubbell, a 3.87 mark. Lefty Grove led the American League with an even 3.00, followed by Wes Ferrell at 3.30. But ERAs of 4.00 to 7.00 were common for top pitchers that season.

One of the most cruelly treated American League pitchers was Jack Russell, who was banged for 302 hits in 230 innings.

IS IT TRUE THAT HORNSBY WAS NEARLY A CASTAWAY FLOP?

Rogers Hornsby, one of baseball's greatest hitters, almost didn't make it to the major leagues—because he was such a rotten hitter in the minors! And, ironically, Hornsby probably would have been expelled from baseball if a scout hadn't made an offhand remark about his hustling abilities.

Hornsby broke into pro ball as an eighteen-year-old in 1914 with Hugo of the Texas-Oklahoma League

Rogers Hornsby taking a cut at a pitch (1937).

and with Denison of the Western Association. He managed only 91 hits, most of them singles, in 393 at bats
for a .232 average. The next season, he hit .277 in 119
at bats with Denison. Team officials were seriously
considering releasing him.

But Hornsby was saved from oblivion by a chance remark by scout Bob Connery to Miller Huggins, then manager of the Cardinals. Connery said Hornsby lacked natural ability, but he certainly was "full of fire and pep. His nickname is Pep, and I tell you he's full of it."

The 1915 Cards were already doomed for a last-division finish, and Huggins was intrigued by Hornsby's enthusiasm. He paid $500 to Denison and brought the young player up to the Cards in late August. Hornsby, whose build could best be described as scrawny, was far from impressive in his first eighteen big-league games.

He choked up high on the bat, crouched low at the plate, and hit only .246. But Huggins thought he detected something in this young man. He suggested that Hornsby put on some weight over the winter. Rog did—he gained twenty-six pounds. Then during spring training, Huggins changed Hornsby's batting style. The crouch and choking up were discarded. Huggins discovered that Hornsby had iron wrists, enabling him to follow through with a free-swinging style.

The "new" Hornsby hit .313 for the 1916 Cardinals and, except for one season, just kept getting better and better. By 1920, Hornsby was ready to begin a six-season stretch of the greatest concentrated period of hitting power by one player in the history of the game.

During that period, he tormented National League pitchers with an average of .397. Starting with .370 in 1920, Hornsby hit .397 in 1921, .401 in 1922, .384 in 1923, .424 in 1924, and .403 in 1925. Each performance yielded a batting title. The closest anyone ever came to Hornsby's six-year spree was Ty Cobb's .394 average for 1909–1914.

And the Rajah made his blows count. His average total-base mileage for each season was 370, and he drove home an average of 120 runs each year for 1921–1925.

Except for his slow start (Cobb had a .338 average for his first five seasons) and a couple of bad seasons later on, Hornsby would have easily exceeded Cobb's all-time high of .387 for a complete big-league career.

The strain of managing the Cardinals to their first pennant in 1926 contributed to the decline of Hornsby's average to .317 that season. He lost one of his most productive years when a broken leg sidelined him for most of the 1930 season. Having batted .387 in 1928 and .380 in '29, he appeared ripe for another year in the lofty .300s before the injury. Operating chiefly as a pinch hitter for the Chicago Cubs, he managed only a .308 average in 104 trips.

In 1931, Hornsby played in 100 games and batted .331. After seven seasons as an occasional pinch hitter, he wound up a twenty-four-year major-league playing term with a composite mark of .358—nine points below Cobb's record.

• • •

When Hornsby hit .424 in 1924, he came up with one of the greatest hitting streaks in baseball history. He got off to a slow season but gradually improved. Nonetheless, he was still below the .400 mark when mid-July rolled around.

A couple of astonishing spurts, including one full week when his average was at the .500 mark, helped Rogers into the .400 range by August 20. And then he simply went wild.

The Cards were playing a doubleheader with Philadelphia that day, and Hornsby was three for three in the first game, including two doubles. He was three for four in the second game. The next day, the Giants were in St. Louis for a doubleheader, and Hornsby had seven hits in seven trips, including two homers and a double. By the time August 29 rolled around, Hornsby had collected an unbelievable thirty-four hits in fifty-one trips for a staggering .667 average! His hits included seven home runs, ten doubles, and one triple. He scored nineteen runs.

By the end of Hornsby's hitting spree, his season batting average had climbed to .432. He batted slightly above .400 for the remaining weeks of the season, but that four-game August production kept his season average from dropping to "only" .424.

HOW COME THEY CALL THAT FUNNY-LOOKING BAT A FUNGO?

The funny thing is, no one is quite sure why the bat with an extra narrow handle and a thick head is called a fungo. Baseball lexicographers have managed to trace the origins of most baseball words and phrases, but the origin of the name of the bat used to hit practice flies has eluded them.

One suggestion is that the wood of the bat is so soft that it resembles fungus. Moe Berg, one of baseball's intellectuals, once proposed that the name was derived from an old children's game, in which the batter yelled out, "One goes, two goes, fun goes," before cracking the ball.

What is known about the term is that it was one of the earliest used in baseball. Its history has been traced back to the mid-1860s, and there are indications that the term was used long before that time.

WHY DO BASEBALL PLAYERS WEAR SUCH FUNNY-LOOKING UNIFORMS?

If you take an honest, unprejudiced look at them, baseball uniforms are rather silly-looking outfits for some of our country's most noted millionaires to wear when performing their daily toil.

Granted, they don't look a bit like what the New

York Knickerbockers wore when they defeated Washington 21–10 on June 3, 1851, a game of historical—perhaps hysterical—significance because it was the first time a team wore uniforms. Until then, regular street attire was the normal costume for baseball games. The Knickerbocker uniforms consisted of blue long pants, white flannel long-sleeved shirts with bow ties, high-top shoes—and *straw hats!*

But before we guffaw too much about those outlandish costumes, take a look at today's modern uniform. First, it's topped off with quaint little billed caps to shield the players' eyes from sunlight, although most games are played at night. There's a little button at the top of each cap that apparently serves no practical function at all.

The players wear shirts with their team's name or nickname boldly emblazoned on the front, and the player's name and number on the back. The shirts are short-sleeved, but sometimes the players wear heavy-duty undershirts that may extend all the way to the wrist or to the elbow area.

The pants end a good six to eight inches above the ground and are reminiscent of the "knickers" sportsmen once wore but abandoned in the early part of this century. Then there are the socks, which baseball spells *sox*. The players wear *two* pairs of them. The top pair has large looping gaps or stirrups in both the front and back to expose the socks underneath. These socks are usually white, although they can be a variety of colors.

Today's uniform results from a compromise between modernization and baseball's resistance to change of any kind. The double knit, lightweight uniforms are sleeker and more modern-looking than the baggy uniforms of years ago.

Yet it's amazing how the basic look of the uniform has remained unchanged during the past 120 or so years. Put a modern-day player in a uniform of the past century, and there would be no mistaking that he was wearing a baseball uniform.

That's because after a whirlwind courtship with changing attire during its first twenty-five years, baseball settled on an idea of what a uniform should look like forever after. Since the 1870s, changes in the uniform have occurred extraordinarily slowly—a change here, an addition there perhaps every decade or so. There have been numerous attempts to deviate from the pattern—such as the checkered uniforms that the Dodgers once wore—but baseball always has returned to the traditional uniform.

After the original Knickerbockers dazzled their fans with their spiffy new uniforms, every baseball team wanted an outfit, and within two decades the basics of today's uniform had evolved.

Trousers crept up the legs to "plus-six" length, and colorful socks became fashionable. Hats were replaced by caps—generally fluffy and padded, with short visors in white or contrasting colors. In most cases, the front of the cap top was snapped down to the visor.

Cleats—made of wood rather than metal—were developed, and as early as 1858 paneled shirtfronts had come into vogue. The Champion Unions of Morrisania, New York, apparently were the first to flaunt the emblem of their club in a conspicuous place: each player wore a large Old English *U* in the center of the shirt panel.

When Cincinnati's Red Stockings became baseball's first professional team in 1869, the players were clad in white padded knickers of flannel and long-sleeved white shirts that laced up the front and carried a large *C* in Old English. Some of the players wore bow ties under their floppy collars—a custom that persisted on some teams until the 1890s. Accessories included red belts, white caps with short visors, stockings that were a *brilliant* red, and white high-topped shoes with red laces. The practice of wearing long pants, bound at the ankles with leather strips, continued into the 1870s—but eventually all baseball teams adopted the Red Stockings' style of pants.

Players for the Forest Citys of Rockford, Illinois, one of the game's early powerhouses, were outfitted in baggy knee britches and all-white uniforms with dark stockings. Shoes were an over-the-ankle type in white with black toe caps. Their caps were patterned after the ones that railroad engineers used to wear, and the belts had dazzling stripes. Contrary to custom, neckties were not worn.

The great Boston clubs of the 1870s introduced the custom of wearing the city's name in block letters upon their chests.

Along the way, there were a few bumps in uniform designing. Before 1882, clubs could utilize any style of uniform that they wanted, and old outfits used by players moving on to different teams were permitted, producing a motley array for most clubs. But then league officials ruled that the identity of separate clubs must be preserved and that the uniforms of each club must match, particularly in color.

The next year, the rule governing the color of the uniform was changed so that it applied only to stockings: red for Boston, white for Chicago, navy blue for Cleveland, brown for Detroit, crimson and black for New York, and so on. The National League officials experimented with another change in the late 1880s—that a different-colored shirt must be worn for each position. That experiment lasted only a month, but out of the chaos it created (players had to switch shirts when they switched positions) came the rule that is still observed today: home clubs were required to wear white uniforms, while visitors could wear a uniform of any color.

In 1886 to 1888, the New York Giants introduced tight, form-fitting flannel knickers, wide belts, and short-visored white flannel caps of a squarish shape. Many people complained that the tight uniforms were downright scandalous.

Detroit introduced stripes to its shirts in 1886 (the team continued to wear solid-colored, dark trousers). The Baltimore Orioles of 1894 were the first team to have their entire off-white uniforms daintily streaked with stripes.

Brooklyn, incidentally, was probably the only major-league club to go the stripes one better. The Dodgers appeared in checkered uniforms in 1916—and won a pennant in them.

While the uniforms were being altered, other major changes were being added to the game. In 1875, Charles C. Waitt introduced a baseball glove. Although it provided scant protection for the hand, the innovation was derided as a sissy touch before catching on later in the decade.

Catchers, who had customarily worked far behind the plate, began acquiring their protective armor when Fred Thayer invented the catcher's mask. He developed it for Harvard catcher James Tyng in 1877, modeling it upon the face protection used in fencing.

A few years later, catchers and umpires both began using chest protectors. The umpires, incidentally, were outfitted in bright, flowery silk shirts for a time until they switched over to the traditional navy blue in the 1890s.

Another major change was the introduction of steel spikes in the 1890s. One sporting goods company advertised its spikes as being made of "hand-forged razor steel."

The formidable Baltimore Orioles of the 1890s (then part of the National League) played a key role in streamlining the uniforms. The Orioles discarded most of the customary padding and started wearing a lightweight flannel. Most of the players cut off their long-sleeved shirts to permit greater throwing freedom. Other teams slowly followed the Orioles' lead. Neckties, shirt pockets, wide and loose collars, high shoes, long shirtsleeves, and baggy pants swiftly faded away.

In 1896, by the way, the complete uniform—shirt, cap, pants, belt, and stockings—cost only $14.75.

Nearly all of the big-league clubs wore dark traveling uniforms during the 1890s, and eight teams still clung to them as late as 1908. Manager John McGraw had a special solid black uniform made for his New York Giants for one World Series, but he adopted chalk-striped suits in 1912. While most teams switched over to the traditional gray road uniforms during the first decade of the century, Chicago's Cubs wore solid blue uniforms until 1922, and the White Sox, which had switched to gray for several years, returned to dark blue with white chalk stripes in 1925 for a couple of seasons.

The sweatshirt, or undershirt as we recognize it today, was introduced by Pittsburgh in the early part of the century, while the Yankees and St. Louis Browns started using emblems on their upper sleeves. Washington introduced the "half-and-half" socks—top half dark, lower half white. The distinctive team emblems on the shirtfront started appearing in 1913.

Detroit was one of the slowest teams to change its uniform. The Tigers stuck with wide roll collars until 1914 and were still wearing inch-high stiff collars until 1921, long after other teams had adopted V-necked shirts. In 1922, catchers, who had adopted shin guards during the first decade of the century, began wearing a new type of mask—two rigid round bars instead of the wire mesh front.

The Yankees are credited with being the first club to number its players, starting in 1929. (That year, Boston's Braves used their backs to display the head of an Indian chieftain.) The Yanks were actually the first team to make the numbering system stick. But Cincinnati had first tried the idea in 1883, and the

Three-I League ordered its clubs to put numbers on the backs of players in 1925.

Baseball traditionalists screamed in anger when the A's and Astros began wearing gaudy uniforms in the late sixties and seventies. Actually, when the A's introduced their gold-and-green uniforms, they were pretty much copying Brooklyn, which wore green caps, socks, lettering, and trim in 1937. For a time in the late 1940s, the Dodgers wore bright blue satin pants for home night games. Cincinnati wore red pants for a number of years after introducing night baseball in 1935.

One other major uniform change was Pittsburgh's 1971 introduction of form-fitting double knits with pullover shirts.

WHY DO UMPIRES RAISE THEIR RIGHT HAND FOR A STRIKE?

Supposedly, the custom of raising the right hand when calling a strike was started in 1888 to accommodate William Ellsworth Hoy, probably one of the least likely candidates to succeed in the major leagues.

Hoy was deaf and mute. Because he couldn't hear the umpire's calls when he was at bat, he requested that the umps raise their right hand when the pitch was a strike. The procedure quickly became a standard feature for all umpires—a tradition that continues today.

Because of his handicap, Hoy was tagged with the unkind moniker of Dummy Hoy—and he's still listed in the record books that way. But Hoy, who was only 5'4", was no dummy on the field. For fourteen years during the last part of the nineteenth century and the early 1900s, he was one of baseball's brightest players.

Contemporaries said he had a lightning fast and deadly accurate throw from the outfield, and he was a daring thief of the bases. He stole 597 bases while playing with seven different major-league clubs from 1888 through 1902. He had a lifetime batting average of .288. Hoy died in 1961—just five months shy of his 100th birthday.

WHY DID BASEBALL IGNORE RUTH AFTER HE RETIRED?

It's often been said that after Babe Ruth had done more for developing the popularity of baseball than any other human, the game's top brass brutally cast him aside. When Ruth's playing days were over, these heartless executives seemingly could find no place in our national pastime for its greatest hero.

In reality, however, it was the impetuous Ruth himself who played a major role in relegating himself to baseball's junk heap. He had several chances to become a major-league manager, and he blew them all.

When the Yankees' beloved manager, Miller Huggins, died suddenly in late September 1929, Ruth actively sought the blessings of owner Col. Jake Ruppert and general manager Ed Barrow as Huggins's replacement. He was turned down, ostensibly because of his lack of experience. In reality, Barrow said later, Ruth's candidacy for the job was never seriously considered. Ruth couldn't handle himself, let alone a mighty team like the Yankees, Barrow said.

Bob Shawkey guided the Yanks to a third-place finish in 1930, before Joe McCarthy was hired for the 1931 season. Ruth took an immediate dislike to his new boss, primarily because he believed the job should have been his. Stories of their altercations dotted the newspapers.

As age continued to whittle away at Babe's abilities on the field, he became more and more obsessed with the idea of managing the Yanks. In 1932, Yankee officials brought up the idea of Ruth managing Newark. Babe, his pride severely wounded, scoffed at the suggestion; it was the big leagues or nothing, said Babe. He derided the suggestion that managing a team in the high minors would prove his managing ability.

Late in the 1933 season, Frank J. Nevin, owner of Detroit, wired Ruth to request a meeting after the season ended to discuss managing the Tigers. Ruth said he couldn't stop in Detroit because he had to catch a ship in San Francisco for an exhibition series in Hawaii. Perhaps because he still had hopes of managing the Yankees, it was weeks before Ruth contacted Nevin and said he had decided he wanted the job. He was jolted to learn that Nevin had already hired Mickey Cochrane.

If Ruth had been a little more patient, he might have achieved his dream of managing the Yanks during the 1935 season. The Yankees were headed for their third second-place finish in four years under McCarthy late in the 1934 campaign, and Colonel Ruppert was slowly becoming disenchanted with his manager. Perhaps, he confided to close associates, the idea of Ruth managing the Yankees was not so bad. The Babe had married Claire Hodgson, a former model and part-time actress, and she had done an amazing job of calming Ruth's rambunctiousness.

Instead of biding his time, however, the Babe made the mistake of confronting Ruppert late in the '34 season and demanding that the Colonel choose between him and McCarthy—immediately. Ruppert was at first flustered, then outraged by what he considered Ruth's impertinence. The Colonel, a stubborn man, angrily responded that he would side with McCarthy. The next winter, when Ruth's contract for the 1935 season arrived via registered mail, it called for a salary of one dollar. It was the Yankee owner's childish way of telling Ruth he was no longer needed—or wanted—by the team.

Just a few months after Ruth's bitter losing showdown with Ruppert, Connie Mack told friends that he had decided to retire as manager of the Philadelphia Athletics—and the number one candidate for his replacement was Babe Ruth.

But, after the end of the '34 season, Ruth, Mack, Lou Gehrig, and a host of major-league stars made an exhibition tour in Japan. It was Mack's first opportunity to observe the Babe close up over a prolonged period—and he didn't like what he saw. It wasn't Ruth who perturbed him; it was the Babe's wife. She was so domineering, he told friends, that if the Babe was named manager, "she'd be running the team within three weeks." Mack quietly gave up his plans to retire.

Ruth started the 1935 season as assistant vice president and player with the Boston Braves, with an unwritten understanding that he eventually would take over as manager. The promise was only a ruse to use Babe's fame to help shore up a financially ailing franchise.

It was clear from the start that the forty-year-old Ruth's playing days were over; his body writhed in pain after every game. Then came the break with Boston owner Judge Emil Fuchs, who ordered Ruth to appear at the opening of a Boston clothing store. Babe, now aware that the judge had no intention of giving him a managing job, bluntly refused.

On May 25, Ruth hit three skyscraper home runs in Pittsburgh, the third his 714th big-league homer. Eight days later, he officially retired.

Ruth played golf, traveled, hit the banquet circuit, and generally loafed until June 1938, when Larry McPhail, the new general manager of the Brooklyn team, called and asked if Babe would like to serve as the Dodgers' first-base coach.

Ruth leaped at the opportunity, although the pay was only $15,000. The Babe, however, was being duped again. His recall to baseball was more for the promotional value of his name than for his coaching abilities. One of his prime functions was to stage hitting demonstrations before games. McPhail also installed lights at Ebbets Field that year, and the combination of the Babe and the novelty of night games lured enormous crowds to the park—quite an accomplishment for a horrendous Dodger team that deservedly finished in seventh place.

Ruth was no great shakes as a coach, but then, of course, he had little talent with which to work. However, he did miss some signals, and there were times when he couldn't recall the names of some of his players.

He also resurrected a feud with Leo Durocher, who was ending his playing days as a Dodger shortstop. Durocher had been a brash, cocky rookie when he broke into major-league ball with the Yankees in 1925—a time when the Babe was at the height of his career. They never were particularly fond of each other, but mutual hatred erupted in 1938, especially when Durocher accused Ruth of missing an important signal that cost the Dodgers a game.

When the season was over, Burleigh Grimes was fired as manager, and Ruth had hopes that McPhail would name him as the replacement. But nary a word came from McPhail. Instead, Ruth read in a newspaper that Durocher had been hired for the job. Ruth's wife said the Babe broke down and sobbed uncontrollably when he read the news. One of Durocher's first acts was to fire Ruth.

The Babe never received another offer to participate in major-league baseball.

• • •

The Babe could easily have surprised baseball's authorities by being a pretty good manager. Yes, he had trouble remembering names, and he did forget signals. But, he was a natural as one of the game's best pitchers and greatest hitters. He knew the game inside and out. As a player, he never made one mental mistake on a ballfield. He loved the game, and his charisma made most people like him. He liked working with young ballplayers. Most important, maturity and the firm hand of his wife, Claire, had transformed Babe into a different person than the raucous youth of his early playing days.

True, he was no mental giant—but other men with less talent have succeeded as managers. Casey Stengel waltzed into the Hall of Fame in 1966 on the basis of a bushel of pennants and World Series titles that the Yankees won while he was manager. But those Yankee teams were superlative; one wonders whether they won because of or despite Stengel. In his playing days, he was far from spectacular, hitting .284 in fourteen big-league seasons. In nine years as a National League manager, his winning percentage was a dismal .403. His teams generally finished deep in the second division.

Writer Bob Considine was one of those who considered Babe unfit to be a major-league manager. In the thirties, Considine maintained that Ruth deserved a spot in baseball—but that the spot should be in the promotional field.

Considine changed his tune, however, when he spent a day observing the Babe work with players at a baseball camp in Florida during the early forties. He was amazed at the patience and maturity Ruth displayed in handling the players—and the quickness with which they picked up the skills that he passed on to them. He had a natural ability, Considine said, for detecting even the slightest mistakes on the field and correcting them.

Ray Doan, the head of the training camp, told Considine that he had never seen a big leaguer who could teach baseball as well as Ruth could, and that, because of his natural abilities, he could teach more in a shorter time than anyone else!

10
MANY MINI BASEBALL LAUGHS

A LITTLE MAN'S BUSY, DIZZY DAY

Not many ballplayers have created the havoc, against both the opposition and their own mates, that Ike Davis wrought one afternoon in 1928. Davis, a tiny shortstop for Toronto's then–International League team, managed to severely injure Maurice Archdeacon of the rival Rochester club, injure his own captain, knock his manager cold, and cause the entire team to miss a train.

During the course of his four-hit day, Davis collided at second base with Archdeacon, who was carried unconscious from the field and was sidelined for a week.

In the clubhouse after the game, Davis got involved in an argument with Eddie Onslow, the team captain. It boiled over into fisticuffs, and Onslow's hand was badly injured. Manager Lena Blackburne stepped in to separate the combatants, but in the confusion, Davis's head struck the skipper's noggin, and Blackburne was out cold.

The Toronto ballpark was on an island in those

days, and by the time the fight was finally stopped, the players had missed the 5:30 P.M. ferryboat and, consequently, the six o'clock train for Buffalo.

YOGI'S HEAD WASN'T IN SHAPE

Lefty Gomez served for a time as a representative of a sporting goods company after wrapping up his brilliant career as a New York Yankees pitcher. One of his duties was to visit players in spring training and measure them for new uniforms.

Yogi Berra was still a catcher for the Yankees when Lefty put the tape measure on him to see what size shirt and pants he required. Then, as Gomez recalled, he asked Berra what size cap he wore. Responded Yogi, "How do I know? I'm not in shape yet."

HOW TO CALM AN ANGRY MANAGER

One of Joe McCarthy's prize anecdotes concerns the fabulous screwball, Jay Kirke, whom Joe managed at Louisville. One day, Kirke muffed a signal, which cost Louisville the game. McCarthy, usually a mild sort of gent, blew his top. He told Kirke to meet him in the clubhouse after the game, and warned him to be prepared for action.

McCarthy paced the floor savagely. He waited and waited, but Kirke didn't show. The longer Joe paced, the more furious he became. Most of the players were dressed when the door opened. There stood Kirke and a priest.

"Come in, Father," said Jay. "I want you to meet my friend."

KID BILL GEHRIG

Babe Ruth always addressed everyone as "Kid," and this used to bother Lou Gehrig, his teammate for ten years with the Yankees. Finally, Gehrig asked Ruth why he didn't use people's proper names. "I can't remember names, Kid," said the Babe.

Gehrig told him he should try. "After all," said Gehrig," it is the polite thing to do. People appreciate the courtesy of being called by their correct name."

Ruth mulled it over for a few minutes. Then, earnestly, he gave Lou his answer: "Maybe you're right. I'll give it a trial, Bill."

IT'S HARD THROWING A CURVE WITH
ONE FINGER

A minor-league baseball club signed a raw young pitcher in midseason. Before the recruit's first game, the veteran catcher talked to him about signals: "I don't want to confuse you, so we'll just use one finger for a fastball and two fingers for a curve."

Eight straight times, the catcher signaled for a fastball, and the pitcher walked the first two batters. The catcher then called for a curve, and the rookie broke it right over for a strike. The pitcher rushed in to thank the catcher.

"I was hoping you'd call for a curve," he said. "It's hard to control the ball with only one finger."

"SHE TALKED MY ARM OFF"

Pete Gray was a remarkable one-armed outfielder who played for the St. Louis Browns during World War II. One sweltering day as Gray came off the field after a strenuous game in another city, he was stopped by a talkative woman. Gray tried to remain polite as the woman droned on about his handicap, overwhelming him with sympathy and sentimentality. "You poor boy—just how did you lose your arm?" the woman finally asked.

Replied Pete, "A woman in St. Louis talked it off"— and he turned and ran for the clubhouse.

THAT'S NOT TY COBB

When Hughie Jennings was managing the Detroit Tigers, he received a letter from a Michigan pitching hopeful who boasted he could strike out Ty Cobb three times in four times at bat. Jennings risked the necessary $1.80 transportation, and the prospect was duly sent in to hurl against Cobb in batting practice.

Cobb whacked the youth's first pitch against the right-field wall. The second he drove over the fence, the third to deep center, and the fourth over the middle barrier.

"Well," Jennings demanded, "what have you got to say?"

"I don't think that's Cobb," replied the pitcher.

THAT SPAHN KID WILL NEVER MAKE IT

Warren Spahn likes to tell the story of his first big-league game—oddly enough against the Brooklyn team that was to hex him eternally. It was 1942, and Casey Stengel was managing the Braves. Pee Wee Reese was up, and he had been blistering Boston. Stengel ordered Spahn to knock Reese down. Spahn threw a pitch inside, but not a knockdown one.

Stengel shouted from the dugout and gestured to Spahn to throw the next one tighter. Spahn pitched inside, but again not a knockdown. Stengel went to the mound, snatched the ball from the young lefty, and snarled, "OK, that's enough. You don't have the guts to be a big-league pitcher."

"The next day," said Spahn "I was in Hartford."

"I'M A CARDINAL TOO"

Hall of Famer Joe Medwick gained his greatest honors as an outfielder for the St. Louis Cardinals in the 1930s. Near the end of World War II, Medwick made

Joe Medwick (1936).

a USO tour of European battle fronts with other baseball players and a troupe of entertainers.

In Rome they were granted an audience with Pope Pius XII. The Pope kindly asked each visitor to name his profession. When it was Medwick's turn, Joe replied with simple dignity, "Your Holiness, I used to be a Cardinal too."

COBB A .200 HITTER?

Dusty Rhodes, whose home runs enabled the New York Giants to win the 1954 World Series over Cleveland in four games but who rarely caught a headline thereafter, appeared on a radio talk show and was asked, "What do you think Ty Cobb would hit against present-day pitching?"

"Oh, about .200," replied Rhodes.

Reminded that Cobb retired with a lifetime major-league average of .367, Rhodes explained, "Yes, but you've got to consider that Cobb is seventy years old now."

JUST WHERE DO YOU WANT THE HOMER?

John McGraw was such a dictator as manager of the Giants that his players looked to him for instructions in almost every situation. One day, McGraw sent in Larry McLean as a pinch hitter with the score tied and the bases full in the ninth inning.

As he picked out his bat, McLean asked, "What do you want me to do, Mac?"

McGraw roared back, "Hit one into the stands, you dope!"

McLean decided that wasn't quite specific enough. He said, "Oh, I figured that, all right. . . . But which seat, Mac?"

BRAVES WERE RED-FACED OVER GREEN SEATS

Braves officials were once red-faced over some green paint. That was when the team was still in Boston, and the paint had been applied to seats throughout the park for opening day. The problem was, not enough drying time was allowed on one section of the seats, and after the game, 330 indignant fans came to the club offices and displayed bright green paint on the seats of their pants. The Braves had two unexpected expenses: a sizable dry-cleaning bill and repainting 330 seats.

• • •

When the Braves later moved to Milwaukee, they once refunded ticket prices to eight very angry persons, because the patrons didn't see Roy Rogers or any other cowboys—just baseball players on the field. Rogers was appearing at a rodeo at a county fair, and by mistake the fans turned up at County Stadium, then home of the Braves.

'TIS EASIER TO GET BLOOD THAN WORLD SERIES TICKETS

The demand for World Series tickets each year far exceeds the capacity of even the largest of the major league's stadiums. Before Boston won the National League flag in 1948, baseball writer John Drohan suffered an illness that required a blood transfusion. Drohan later sought out the donor and said he would like to return the favor some day. When Boston finally clinched the pennant, the donor called Drohan to suggest that he could repay him with a couple of seats to the World Series.

"It would be easier to give back the blood," said Drohan.

RUN AROUND THE BASES AGAIN!

Babe Herman liked to recall the first time his mother, whose baseball knowledge was limited, saw him play. It was in a semipro game in California, and on his first trip to the plate, Herman tagged a tremendous homer. After he circled the bases and came back to the bench, he said he could hear his mother yell out over the crowd noise, "Run around again, Son, the ball's not back yet!"

Stan Musial.

STRIKEOUT HOLDS MUSIAL TO TWO BASES

When St. Louis's Stan Musial was at the height of his career in 1949, Cincinnati's Ewell Blackwell struck out the Cardinals' superstar. However, the third strike was a curve that eluded the catcher, and Musial was able to race all the way to second base.

Reds manager Bucky Walters shook his head in disbelief. "That guy is so good," he moaned, "that even when he strikes out, a team is lucky to hold him to two bases."

YOUNG WAS KNOCKED OUT OF THE BULLPEN

Cy Young was pitching for Cleveland in the gloaming of his historic career when, one afternoon, manager Jimmy McGuire—who was noted for changing his mind often and strangely—dispatched Cy to the bullpen to limber up. While Young was warming up, the Indians' pitcher who had been in trouble settled down and retired the side.

Young continued to warm up for a couple of innings, however, and suddenly the pitcher got into trouble again. But instead of bringing in Young, McGuire rushed in another pitcher. Young was at first astonished, and then enraged.

"This takes the cake," he said as he stalked up to McGuire. "I've been pitching for twenty-two years, and this is the first time I've been knocked out of the bullpen."

A CHANGE OF DIRECTIONS

George Earnshaw, one of the Philadelphia Athletics' better pitchers back in the 1920s, ran into problems one day against the Yankees. After Lou Gehrig lofted a homer into the right-field seats, manager Connie Mack yanked Earnshaw. Instead of sending him to the showers, Mack ordered him to sit on the bench to see how his replacement handled the mighty Yankees.

Earnshaw reluctantly sat down. Soon Gehrig came to the plate again, and Earnshaw obediently paid strict attention as his replacement turned on the power. Gehrig responded with a home run into the *left-field* stands. There was a long pause, then Earnshaw turned to Mack: "I see," he said, "Made him change directions."

PITCHER REFUSED TO GIVE UP BALL TO MANAGER

Gene Alley, who played eleven seasons with Pittsburgh, broke into pro ball in 1959 with Dubuque, Iowa, of the Midwest League. Alley said he was amazed at the meekness of the manager and his lack of control over the players.

In one game, Alley recalled, the starting pitcher

was being hit hard, and the manager walked out to the mound to pull him from the game. The pitcher refused to give the ball to the manager, and before anyone knew what was happening, the manager and the pitcher were wrestling on the ground for control of the ball!

IN THE WAY

Burleigh Grimes loved to tell of the time he was managing Brooklyn in 1937 and the Dodgers acquired veteran pitcher Waite Hoyt during midseason. At the time, Grimes was flashing his signs directly to Watty Clark, the first-base coach, or using a utility man to relay them in an effort to fool the opposition. Grimes recalled that the day Hoyt arrived, he was sitting in the dugout between Waite and Watty.

He forgot, however, that he was sitting next to Watty Clark's deaf ear. Watty kept staring at the field as Grimes explained to Hoyt how the signs were relayed. Grimes said he'd like to have Hoyt stand in front of him that day and relay the signs to Clark at first.

Brooklyn's sign for a steal then was a tug at the cap bill. An opportunity for a steal developed in one of the early innings, and Grimes ordered Hoyt to relay a steal sign to Clark. Watty looked over again and again, and Hoyt repeatedly yanked at his cap. The runner stayed glued to first. When the inning was over, Grimes ran up to Clark and jumped on him for not sending the runner down on the signal.

Said Watty, "How could I get your sign when this stupid jerk was standing right in the way?"

THE GROUNDS WERE VERY WET

Judge Kenesaw Mountain Landis didn't like to quibble over trivialities during his long tenure as baseball's commissioner. After the judge inspected the soggy Polo Grounds on the morning of the scheduled second game of the 1936 World Series, he announced, "The game is off because of wet grounds."

When he returned to his hotel, several newspaper writers asked him to elaborate on this announcement. "Elaborate on wet grounds, why that's ridiculous," he said.

But the writers persisted. "All right, I'll elaborate," said the commissioner. "You may say the game is off because of *very* wet grounds."

EMBARRASSING POSTPONEMENT

Back in the mid-1960s, Ken Nicolson had two jobs. He was president of Detroit's Duluth, Minnesota, farm club and also was the chief meteorologist of the area's U.S. Weather Bureau.

One day in early August of 1963, he ordered the groundskeeper to water the field, because he had predicted a spell of dry weather. Then the heavens opened, and torrents of rain forced the game to be called because of wet grounds!

"I'M BATTING FOR MYSELF"

Pinch hitting was not a widespread practice when Wally Rehg reported to the Boston Red Sox late in the 1911 season. When the cocky youngster was sent in to bat for the pitcher, the umpire asked him who he was batting for.

"I'm batting for myself, you old fool," replied Rehg. He didn't, though. The ump tossed him out of his first big-league game before he even got into it.

SEASICK SIT-OUT

Over the years, ballplayers have been forced to sit out games for a variety of reasons, ranging from injuries to a simple case of the flu. But former Milwaukee shortstop Johnny Logan had one of the most unusual excuses for missing a game: seasickness. When the Braves made a trip to Los Angeles in 1958, Logan took advantage of an off day to go deep-sea fishing and developed such a violent case of seasickness that he was immobilized the next day.

DOBY'S DINNER WAS A BIT LATE

After the 1957 season, the Chicago White Sox traded outfielder Larry Doby to Baltimore. To make him feel welcome, a number of Orioles supporters sold tickets for a special dinner honoring Doby. It was scheduled to be held after the season started in April. Ticket sales for the dinner were brisk—until Baltimore traded Doby to Cleveland on March 31.

OUTFIELDER DELIVERED TWO HITS—AND TWO BABIES

Dr. Keith Oliver, an outfielder on a semipro team in Purcellville, Virginia, delivered two babies one summer afternoon in 1958. That's not unusual for an obstetrician—but the two deliveries interrupted Dr. Oliver while he was playing a game against Warrenton, Virginia. He also had to leave the game to treat a spectator who suffered a heart attack.

Despite the interruptions, the doctor managed to slug out two hits!

WHAT GEHRIG DIDN'T SAY IN HIS FAREWELL SPEECH

Lou Gehrig had a gentle and wry sense of humor— humor that didn't fail him even after he learned that he was dying of the disease that now carries his name.

When Gehrig was in his prime, he was interviewed on a radio program sponsored by a breakfast cereal named Huskies. He stunned the interviewer and the sponsor and drew national attention by noting that he ate a bowl of Wheaties every morning.

In 1939, when the Yankees staged the famous Lou Gehrig Appreciation Day on July 4, Gehrig made one of the most moving speeches in baseball history, noting that although he was facing death, "I consider myself to be the luckiest man on the face of this earth."

A few weeks after the speech, Gehrig told a friend, a newsman, that at the last minute he had deleted one paragraph from his speech.

"What I was going to say," smiled Gehrig, was, "A couple of years ago, I was on the Huskies radio program and accidentally mentioned Wheaties. Today, I understand these ceremonies are being broadcast by the Wheaties company, and I just want to say this one word: *Huskies.*"

GREAT PLAY LED TO APPLAUSE—AND THREE STRAIGHT STEALS

One of baseball's most unusual steals—three straight bases without a stop—took place when a player was accepting plaudits from a crowd for an outstanding catch. One afternoon in 1880, Miah Murray was catching for Worcester, Massachusetts. There was a runner on first when the batter cracked a high foul back toward the stands. Murray raced back and made such a dazzling catch that the hometown fans leaped to their feet with shouts of glee and loud applause.

Murray accepted the adulation by removing his cap and repeatedly bowing right and left to the crowd. The runner on first, meanwhile, saw what was going on and raced to second. Murray kept bowing, and the runner raced to third. The bowing continued—and the runner raced home.

LEGISLATION TOOK SECOND PLACE

John K. Tener was a pitcher for Cap Anson's White Stockings in the 1880s before launching a career that brought him the governorship of Pennsylvania, the presidency of the National League, and a term in the U.S. Senate.

As governor, Tener succeeded in pushing three important reform bills through the legislature. When it came time to sign them, an overjoyed observer remarked, "Governor, this must be the biggest moment of your career."

Tener angrily retorted, "Man, what are you saying? Why, I once shut out the Giants!"

THE OUTFIELDERS DON'T NEED THE WORK

Milwaukee's Lew Burdette once was being pelted with abandon by Los Angeles in a late spring exhibition game, and coach Billy Herman was dispatched to the mound to pull Lew from the game. Lew wasn't very happy about the idea, pointing out that it was only an exhibition game and "I need the work."

Red Schoendienst, then the Braves' second baseman, who had joined the conference on the mound, cracked, "Maybe you do. But the outfielders are getting more than they can use."

A TOAST OF AN ANNOUNCEMENT

There was once a shortstop named Woody Bottoms in the old Georgia-Alabama League. Whenever Woody came to bat, league public-address announcers drew a laugh from the crowd by cheerfully announcing, "Bottoms up!"

"MY SPITTER'S FREEZING"

Dick (Turk) Farrell, who toiled fourteen years for Philadelphia and Houston in the fifties and sixties, once drew a pitching assignment in an early-spring game when the temperature was barely above freezing. After a stint on the mound, Farrell returned to the dugout to complain that it was "so cold that my spitter is freezing on the way to the plate."

UNZIPPED

Kansas City's Jim Nash was pitching a superb game against California one night, when the third baseman, for no apparent reason, called time and raced to the mound. "What's the matter?" asked the bewildered Nash.

The third baseman leaned over and whispered into Nash's ear, "Your zipper is unzipped."

GIBSON WAS LUCKY

Catcher Tim McCarver once cracked that St. Louis pitching great Bob Gibson was an extraordinarily lucky pitcher. "He always pitches when the other team doesn't score any runs," smiled McCarver.

"IT'S HOT—BUT I LIKE IT!"

Charlie Metro was the "head coach" of Chicago in 1962, when the Cubs made a pre-Astrodome visit to Houston. The temperature was near 100 degrees, and the humidity was equally stifling. Cubs players complained constantly about the terrible weather while losing three straight games. Metro became fed up with the complaining and said he'd slap a fifty-dollar fine on any player who mentioned the sizzling heat.

A little later, Ernie Banks returned to the dugout, exhausted after a long run-down, and said, "Man, it's sure hot out there." He looked up to see Metro, and quickly added: "But that's the way I like it!"

"LET ME LEAD YOU TO FIRST"

Los Angeles' Sandy Koufax was one of baseball's greatest pitchers, but he was also one of baseball's most miserable batters. One night, Koufax drew a walk, and Jake Pitler, then a Dodger coach, called time and went over, grabbed Koufax's hand, and started walking him to first base. "It's been so long since Sandy has seen first base, I don't think he remembers the way," joked Pitler.

"DON'T KICK THE BUCKET—I MAY NEED YOU"

Casey Stengel was managing Brooklyn one day when Walter (Boom-Boom) Beck was knocked out of the pitching box. Boom-Boom stormed into the dugout and gave the water bucket a healthy kick.

"Here, here," admonished Stengel. "Cut that out. If you break your leg, I can't trade you."

THE BALL IS SLOWING DOWN

Lefty Grove once had a simple explanation for why he was encountering difficulties as his pitching career was coming to a close with the Boston Red Sox: "I'm throwing just as hard as I ever did. The ball's just not getting there as fast."

YOUR SIGNS DID YOU IN

At one time, Milwaukee's minor-league team was on such a prolonged losing binge that manager Marty Berghammer called a special clubhouse meeting to announce a new bit of strategy. Berghammer said the players had been missing so many signs that he had decided the team would simply not use any signs at all that day. Despite the lack of signs, Milwaukee turned in a fine performance, but the team still lost a close one to Toledo.

After the game, Toledo's Bruno Haas, who had been a former teammate of Berghammer's, ran into Marty and tried to offer some consolation for the loss. "Your guys did all right today," said Haas, adding, "You might have won but for one thing, and I'll tell you what it was. The Toledo club had all of your signs."

GLOVEY SARCASM

When Bucky Harris was managing Detroit, his out-fielder, Roy Johnson, dropped a fly to center. After the inning, Johnson came to the bench with all kinds of apologies for his error.

"Forget it," said Harris. "It hit you in a bad spot— right in the middle of your glove."

PRETEND YOU'RE FACING HARVARD

Back in the early 1960s, when the New York Mets were achieving new heights of mediocrity each day, man-ager Casey Stengel decided to try out rookie pitcher Ken McKenzie, who had graduated from Yale. McKenzie proved to be a true Met of the times—he walked the first five batters he faced.

Stengel wandered out to the mound, muttering to himself over what he should say to a pitcher in a situation such as this. An inspired look crept across Stengel's face, and he told the young rookie, "Make believe them guys is Harvards!" Then he sauntered back to the dugout.

BATBOY ASSISTANCE

The old Philadelphia Athletics were playing a home game many years ago, when a visiting player on second tried to score on a wild pitch. The Athletics' batboy, consumed by concern that there was no Philadelphia player near the ball at the backstop, raced over, picked it up, and threw a perfect toss to the pitcher covering home. The ball arrived in time to retire the runner—but, of course, the batboy's impulsive assistance was ruled ineligible.

SKUNKED

Jamestown was playing at Wellsville in the old Pennsylvania-Ontario-New York League, when both teams literally got skunked. About a dozen players were taking part in a boisterous argument near the mound in a late inning, when suddenly all became quiet. A skunk had wandered from under the grandstand onto the field—and was headed straight for the mound.

The argument was forgotten as the players frantically scampered away, while the skunk sauntered right across the mound, past second, and through the outfield, then disappeared under the fence.

DENTING THE DOME

When Houston's famed Astrodome first opened for business in 1965, club officials confidently proclaimed that there wasn't a chance in the world that anyone could hit a ball high enough to strike the roof. But, in June 1967, the Astros' Jimmy Wynn cracked a shot that hit the dome in a game against St. Louis. The ball struck in foul territory. Although it rebounded into fair territory on the field, it was ruled a foul ball because of local ''roof'' rules.

Manager Grady Hatton was asked if anyone attempted to catch Wynn's shot off the dome. "Gosh no," replied Hatton. "Everybody scattered."

GOLF, UGH!

After Rogers Hornsby retired from baseball, a friend remarked that now he would have time for leisurely pursuits, such as playing golf.

Replied Hornsby, "I don't want to play golf. When I hit a ball, I want someone else to go chase it."

WEAK ON GROUND BALLS

When the New York Mets first came into existence, they were so desperate for talent that they staged a special tryout camp for young hopefuls. Manager Casey Stengel noticed that one young man was wearing a pair of shin guards, so he invited him to get behind the plate and show what he could do. The youth said he wasn't a catcher—he was an infielder.

Why the shin guards? "Well," he replied, "I am a little weak on ground balls."

HIS FEET ARE IN THE WRONG PLACE

When Tony Kaufmann was a pitching coach for the St. Louis Cardinals, he had a particularly exasperating spring-training afternoon trying to teach a cocky young rookie how to stand on the rubber. The young player repeatedly resisted Kaufmann's suggestions.

Finally, the exasperated Kaufmann called to Mike Kelly, a veteran baseball executive who had been watching the demonstration. "Isn't this boy's right foot in the wrong place, Mike?" asked Kaufmann.

"I'll say it's in the wrong place," replied Kelly. "And so is his left foot. They ought to be in Keokuk." And, in a few days, they were.

SORRY FOR YOUR SUICIDE ATTEMPT

Frankie Frisch and Casey Stengel carried on a prolonged mock feud when the two were managing in the National League more than a half-century ago. Stengel was boss of the woefully weak Boston Braves and suffered a broken leg when he was struck by a taxi while attempting to cross a street. The first telegram to reach him at the hospital was from Frisch. It read, "Your unsuccessful attempt to commit suicide is deeply lamented."

HOPEFULLY, THAT PITCH WAS A MISTAKE

The fiery Ty Cobb was such an excellent place hitter that he could carve out quick revenge against any pitcher who deliberately threw at him. Cobb could whistle a line drive directly toward the pitching mound or lay down a soft bunt, then clobber the pitcher when he rushed over to field it.

When Red Ruffing broke in with the Boston Red Sox,

Ty Cobb (1950).

he delivered a pitch that sailed just inches from Cobb's cap bill. Cobb shook his finger at Ruffing and said, "Young man, for your sake, I hope that was a mistake."

THOSE SHINY FINGERNAILS

Baseball players always have an excuse for their errors. But no one has topped an alibi offered by Josh DeVore, a one-time outfielder with the New York Giants, after he dropped a routine fly ball. "I had a manicure this morning," DeVore explained, "and I was blinded by the reflection of the sun on my fingernails."

PITCHER ZINGS SPORTSWRITER

Wilmer (Vinegar Bend) Mizell was an unpolished Mississippi country boy when he broke into the majors with the St. Louis Cards in the early 1950s. But he was sharp enough to squelch a sophisticated sportswriter. Mizell liked to sing country music, and the sportswriter sarcastically asked him one day if he eventually planned a singing career on the stage or television. "Shucks no," replied Mizell. "I can't sing no better than you can write."

FAN LEARNS NOT TO BE FIRST IN LINE

Robert Hunt was such a loyal St. Louis fan that when the Cardinals won the 1964 National League pennant, he turned up at the ballpark days before the World Series to be first in line for tickets.

Hunt got his tickets. But he also received so much publicity that he was fired from his job for skipping work, a bill collector saw his picture in the paper and nailed him, and he was later arrested for nonsupport of his family.

HE WOULDN'T HAVE MISSED

Frederick (Crazy) Schmidt, an old-time pitcher, once got into a fight with a fan in Macon, Georgia, and was accused of throwing a brick at the fan. The fan filed suit, but the judge tossed the case out of court when Schmidt confidentially explained, "The fact that the plaintiff is alive today is evidence that I did not throw a brick at him. Everybody knows I have perfect control. If I'd thrown a brick at this fellow, I would have killed him dead!"

A REAL BREAKING PITCH

Arthur (Bugs) Raymond, a major-league pitcher in the early part of this century, was noted for his sharp curveballs. Once, while Raymond was dining in a restaurant, a group of fans asked him to show them how he was able to make the ball break so much.

Raymond picked up a water glass, proudly displayed his grip, then to the amazement of all, hurled the glass against the wall. It shattered into a hundred fragments. "There," said Raymond, "did you notice the break?"

HAMBURGER HOMERS

A restaurant owner in Fort Collins, Colorado, didn't know what he was getting into one summer when he offered a free hamburger, french fries, and soft drink to any child hitting a home run in a local Little League. The year before, the eighty-two teams in the Little League had averaged only about forty homers for the entire season, so the owner figured his offer would be only mildly costly.

But the free food provided stirring inspiration for the young players. The youngsters started crashing homers faster than the restaurant could cook up their orders. One boy hit five homers in a single game.

When the Wolves trounced the Foxes 77–18 in another game, forty-four of the ninety-six hits were homers!

WORN OUT FROM EATING

For such a lanky man, Satchel Paige used to amaze his teammates with the prodigious amount of food he could consume in one sitting. Once, after he had downed the equivalent of three meals at a restaurant, the waitress asked Paige if he wanted any more food. "No, ma'am," replied Paige. "Not that I'm not hungry—just tired of eating."

WHAT ENCOURAGEMENT? WHAT ADVICE?

Yankee great Lefty Gomez once recalled the time he was pitching and loaded the bases with nobody out. Infielder Tony Lazzeri took the ball and walked over to the pitcher's mound. "This is a heck of a mess, isn't it?" he asked, then tossed the ball to Gomez and said, "Well, you got yourself into it—now get yourself out."

Gomez did manage to work out of the jam and went on to win. The next morning, he was startled to read in the newspaper how Lazzeri's "encouragement and advice helped him out of that tight spot."

LET'S NOT TALK BASEBALL

When Bob Gibson was a superstar pitcher for St. Louis, he had one major complaint: "Ninety-nine percent of the people I meet only want to talk about baseball," said Gibson, who had a 251–174 record in seventeen years with the Cardinals.

"Just suppose, for example," said Gibson, "you were a garbage collector, and every day about a hundred people stopped you and asked you how much garbage you collected that day—and how much you expect to collect the next day."

GOOD AND BAD NEWS

When the Padres were once rumored to be moving out of San Diego, then-club president Buzzie Bavasi told a news conference, "The good news is that we may stay in San Diego. The bad news, I guess, is the same thing."

YOU'RE THE BRAINS—YOU TAKE THE BALL

There was a reason why Lefty Gomez, one of the Yankees' leading pitchers during the 1930s, quickly picked up the nickname Goofy. One of Tony Lazzeri's favorite stories about the New York southpaw involved a game in which the Philadelphia Athletics had managed to get a runner on third against Gomez before Mule Haas laid down a beautiful squeeze bunt.

Gomez raced to the ball and looked at home. It was too late for a play. Then he looked at first. Again, too late for a play. So, for no apparent reason, Gomez whirled and fired the ball to an astonished Lazzeri at second base.

Lazzeri called time and walked over to the pitcher. "What's the idea of throwing the ball to me?" he asked. "There was no play at second."

Gomez shrugged. "I know," he replied, "but I didn't know what to do with the ball, so I threw it to you. They all tell me you're supposed to be the brains on this team."

SIXTY DAYS FOR SPITTING

Stanley (Frenchy) Bordagaray served a brief tenure as manager of a Brooklyn farm team after eleven years in the majors. One day, Frenchy got into a furious argument with an umpire and spat in the ump's face.

He was astonished when the league president suspended him for sixty days. But he didn't lost his sense of humor. "OK, maybe I did wrong," he said, "but it's a little more than I expectorated."

NO ONE IS BETTER THAN YOU

When Clark Griffith was running the old Washington Senators, he had a pitcher named Joe Engel, who was so wild that he'd sometimes miss the plate by ten feet or more. Finally Griffith called Engel into his office to tell him he was being sent to Minneapolis.

"For whom?" Engel inquired.

"For nobody," replied Griffith. "It's an even trade."

WHAT, NO RADIO?

There was a time when automobile companies would award new cars to baseball players who were particularly popular or had achieved remarkable accomplishments. Lefty Grove, who won twenty-eight games for the Philadelphia Athletics in 1930 and had a 31–4 record in 1931, was selected to receive a car in a ceremony at the A's park.

After being presented the keys, Grove walked over to his new car, opened the door, and leaned in to take a look. Suddenly he slammed the door shut with a crashing bang and yelled, "What the hell—no radio?"

WHAT DOES A CATCHER HAVE TO BE PROUD OF?

A number of years ago, the publicity department of the International League sent out questionnaires to all league players, asking them to write in their ages, weights, heights, and so forth. The questionnaire also asked each player, "Of what feat are you proudest?"

Pat Collins, who later caught for the Boston Braves, provided the frankest answer: "I'm a catcher. I've got nothing to be proud of."

"I ONLY HAD ONE GLASS"

Charlie Grimm liked to recall the time he was managing the Chicago Cubs and a young player came up and inquired about Grimm's feelings about a player having an occasional glass of beer. Grimm said he thought it was all right, as long as the player observed moderation.

About an hour later, Grimm said, he was in his Wrigley Field office and happened to glance out the window. Walking out of the tavern across the street was his young player, in full uniform, spikes and all. Grimm rushed down and started screaming at the rookie, who immediately drew himself up in indignation and asked, "Hey, what's all the fuss? I only had one glass."

THE ONLY GAME

The late Bill Veeck, one of baseball's most colorful executives, joked that baseball is the only game left in America for normal people: "To play basketball now, you have be 7'6". To play football, you have to be the same width!"

Bill Veeck, one of baseball's most colorful owners.

11
THE FOUR MOST IMPORTANT EVENTS IN MODERN BASEBALL

Few of today's fans realize it, but our national pastime has come perilously close to obscurity several times during this century. The two world wars, the Black Sox scandal, and the Great Depression all could have quashed fan interest in baseball, eventually making our ballparks as popular for sport as the Roman Colosseum.

But baseball is a lucky sport. Four separate events between 1920 and 1946 played incalculably important roles in saving the game and propelling it to new heights of prosperity and popularity.

LET THERE BE LIGHT: THE FIGHT OVER NIGHTTIME BASEBALL

A mild-appearing man with rimless glasses, E. Lee Keyser looked more like a bookkeeper than a monster. But in early 1930, that epithet—along with a number of derogatory, unprintable remarks—were directed toward Keyser, the owner of the Des Moines, Iowa, team in the Western League.

A photograph of some children playing a pickup game of baseball at night on Boston Common provided Keyser with the inspiration for one of baseball's greatest and most important innovations—and at the same time made him a target of one of the sport's most vociferous attacks.

At the 1929–1930 winter minor-league meetings, Keyser shocked his fellow executives with the announcement that he planned to install permanent lights at his park for the 1930 season.

Night baseball! Preposterous, screamed most of baseball's executives and sportswriters. Didn't this "monster" Keyser have any idea of the potential harm he could do to athletes playing under lights? one minor-league executive asked, adding that God knows how many players would have their careers shortened or terminated by nocturnal contests.

Sportswriters confidently predicted that night baseball would completely change the tone of the game: Pitchers would have a substantial advantage under the lights. Players would suffer eyestrain—perhaps even permanent eye damage—trying to follow the ball. And undoubtedly there would be a plague of injuries to players who had trouble picking up the ball without the benefit of good old-fashioned sunlight.

Didn't Keyser know that there had been several experiments with night baseball—including one night game at Chicago's Comiskey Park during the early years of this century—with less than spectacular success?

The wily Keyser knew exactly what he was doing. Minor-league attendance had been slipping slowly since the mid-1920s, and now that the Great Depression was beginning to heat up, he was convinced patronage would drop even more.

The problem was that the unemployed couldn't afford even the modest cost of a seat for a daytime baseball game, yet folks who could afford it were hard at work while the games were being played. With lighted games, the working stiff could come home, eat supper, then go out to a ball game.

Keyser said his idea for lighting came from two sources. The local college football team, which had played night games as early as 1900, started playing most of its games under the lights around 1927—and the games were well attended. Also, General Electric had experimented with powerful lights for sporting events and had even lit a ballfield on an experimental basis during the 1920s.

But it was another brochure put out by General Electric that sold Keyser on night baseball, he once recalled. GE "had been given an order by the Commonwealth of Massachusetts to light up the Boston Common. The order had been 'to make it as nearly like daylight as possible,'" Keyser said. To illustrate that success, he said, the GE brochure "included pictures of youngsters playing ball on the Common."

He immediately contacted GE officials, who provided the expertise in setting up a lighting system. "We didn't have too much money to spend, but we begged tower poles from the telephone company and the light and power company," said Keyser.

"I even went up to a windmill manufacturer in Wisconsin to get help on how to set up the towers. We settled on burying them in ten feet of concrete. Then it was decided to raise the towers over a hundred feet in the air instead of sixty-five or seventy feet, to cut the glare on both the players and the spectators."

Ironically, Keyser was beaten to the punch in presenting pro baseball's first regular league-play night game. Des Moines opened the season on the road, and the debut night game was scheduled for May 2, 1930. A few days before Des Moines' opener, Independence, Kansas, of the Western Association hastily threw up a set of lights, far inferior to Keyser's lighting standards. Only about 1,000 fans turned out for that first night game, when Muskogee whipped the locals 13–3. The dimly lit field drew bitter complaints from most of the players.

It was a different story at Des Moines on May 2. The local paper reported:

> One hundred and forty-six projectors diffusing fifty-three million candlepower of mellow light and the amazing batting of Des Moines' nocturnal-eyed players made the opening of the local baseball season a complete success Friday night.
>
> Baseball was played successfully after dark on an illuminated field and the Demons won, 13–6, from Wichita in a contest that was normal in every respect so far as the playing was concerned.

The game attracted a crowd of more than ten thousand, and the paper noted that none of Des Moines' four errors "could be charged to the lack of light or glare.... On the other hand, many brilliant stops and catches were made and most of the skeptics' questions were answered by things which occurred." The paper then listed numerous instances where towering flies and pop-ups were easily snared.

Keyser's lighting experiment was an unqualified success—and it drew worldwide attention. The National Broadcasting Company aired the latter part of the game nationally, and the game was rebroadcast via shortwave to Europe, South America, South Africa, Australia, and the Orient.

In following games, the lights continued to attract crowds. Des Moines played eleven of its first nineteen games at night. Despite miserable spring weather, attendance was staggering. Keyser attempted to obtain a patent or copyright on his innovation, but without success.

In the meantime, minor-league executives—in-

cluding many who had sharply criticized Keyser—
began installing lights and experiencing a corres-
ponding increase in attendance. By the end of the
season, teams with lights were reporting attendance
figures double or triple those of 1929.

Within three years, the vast majority of minor-
league parks were lighted—and there's little doubt
that night baseball prevented scores of minor-league
teams from becoming casualties of the Depression. By
1934, some leagues demanded that members either
light up or light out from the league. Since then, minor-league baseball has become virtually a nighttime activity, with day games a rare weekend occurrence.

Despite the success of lights in the minors, baseball's conservative major-league owners and executives remained united in opposition to nighttime play
in the big leagues—until the entrance onto the scene
of the controversial Larry McPhail, who had seen
attendance soar when night baseball was introduced while he was with Columbus of the American
Association.

At the annual National League meeting in December 1934, McPhail, then general manager of Cincinnati, formally requested permission to play night
baseball in 1935. His fellow executives were flabbergasted but eventually granted McPhail's request because of the Reds' ailing financial condition. It was
only an experiment, they said, and they permitted
just seven night games.

On May 24, 1935, President Franklin D. Roosevelt
pushed a special button that had been installed in
the White House, and instantly more than 600 flood-
lights illuminated the Reds' old Crosley Field. A huge
crowd turned out for the first major-league night
game, in which Cincinnati edged Philadelphia 2–1.
By the end of the season, the Reds had attracted
130,000 customers for its meager allotment of night

games—enormous crowds compared to normal day-time attendance.

Suddenly McPhail's nighttime games were no longer classified as an experiment. When he took charge at Brooklyn in 1938, he immediately installed lights at Ebbets Field. The Dodgers' first night game on June 15 was a success in more ways than one. A total of 38,748 customers saw Cincinnati's Johnny Vander Meer toss his historic second straight no-hitter, blanking Brooklyn 6–0.

Connie Mack was seventy-six and was still managing the Philadelphia Athletics in 1939, but his aged brain grasped the significance of the attendance surges at Cincinnati and Brooklyn. Mack installed lights at Shibe Park, and on May 16, 1939, nighttime baseball made its debut in the American League, when Cleveland stopped the A's 8–3 in ten innings before a crowd of a little more than fifteen thousand. The Phillies also used Shibe Park and played seven night games that season.

The rest of the major-league teams started lighting up faster than smokers emerging from a movie theater. By 1941 only Boston and Chicago of the National League and New York, Boston, and Detroit of the American had parks without lights. World War II prevented the Yankees and Braves from installing lights until 1946. The next year, Boston joined the crowd, and the lights went on in Detroit in 1948.

The Cubs' Wrigley Field ended the last holdout with seven night games in 1988—a compromise permitted by city officials to prevent the team from moving outside the city limits. The Cubs had been praised for years as the last bastion of daytime ball, but former owner P. K. Wrigley originally had planned to install lights during the early 1940s. When World War II broke out, Wrigley donated the steel he had purchased for the lighting towers to the war effort.

The All-Star Game became a nighttime affair during the 1960s in order to hype TV ratings. (Most fans, however, would be surprised to learn that the first nighttime All-Star Game was played at the Polo Grounds in New York on July 6, 1942. It wasn't supposed to be a night game, but a steady afternoon rain delayed the start until 7:22 P.M.)

Then, again to accommodate TV ratings, the World Series became a nighttime event on October 13, 1971, when Pittsburgh nipped Baltimore 4–3 in game four at Three Rivers Stadium.

ROBINSON PAVED THE WAY FOR EQUALITY— AND BASEBALL EXPANSION

On a crisp, sunny April day in 1946, a young rookie nervously stepped to the plate at Roosevelt Stadium in Newark, New Jersey, and promptly grounded out to the infield.

It would have been a routine play, except that the batter was Jackie Robinson and his plate appearance was the first by a black man in professional baseball—white man's version—during the twentieth century.

That modest groundout signified the beginning of the end of baseball's unforgivably shameful years of racism—but it also blazed another trail that eventually led to the expansion of the major leagues in the sixties and seventies.

The taunts, the jeers, the racist remarks that Robinson courageously endured during that '46 season with Montreal of the International League and the next year when he broke into the majors with Brooklyn have been well documented. Less well known is that the Dodgers originally had assigned two black men to the Montreal team. Robinson gallantly shrugged off the torments; his fellow black player crumbled under the insults and fled pro baseball to return to the Negro leagues.

Nor is it well known that Robinson's debut in the majors was the culmination of a secret five-year master plan conceived by Branch Rickey to integrate baseball.

● ● ●

Few realize it, but baseball was integrated—at least to a limited degree—during the last century, until the game's executives systematically drove blacks from the sport during the late 1880s and 1890s.

History has recognized Adrian Constantine Anson, the famous player-manager of the Chicago White Stockings during the last quarter of the nineteenth century, as the man most responsible for establishing baseball's unwritten whites-only rule. Anson was the most famous and vocal proponent of the "inferiority" of blacks. In reality, however, racism was rampant among baseball's leaders virtually from the start, but they used quieter and more devious methods in making baseball a game for whites only.

In 1867, the National Association of Professional Baseball Players—then baseball's chief governing body—passed a rule saying that any club with one or more "colored persons" would be barred from the association. The reason given was politics. It's true that the role of blacks was still a hotly debated political issue two years after the Civil War had ended.

But the real reason for the exclusion of blacks was that nearly all of the members of the baseball organization were composed of "gentlemen's clubs." Even in the North, it was considered most inappropriate for a "gentleman" to associate or play with a black in 1867. Baseball was considered strictly a social event in those days.

The "gentlemen's agreement" continued through successive baseball organizations and stuck around when the National League was formally organized in 1876. It's estimated, however, that at least twenty to thirty blacks cracked the color line in the minor leagues, and at least two blacks were major leaguers.

John Fowler, who played for a white team in New Castle, Pennsylvania, in 1872 apparently was the first black to be paid by a white team. Fowler eventually played with many other minor-league teams, including entries in the Western League, Northern League, and Northwest League. Slowly other blacks were quietly acquired by minor-league teams in the 1870s and early 1880s.

Then, in 1884, Moses Fleetwood Walker became the first black major leaguer when he signed with Toledo of the American Association, then considered a major league. Fellow players and hometown fans raised not a word of dissent when he joined the team as a catcher.

Things were different, however, with the league's two southern entries, Louisville and Richmond. Walker was showered with racist remarks and hisses at Louisville. (When Louisville turned up to play its next games at Toledo, the local fans loudly booed and hissed their rivals!)

At Richmond there were threats that if Walker appeared on the field in uniform, he would be lynched. By the time Toledo traveled to Richmond, however, it was a moot problem. Walker suffered a broken rib after being struck by a foul tip and was released for the season. Toledo's franchise folded at the end of the campaign.

Walker's younger brother, Welday, was the second black to play in the majors. He appeared in a handful of games as an outfielder during midsummer 1884, when Toledo was severely crippled with injured players.

Meanwhile, a number of blacks were performing admirably in the higher minors. In 1887, for example, the International League had several outstanding blacks, including Frank Grant, who topped Buffalo with a .366 average; George Stovey, who had a 33–14 record for Newark; Bob Higgins, who was 20–7 with Syracuse; and John Fowler, who hit .350 for Binghamton.

Today one would assume that these outstanding performances would lure more and more blacks into baseball. But prejudice was especially strong in that era, and the expansion of black players in the minors apparently intensified the racism.

Many white players suddenly became vocal about playing with blacks. The discontent reached such a level in the International League that loop directors called an emergency midsummer meeting in 1887 and issued a written edict barring all league teams from signing future contracts "with colored men." Baseball's unwritten agreement was now a written agreement.

A few days later came the Anson incident—the one that is credited with launching baseball's half-century affair with segregation. Anson, one of the greatest ballplayers of all time, was scheduled to match his mighty White Stockings in an exhibition at Newark. Stovey, the ace of the Newark pitching staff, was the natural pitcher to go against Anson's major leaguers—but the crusty Chicago manager said he wouldn't field his team if the black was allowed to play, and Stovey was held out of the exhibition.

No one is quite sure why Anson was such a staunch racist. He was the first white child born in Marshalltown, Iowa, and Indian children were among his early playmates. Many of his teammates on the Marshalltown team, where he got his baseball start, had fought for the North in the Civil War. Anson had always lived in the North, and in the 1880s Chicago was considered one of the most racially liberal cities in the country.

Yet Anson made no secret of his hatred of blacks. In his autobiography, written in 1900, he made numerous bigoted remarks about the White Stockings' black mascot, calling him a "no account nigger" and a "coon." He did not mention black players or offer any explanation of why he held blacks in such contempt.

Because of his stature in baseball, word of Anson's successful stand against Stovey spread quickly, giving the game's bigots all the impetus they needed to expel blacks from the game. A few months after Anson's stand, the St. Louis Browns, winners of the American Association pennant, backed out of an exhibition against a black Cuban team. Eight of the Browns' players—including four native Northerners and one from Canada—had presented team officials with a petition saying they would refuse to play against the black team.

Late in the 1887 season and during most of the 1888 season, blacks one by one were quietly dropped from minor-league teams. By 1892 pro baseball was strictly white.

Blacks did experience one last, brief fling playing against whites in 1898. An all-black team, called the Acme Colored Giants, started the year representing Celoron, New York, in the white Iron and Oil League. Although the team apparently was well received, it was a loser; by the end of June, the team held a firm lock on the league's cellar.

The team folded on July 8—after winning only eight of forty-nine games. Two weeks later, the Iron and Oil League itself collapsed because of sparse attendance.

The era of blacks in white man's baseball was over until 1947.

● ● ●

There were several attempts before 1946 to break baseball's color line. One of the earliest involved an effort by the Giants' John McGraw, who signed a talented black in 1901 and planned to pass him off as an Indian named "Tokohoma." But White Sox owner Charles Comiskey got wind of the plan and raised such a ruckus that McGraw had to abandon the idea.

McGraw also apparently toyed with the idea in 1906 of signing William Matthews, a standout football and baseball player at Harvard. Matthews at the time was playing in the Vermont League, which was not a recognized pro league. But Matthews's chances of joining the Giants were eliminated when fellow members of the Vermont League angrily protested his presence, and Matthews soon departed from baseball.

Connie Mack reportedly considered the idea of signing a black player or two for his Athletics in the late twenties or early thirties but backed down under quiet but powerful pressure from fellow executives.

Several serious attempts were made to break baseball's color line during World War II, when there was a serious shortage of competent talent. In 1943, Clarence (Pants) Rowland, then president of Los Angeles of the Pacific Coast League, let it be known that he planned to try out at least three black players. Rowland said later that he was forced to back down on the proposal because of stern pressure applied by other league leaders. In Oakland that same year, owner Vince Devincenzi told Manager Johnny Vergez to try out two blacks. Vergez stubbornly refused. Devincenzi then dropped the matter.

● ● ●

Meanwhile, in 1944 Bill Veeck and Abe Saperstein, owner of the Harlem Globetrotters, cooked up a plan to integrate baseball—and they almost got away with it!

Veeck had raised the necessary funds to purchase the financially troubled Philadelphia Phillies, who had finished next to last in '43. Then, with Saperstein's help, he planned to liberally stock the team with players from the Negro leagues, including Roy Campanella, Luke Easter, Satchel Paige, and Monte Irvin, said Veeck in his autobiography, *Veeck—as in Wreck.*

But Veeck said he made one terrible mistake. Because of his long respect for Judge Kenesaw Mountain Landis, he told the aged commissioner of his plan. Suddenly the National League took over the Phillies' franchise, and league president Ford Frick sold it to William Cox for about half of what Veeck had intended to offer.

● ● ●

While baseball was fumbling around with integration, shrewd Branch Rickey had quietly developed in 1942 a plan to integrate baseball. A devout Christian fundamentalist, Rickey had been a schoolteacher, a pro player, a college coach, and an attorney before becoming a baseball management wizard.

He had developed St. Louis into a National League dynasty, and he undoubtedly was baseball's best-known executive in 1942, when, at the age of sixty-five, he became president and general manager of the Brooklyn Dodgers. The Dodgers won the pennant in '41 and finished second in '42, but Rickey knew the team was aging and future prosperity was precarious.

He told fellow team executives that the Dodgers would have to start signing young players—and that might include the signing of blacks. Rickey's proposal to sign blacks was backed by two motives: his religious compassion and firm beliefs about the equality of man, and, more important, his conviction that blacks could play major-league ball—and that they represented a vast, untapped source of talent for the Dodgers.

Rickey obtained the blessing—or at least the approval—of the other Dodgers officials and immediately drew up a list of specifications for the first player to break the color line. Rickey said he would

have to select a player who was the "right man" both
on and off the field, one who would be well received
by the media and public, and one who would be
accepted by his teammates.

Then the search began. Rickey even financed a
third Negro league, which fielded a team called the
Brown Dodgers at Ebbets Field, in a secretive attempt
to scout black players. Scouting reports on black prospects poured in, but none met Rickey's criteria for one
reason or another—until 1945, when he learned that
the Red Sox had given a trial to a young player
named Jackie Robinson. The young Robinson, a football, baseball, track, and basketball star at UCLA,
was rejected by Boston. But Rickey's ears perked up
when he kept hearing about the fine qualities of the
soft-spoken, articulate Robinson, then playing for the
Kansas City Monarchs.

Rickey dispatched scout after scout to look at Robinson before he personally inspected the young prospect. Rickey knew at once he had the man he was
seeking.

On August 28, 1945, Rickey summoned the twenty-
five-year-old Robinson to his office. Jackie thought he
was being called in to sign a contract for Rickey's
black team in Brooklyn. Instead, he was stunned with
the news that Rickey intended to sign him with the
Brooklyn Dodgers.

The two spent more than three hours discussing the
formidable problems that Robinson would face: the
opposition from other players and owners, the insults,
even efforts to deliberately injure him on the field.
And, Rickey said, he wanted a player with the "guts
not to fight back," no matter how much torment he
received. Robinson agreed to the conditions.

At the end of the long talk, Jackie signed an agreement calling for a $3,500 bonus and $600 a month for
signing a contract with Montreal, the Dodgers' top
minor-league team. On October 23, 1945, Robinson

formally signed a contract to play the '46 season with Montreal.

This, of course, was the biggest sports story of the year. Many newspapers wrote glowing editorials praising Rickey's historic effort. But numerous white major leaguers from the South decried the move and vowed they'd never play on a team with a black. Other players, such as Bob Feller, said they doubted Robinson had the talent to play in the majors.

● ● ●

Although Robinson's initial plate appearance was a dismal bust at Jersey City that April 18, he finished the game with four hits, including a home run, and two stolen bases in a 14–1 romp.

Robinson was one of two black men in uniform for Montreal that day. Sitting in the dugout was twenty-seven-year-old pitcher John Wright, whom Montreal had signed in February.

Throughout spring training in Florida, the two had endured daily bouts of racial prejudice, had been pulled from exhibition games because of local ordinances barring blacks and whites from playing together, and had faced the pressure of the nation's press keeping a watchful eye on their every activity.

Their situation worsened once the International League season began. Baltimore residents threatened to boycott any games in which Robinson and Wright appeared. Although there were no problems in many league cities, the two players received liberal doses of racial taunting in cities as far north as Syracuse.

In what must surely be one of the most impressive accomplishments of a human being, Robinson obeyed Rickey's orders and quietly endured the terrible strain. What makes Robinson's effort even more remarkable is that, despite the savage, brain-numbing attacks, he led the International League with a .349 average, finished second in stolen bases with 40,

tied the league mark of 113 runs scored, and had a
.985 fielding average, the best of any second baseman in the league.

The talented Wright couldn't match Robinson's endurance of the racism. He managed only two relief
appearances for the Royals before he was optioned
to Three Rivers, Quebec, of the Class C Border
League. But the strain had already destroyed Wright.
At the end of the season, he was released by the
Dodgers and returned to Negro league play.

Meanwhile, the Dodgers, benefiting from their
years of scouting blacks, were continuing to add
blacks to their roster. They signed catcher Roy Campanella and pitcher Don Newcombe, assigning both
to Nashua of the Class B New England League. They
also signed Roy Partlow to the Royals, optioning him
later in the season to Three Rivers.

During the summer, shortstop Manny McIntyre was
signed by a St. Louis Cards farm team, Sherbrooke,
Quebec, of the Border League.

●   ●   ●

In 1947, Brooklyn moved its spring-training camp
to Cuba in an effort to make life easier for Robinson,
and announced that he would play with the Dodgers
that season.

Rickey, the careful taskmaster, wanted to make
Jackie's transition to the majors as easy as possible.
He met with leaders of the black community in Brooklyn to encourage them to avoid making a major fuss
over Robinson's big-league debut. In effect, he said,
leave him alone, and let him play baseball.

A minor uprising arose during spring training
among some Dodgers players who said they would
not play with a black. The uprising was quelled after
Rickey met face to face with the belligerents.

But players from two other teams—Philadelphia
and St. Louis—quietly laid plans to leave the field
against Brooklyn if Robinson was in the lineup. Ford

Frick, the league president, halted that threat with a warning to the Cardinals that if they carried through with the plan, the team would be suspended from the National League—even if it wrecked the league for years. Said Frick, "This is the United States of America, and one citizen has as much right to play as another. The National League will go down the line with Robinson, whatever the consequence."

Robinson made baseball history again on April 15, 1947, when he played first base against the Boston Braves in the season opener at Ebbets Field. It was the first time ever that a black had played in a National League or American League game. Jackie got off to an inauspicious start. He went hitless in his major-league debut, although he did score a run in the 5–3 victory. In his first five games, he was hitless in twenty trips.

He also had to endure a torrent of racist remarks, including a barrage from the Philadelphia Phillies that later required an apology from Phils manager Ben Chapman.

After that slow start, however, Robinson was phenomenal. Despite hate mail, death threats, racial slurs, and taunts from opposing players and fans, he was the National League Rookie of the Year. He hit .297, had a team-high twenty-nine stolen bases, and rapped twelve homers. The Dodgers also won their first pennant since 1941.

Robinson eventually played ten seasons for the Dodgers, with a lifetime average of .311. In six of those ten seasons, he appeared in a World Series—another tribute to Rickey's management style.

● ● ●

Baseball integration came slowly but surely after 1947. Later that summer, Bill Veeck of Cleveland signed the first American League black: hard-hitting Larry Doby. Campanella moved up to the Dodgers in 1948, and Veeck signed the aged Satchel Paige.

By 1949 baseball's black population had increased to thirty-six, and within four years, there were twenty blacks on seven major-league clubs. By 1957, ten years after Robinson's debut, fourteen of the sixteen major-league clubs were integrated.

It wasn't until 1959 that the final holdout, Boston, signed a black player.

● ● ●

Rickey and Robinson brought an end to discrimination on the playing field, but major-league baseball still can't fully lift its head from shame. Blacks such as Frank Robinson, Maury Wills, and Larry Doby have received opportunities as big-league managers, but most major-league teams are still woefully weak in black representation in the front office and among executives.

Perhaps the saddest aspect of baseball's racism is the unanswered question of how some of the great black players of the Negro leagues would have fared in major-league baseball.

How many victories would Satchel Paige have won in the majors in his prime? Paige, who didn't make the majors until he was in his late forties, was dazzling in his prime in exhibitions against major leaguers. He threw some 100 no-hitters during his barnstorming days. How many no-hitters would he have thrown in the majors?

Then there was catcher Josh Gibson, who hit more than seventy homers in black baseball. In one game at Yankee Stadium in 1930, he hit a fair ball *over* the stadium roof. He was only nineteen. How would Gibson, who had batting averages as high as .457 one year and .440 another, have fared in the big leagues?

How would John Beckwith, who hit an astonishing .546 in the Negro leagues in 1930, have stood up against major-league heroes of the era?

There are dozens of other blacks who undoubtedly

Satchel Paige, *left and right.*

would have surpassed some of the big leagues'
greats. Unfortunately, we'll never know.

• • •

Millions of fans are enjoying baseball today because of one aspect of Rickey's plan to integrate the
game. Rickey knew that blacks offered an important
source of major-league talent.

This additional talent enabled baseball to expand
from sixteen teams to today's twenty-six teams. Without blacks, that expansion would have been impossible. There simply wouldn't have been enough major-
league talent available for that many cities.

Without Rickey's master plan, residents of such cities
as San Diego, Kansas City, Montreal, Milwaukee, Toronto, Seattle, Houston, and Dallas would have to
drive hundreds—perhaps thousands—of miles to see
a major-league game.

Thank you, Mr. Rickey.

Babe Ruth with famous radio announcer Graham McNamee.

OWNERS FOUGHT TO KEEP RADIO ANNOUNCERS OUT OF THEIR PARKS

When baseball executives heard the voice of Graham McNamee describing a World Series in the early 1920s, many of them felt shivers zipping up their spines. It wasn't McNamee's distinctive gravelly voice that produced the sweaty palms and nervous twitches, it was where McNamee's voice could be heard: outside the ballpark, in homes, restaurants, and saloons.

If potential patrons could twist a few dials on that newfangled invention called radio and listen to the exploits of their favorite teams in the comfort of their homes, why would they bother visiting the ballpark?

At the same time, baseball fans were overjoyed with this new contraption that could tell them instantly how their teams were faring. Before radio, they usually knew nothing about their heroes until the next morning's papers arrived, or they were forced to wander the streets, looking in the windows of the many businesses that posted inning-by-inning scores.

Today, of course, we take radio baseball—and its offspring, baseball on television—for granted, but in the twenties and early thirties, broadcasting was the subject of one of the most heated debates in baseball. There seemed to be no middle ground: fans and some baseball executives loved it, while most baseball officials and many sportswriters deplored it, savagely warning that it eventually would lead to the demise of the national pastime.

● ● ●

Baseball broadcasting made its debut when Philadelphia visited Pittsburgh on August 5, 1921. The first regular radio station in the nation, KDKA, had been launched in Pittsburgh a year earlier by Westinghouse, and station officials had experimented with broadcasting other sports. Now they felt it was time to give baseball a try. Harold Arlin, a Westinghouse foreman, was selected to broadcast that first game, primarily because he knew more about the sport than anyone else at the station.

The broadcast, picked up on crude crystal sets by thousands of people hundreds of miles away from Pittsburgh, was an immediate success. It was so successful, in fact, that Westinghouse linked KDKA with two of its other affiliates, WBZ in Massachusetts and WJZ in New Jersey, to broadcast the 1921 World Series between the Yankees and the Giants. Famed sportswriter Grantland Rice handled the play-by-play.

The broadcast was received with such wide enthusiasm among listeners that the experiment was repeated the following year when the same clubs met.

Sportswriter Bill McGeehan joined Rice in handling the broadcast. A year later, New York's WEAF (later to become WNBC) hired McNamee, who quickly became the foremost broadcaster of his era.

Then, in 1925, WMAQ of Chicago set the baseball world buzzing with the announcement that it planned to broadcast *all* home games of the White Sox and Cubs. Stations in other major-league communities quickly announced similar plans. Baseball hadn't dreamed up the idea of exclusive rights yet, so three, four, or more stations in a city might broadcast the same game.

Radios had become more than just amusing toys. They were in millions of homes—and the debate over baseball broadcasting quickly heated to full-scale controversy.

Some baseball executives argued that radio actually helped attendance, because it created a broader interest in teams. Baloney, countered other baseball executives, who contended it caused fans to desert the ballparks. The executives of the Yankees, Giants, and Dodgers feared radio so much that they inked an agreement that all three would bar the broadcasting of their games. Still others argued that it was a novelty that would soon wear off.

Meanwhile, sportswriters began launching vicious criticisms of radio broadcasts. Many stations selected broadcasters on the basis of the sound of their voices, rather than their baseball knowledge, and sportswriters dutifully and efficiently reported their horrendous on-the-air miscues. One writer noted that a broadcaster mispronounced the name of every player on the team; another writer told of the confused broadcaster who credited a team with four outs in one inning; another story was told about a broadcaster who got behind in a fast-moving game and announced three quick, nonexistent strikeouts to enable him to catch up with the play-by-play.

Broadcaster Mel Allen with Roger Maris, who was turned down by the Cubs because he was too small.

One writer even demanded that teams thoroughly test the baseball knowledge of their broadcasters' before these people were permitted to go to work.

The broadcasting controversy came to an abrupt stop, however, when the owners suddenly woke up to the idea that they could charge radio stations for the right to broadcast their games.

During the twenties, team owners didn't require a fee for the broadcasting, and few games were sponsored. Even the World Series wasn't sponsored until 1934, when the Ford Motor Company signed a four-year, $400,000 pact.

Once baseball execs found out that broadcasting rights brought in a lot of money, radio suddenly seemed less ominous. Even the famous New York–Brooklyn pact crumbled in 1938, when the Giants were offered $150,000 and Brooklyn received $77,000 for exclusive broadcast rights.

• • •

The first major-league baseball game was televised at Ebbets Field in 1939, but the telecast caused hardly a ripple of notice, because there were only a few televisions in the world at the time.

After World War II, as television slowly invaded the American household, many baseball executives started fearing the great eye as much as their counterparts had feared radio in its infancy.

Again money settled their fears. As television continued to blossom, teams made more and more money peddling TV rights. The All-Star Game and the World Series eventually became nighttime affairs, thus producing higher TV audiences, resulting in higher advertising revenue—and more money for baseball.

Late in the fall of 1988, baseball signed a $1 billion contract with CBS, thus assuring virtually every major-league team a profit during the early 1990s. Baseball's original fear of broadcasting had developed into a love affair.

BABE RUTH—NOT JUDGE LANDIS—SAVED BASEBALL

Hugh S. Fullerton, Sr., had only a feeling in his gut that something was wrong. The veteran sportswriter didn't have a shred of evidence to prove it, but he was positive that some members of the 1919 Chicago

White Sox had conspired with gamblers to throw the World Series to Cincinnati.

Fullerton adored statistics, and he was a knowledgeable observer of virtually every player's capabilities. He had even developed an elaborate statistical system that was amazingly accurate in predicting World Series winners. That's why Fullerton was so convinced that the White Sox had thrown the Series: their performance deviated so drastically from his "prediction" assessment.

Other sportswriters had the same convictions, influenced by the erratic play of some White Sox players during the fall classic. But like Fullerton's editor at the *Chicago American*, other editors and publishers feared libel suits if they printed a word about the possible scandal without positive evidence.

Fullerton was so convinced that he was right—and so disillusioned over his inability to expose the truth—that he gave up writing about baseball that winter. Instead, he wrote a fictional story about a crooked baseball series that was uncovered by a sportswriter using an elaborate mathematical formula.

That spring, Fullerton took his ideas about the Series to the editor of the New York *World*. After listening to the detailed explanation of Fullerton's reasoning, the editor became convinced that Fullerton was right. In spite of the legal risks, he ordered Fullerton to write a series of articles in the spring of 1920.

Once the subject had been broached, other sportswriters started producing stories and columns questioning the honesty of the Series. The possibility of a fix was mentioned so many times that the American League's president, Ban Johnson, was forced to launch an investigation.

In September 1920, Johnson's detectives brought him the dread news: eight Chicago White Sox had indeed made a deal with gamblers to throw the 1919 World Series.

• • •

Charles Comiskey, owner of the Chicago White Sox, didn't have to wait around until the news stories and Johnson's investigation revealed the scandal. Joe Jackson told him all about it a few days after the Series.

Like any dedicated, unscrupulous owner, Comiskey did the natural thing: He covered up the problem. He laughed off all notions that the Series had been fixed and even offered a $10,000 reward to anyone who could prove anything to the contrary. Meanwhile, Comiskey continued business as usual and fielded his eight crooked players in the 1921 season.

The White Sox were well on their way to winning another flag in 1921 when Johnson learned of the fix. He immediately suspended the eight players—seven of them regulars. The drastic depletion of Chicago's talent enabled the Indians to overtake the White Sox and win the pennant in the closing days of the season.

At this point, history tells us, alarmed baseball owners, fearing that the public would cast aside all interest in their scandal-plagued sport, immediately hired Judge Kenesaw Mountain Landis as baseball's first commissioner—and the stern-faced judge's scrupulous honesty and decorum promptly restored the public's trust in our national pastime.

But the truth was that Landis, who knew very little about baseball, was a pawn in a power struggle among team owners—a struggle that backfired handsomely on Landis's behalf. The judge wound up earning nearly $1.5 million during his twenty-four-year tenure as commissioner, and no one ever knew just what happened to the $3.2 million the commissioner's office received as its share of World Series receipts from 1921 until Landis's death in December 1944.

Although the judge's dictatorial powers led him to

make many highly controversial decisions that angered owners, there was never a word of criticism—because he had craftily backed the owners into signing a pact forbidding them to say anything naughty about him.

The judge did bring dignity and decorum to baseball, but it's doubtful that dignity and decorum ever lured a single patron through the turnstiles!

●   ●   ●

Before the job of commissioner was created, baseball was ruled by a three-member National Commission, which included the presidents of the National and American leagues. Ban Johnson was an honest man, but he had a lot of enemies. His launching of the American League in 1901 had created many bitter foes among owners in the elder circuit. He'd angered many of his own league's owners—especially Comiskey—with rulings as league president and as a member of the National Commission.

At a joint meeting of the two leagues in late 1920, all of the National League clubs and three American League clubs joined forces to kill the National Commission, thus eliminating a large chunk of Johnson's power. Instead, they decided that one man should be named supreme ruler over baseball.

Judge Landis quickly surfaced as the leading candidate. Landis had gained national fame in 1907, when he fined the Standard Oil Company a then-staggering $29 million in a freight rebate case. Baseball owners knew the judge well because he had withheld an opinion on an antitrust suit spawned by the collapse of the old Federal League. Here was a man, they felt, who would serve the best interests of baseball owners and be a model of honesty for the game. Oh, how wrong they were.

The judge's name was leaked to the press, so Landis was one up on them when baseball's executives asked him to take the job.

The owners offered him a $25,000 annual salary. Nope, he wanted $50,000—to start. (His salary quickly was increased to $65,000, although Landis did take a pay cut during the Great Depression.) When the eleven clubs that had supported him at the joint meeting nervously agreed to the salary stipulation, the judge reeled off a list of other demands.

First, the owners were to give him a seven-year "iron-clad" contract, which Landis personally drafted. When the owners got around to signing the contract in January 1921, they discovered the new commissioner had inserted an interesting clause: The owners pledged that they would not "publicly criticize or find fault with me or any of my decisions, even in cases where they disagree with me or think I am wrong."

The owners believed they had no choice but to accept the terms in order to regain the confidence of the public.

Landis's first decision was to ban the eight "Black Sox" players from baseball for life. He even forbade them to ever buy a ticket to a minor- or major-league game. Their records, including Jackson's .356 lifetime batting average, were removed from the official record books.

Meanwhile, the man who was supposed to be the owners' friend wound up befriending the players with scores of rulings favoring them against the owners. Repeatedly the owners were stunned and upset by Landis's rulings—but because of that special clause, all they could do was gnash their teeth and smile!

• • •

As for the true hero who saved baseball after the Black Sox scandal, there's only one nomination: Babe Ruth. The Babe so captured the hearts of baseball fans with his home-run bashing that the Black Sox scandal quickly faded from memory without adding a bit of permanent injury to the fans' addiction to the game.

Ruth, a former Baltimore street urchin, first gained national fame as an outstanding pitcher with the Boston Red Sox, starting in 1914. But it was the bat—coupled with a Ruth obsession—that made the Babe the darling of baseball.

Like most hitters in the era when Babe was getting his start, Ruth was at first a line-drive hitter. But he was a very nervous line-driver because of his pitching knowledge and his awareness of his own batting strength. The Babe developed a terrible fear: that someday he would kill a pitcher!

He knew that he could return a delivery to the mound faster than the pitcher could react to it. He even had nightmares of slamming a ball into the head of a hurler unable to duck quickly enough.

So the Babe, who had amazing control over his cudgel, began purposely lofting his hits—and pretty soon those lofts started sailing into the outfield stands. In 1918, when the Red Sox first used the Babe more as a hitter than as a pitcher, he led the league with eleven homers. The next year, he hit twenty-nine home runs, then considered an unbelievable achievement.

But the best was yet to come. In one of baseball's biggest blunders, the financially strapped owner of the Red Sox sold Ruth to the New York Yankees for $125,000 plus a $350,000 loan. Boston fans were stunned and angered over the loss of their hero, and Ruth himself wasn't particularly pleased with the idea of playing with the Yankees, who at the time were distant cousins in popularity to the Giants in New York.

In his first year as a Yankee, however, Ruth turned the sports world inside out with fifty-four home runs. The next year, he hit fifty-nine. Baseball fans, who had been used to seeing baserunners slowly and methodically advance one, two, or three bases at a time, were stupefied with excitement over the new dimension Babe's homers added to the game. Now a lead by the enemy could be wiped out with one brutal blow. A tight game could become a rout in seconds.

The Babe became the biggest draw in baseball, at home and on the road. He led the Yanks to their first pennant and to the start of baseball's greatest dynasty.

When the word *baseball* was mentioned, it generally was in connection with Ruth's name. Hardly anyone talked about the Black Sox scandal. There was virtually no discussion of the "honesty" Landis had returned to the game.

And the owners? With the authoritarian Landis in office for nearly two and a half decades, they did a lot of smiling—and teeth gnashing!

12
MYSTERY, MAYHEM, AND MORTALITY

DEATH AT PLAY

James Phelps was patrolling the outfield for the Rayville town team during a hot afternoon game at Monroe, Louisiana, on July 27, 1909, when he literally made a dying gesture for his club.

An opposing player looped a long, high fly that threatened to go for a home run and wipe out Rayville's slim lead. Phelps raced back . . . back . . . back into the bog bordering the outfield and made a leaping, spectacular catch. At the same instant, he felt a sharp pain in his leg and looked down to see a water moccasin wriggle away.

His leg began to swell, but Phelps paid no heed, bravely finishing the game, although the swelling increased so much he could hardly walk. Within twenty-four hours, he was dead.

Phelps is one of hundreds of amateur and semipro players who have perished, sometimes in grotesque and ghastly fashion, while playing our national pastime.

At St. Louis in 1909, an amateur named John R.

Perry put such effort into a long throw from the field that he burst a blood vessel in his brain—and fell dead on the spot. He never knew that his superhard throw was directly on the mark to the catcher, who nabbed a runner trying to score.

In that same era, Charles Black, a twenty-year-old pitcher for the Big Bone Springs, Kentucky, town team, leaped high for a sizzling liner. He caught the ball and fell headfirst to the ground, while the crowd let loose a lusty cheer for the play. But Black didn't move. Players from both teams rushed to his assistance, and a physician was called. The doctor discovered that Black had died of a broken neck.

Lightning bolts have killed several players in the minors and amateur ranks. One of the strangest such incidents involved a player in a game at Atlantic City, New Jersey. The bolt struck the field some distance from him—but the powerful electrical current traveled along the ground and ran through his spikes and into his body.

In a 1901 game at Monroe City, Illinois, semipro first baseman Morris Carlson was in position awaiting the pitch. Suddenly there was a boom and a flash of lightning—and Carlson spun around several times and dropped dead.

Spectators have not been immune from tragedy. The most grotesque involved Stanton Williams, who was serving as the official scorekeeper at a town game at Morristown, Ohio, one afternoon in 1902. To sharpen his pencil late in the game, he borrowed a knife from the person sitting next to him. He was adding the new point when a brutal foul sailed back from the plate, struck Walker's hand—and drove the knife blade into his heart.

• • •

The only player to die in a major-league game was Ray Chapman, a popular twenty-nine-year-old shortstop for Cleveland, who was beaned by a Carl

Mays's pitch at New York on August 17, 1920. Chapman had come to bat in the fifth inning and assumed his usual slight crouch as he faced Mays, a surly looking hurler who had a reputation for throwing knockdown pitches. Mays delivered a fastball that suddenly broke toward Chapman. In trying to move out of the way, the shortstop bent forward, and the ball struck him sharply on the side of the forehead.

Observers said the sickening sound of ball colliding with bone could be heard hundreds of feet away. Chapman immediately dropped. Teammates rushed to help him to his feet. They said Chapman's eyes were open, and he appeared only slightly dazed. But when they moved him into the shade, he lost consciousness. When an ambulance arrived, Chapman regained consciousness briefly and said softly, "Tell Kate [his wife] I'm all right."

The game continued, but when it was over, Chapman's teammates rushed to the hospital for an all-night vigil. At five o'clock the next morning, they were told that Chapman had died of a fractured skull. Many of the players openly wept.

Doctors said later that there had been no hope for Chapman's survival. The blow was so powerful that it had split his skull an inch and a half, and his brain had been shoved against the bone on the other side.

Meanwhile, the district attorney's office stepped into the case. After a long visit with Mays, the investigators exonerated the Yankee pitcher. Death was attributed to "accidental blow by a baseball."

Nonetheless, a large number of fans and players began calling for Mays, a particularly unpopular player, to be barred from baseball for life. Many players, including Ty Cobb, threatened to strike unless Mays was exiled.

Surprisingly, Tris Speaker, Cleveland's manager, who had been especially fond of his young shortstop, came to Mays's defense. Speaker said the incident was an accident and told fans and players that indicating it was anything else was unfair to Chapman's memory. Fans and players immediately acquiesced to Speaker's request.

Chapman was buried in Cleveland on August 20, and local papers reported the funeral was one of the largest in the city's history. The lengthy funeral cortege blocked streets for miles. All flags in the city were at half-mast, as they were at all ballparks in the country.

When Chapman was laid to rest, a blanket of 20,623 flowers, donated by fans, was laid over his grave. Tris Speaker and outfielder Jack Graney, who had been Chapman's best friend, were so overcome with grief that they did not appear at the funeral.

Mays continued his big-league pitching career through 1929, finishing up with Cincinnati and the Giants. But friends said the death of Chapman haunted Mays until the day he died in 1971.

● ● ●

Chapman might not have been killed if he had been wearing a batting helmet, which was available in that era. Many other players as well would not have had their skulls and careers broken by beanballs.

In the wake of Chapman's death, the 1921 *Spalding Guide* issued a call for players to wear batting helmets. "A head helmet for the batter is not to be despised," the guide reported, adding:

> There is nothing 'sissy' about it. The first time a catcher wore a mask, he was hooted. The first time a catcher wore shin guards, he was jeered. Both of them are accessories to the game now and very useful.
>
> For a long, long time, batters as a class had boasted that no pitcher could hit them. Then there came faster pitching. After that came curves which deceived. After the curves came the new-

fangled devices of pitching in which the pitcher himself had doubt as to the final destination of the ball.

• • •

Players ignored the advice—until Branch Rickey stepped in. When Rickey was general manager of the Pirates, he insisted that his players wear the fiberglass hats lined with airfoam. Before long, everyone in baseball was wearing the protective headgear.

Rickey's order involved a bit of a conflict of interest: at the time, he was head of the American Cap Company, which manufactured the helmets. Nonetheless, Rickey's action undoubtedly has saved scores of players from serious head injuries or possible death in the minors and the majors.

DEATH STALKS PLAYERS OFF THE FIELD

Although only one player has been killed in the more than a quarter-million big-league contests, one of the sad statistics of baseball is the death rate of players off the field. The chance that a big-league player will suffer a premature death—generally in an accident—is more than *four times* as high as it is for the public in general.

More than three dozen established major leaguers have died in their prime since the turn of the century, scores of promising rookies have perished before becoming established stars, and hundreds of others have suffered near-death or career-ending injuries.

It is indeed a strange paradox. On the field, these men defy death daily, earning a living playing with a spheroid that repeatedly travels at deadly speed; off the field, they suddenly become some of the most accident-prone members of any profession. Part of the cause could be that their confidence in their skills and reflexes on the field produces a sense of security off the field that prompts the players to take more chances than the average person.

• • •

Airplane crashes have robbed baseball of some of its most promising stars.

Roberto Clemente, Pittsburgh's superstar right-fielder for eighteen seasons, perished in a December 1972 plane crash while attempting to ferry supplies to victims of a Nicaraguan earthquake. The thirty-eight-year-old Clemente had rapped out the three-thousandth hit of his career in the last game he ever played for the Pirates. The popular Pirate was inducted into the Hall of Fame the following year.

The Yankees' team captain, Thurman Munson, died in a private-plane crash in August 1979, during the height of his career. He was only thirty-two when he lost his life in the accident near Canton, Ohio.

Ken Hubbs, a young second baseman for the Chicago Cubs, died when the private plane he was piloting crashed near Salt Lake City in February 1964. The twenty-two-year-old Hubbs, named Rookie of the Year in 1962, was flying home to California after signing a new contract with the Cubs in Chicago.

Thomas Gastall, a twenty-three-year-old bonus catcher of the Baltimore Orioles, died when the single-engine plane he was piloting crashed into Chesapeake Bay in September 1956.

Outfielder Charlie Peete played only twenty-three games with the 1956 Cardinals, but the twenty-five-year-old looked like a potential major leaguer. That winter, he planned to play ball in South America to gain additional experience. Peete and his wife and children were killed when their commercial flight crashed near Caracas, Venezuela.

Baseball's first victim of an air crash was Marvin Goodwin, manager of Houston's Texas League club that had just been purchased by Cincinnati. The thirty-three-year-old Goodwin, previously a pitcher for the Senators, Browns, and Reds, died in the crash of a plane he was piloting on October 22, 1925.

• • •

Unexpected and sudden illnesses have contributed to the deaths of a large number of major leaguers. The most famous and poignant case involved the Yankees' ironman, Lou Gehrig, who quit after eight games of the 1939 season, when his batting average dropped to .143. He was already in the grips of the wasting disease that now bears his name and that claimed his life two years later.

Cancer claimed the lives of two other Yankees, who hit more home runs in one season than anyone in major-league history. Babe Ruth, who hit sixty homers in 1927, died at the age of fifty-three in 1948. Roger Maris, who hit sixty-one homers in 1961, was only fifty-one when he died December 14, 1985.

The baseball world was saddened by the early deaths of two of its most popular managers. Dick Howser, who guided the Yankees to the pennant before making Kansas City a powerhouse and World Series champ in 1985, began suffering terrible headaches during the 1986 season. A few days after the All-Star Game, he underwent surgery for removal of a brain tumor. Howser valiantly returned to the Royals at the start of 1987 spring training, but after two days, illness forced him to resign. He died on June 17 at age fifty.

Miller Huggins, popular manager of the Yankees from 1918 to 1929, told Yankee acquaintances late one September afternoon that he was going home because he didn't feel well. When someone expressed hope that he would be feeling better soon, Huggins sadly replied, "I don't think I'll be coming back." He died September 25 from a combination of influenza and erysipelas at the age of fifty.

Manager Pat Moran was a topflight catcher in fourteen National League seasons with the Braves, Cubs and Phils. He managed the Reds for four seasons after serving as the Phillies' boss from 1915 to 1918, winning pennants for the Phillies in 1915 and Cincinnati in 1919. Moran died suddenly of Bright's disease at spring training camp in Florida. His death on March 7, 1924, followed only a four-day illness.

Ken Boyer spent most of his fifteen years in the majors with St. Louis and managed the team in 1978, 1979, and part of 1980. On September 7, 1982, he died of cancer at the age of fifty-one.

Harry (Golden Greek) Agganis was beginning to display great potential in his second season with the Boston Red Sox in 1955. The twenty-five-year-old Agganis was hitting .313 when he suddenly developed pneumonia in late June. He seemed to be making a satisfactory recovery after a brief hospitalization, but complications developed, and he died.

Star hurler Urban Shocker pitched only two innings for the 1928 Yanks before he was forced to quit because of heart trouble. Several months later, he developed pneumonia and died on September 9. He was only thirty-eight.

One of the New York Giants' most popular players, outfielder Ross Youngs, was only twenty-nine when he developed health problems during spring training of 1926. A worried manager John McGraw sent Youngs to a physician, who tipped off McGraw that his veteran outfielder had a serious stomach ailment (probably cancer).

But Youngs never complained. He constantly bore down, admitting only occasionally that his "stomach bothers me a little." During the 1926 season, a physician examined him every day the Giants were home, and a male nurse traveled with Youngs on the road. He appeared in ninety-five games that season and managed a .306 average. But he was too sick to return for the 1927 season and died in October of that year.

Bill DeLancey, who showed great possibilities as a catcher for the St. Louis Cardinals in 1934–1935, was sidelined when he suddenly developed tuberculosis. Five years later, he made a comeback effort but was capable of playing in only fifteen games. He died in 1946.

Pitcher Roy Meeker was only twenty-eight when he died of a heart attack at Cincinnati's spring-training camp on March 25, 1929. He had played one full season in the majors with the Athletics and parts of two others in the big leagues when he was cashing in on a new opportunity with the Reds.

Austin McHenry hit .350 with the 1921 Cardinals, but the next season he suddenly ran into difficulties following fly balls. Manager Branch Rickey sent Austin to a doctor, and a brain tumor was discovered. An operation was unsuccessful, and McHenry died at the age of twenty-seven on November 27, 1922.

It was the second tragedy of the year for the Cards. Catcher William Dillhoefer died of typhoid fever at the age of twenty-seven in February of that year.

One of the big leagues' top pitchers, Adrian Joss of Cleveland, died on April 11, 1911, of tubercular meningitis. Joss had fainted on April 3 in an exhibition at Chattanooga, Tennessee, and was rushed to a hospital. He insisted on rejoining the team that night, but a few days later he admitted that he was really sick and again was rushed to a hospital, where his illness was diagnosed. A week later, he died at the age of thirty-four.

Pitcher Leonard (King) Cole jumped off to a brilliant start with the Chicago Cubs, posting a 20–4 record in 1910 and 18–7 in 1911. But he developed a lingering illness and soon disappeared from the majors. He was brought back to the big leagues by the 1915 Yankees but had only a 2–3 record in ten appearances. He died the following January, only three months shy of his thirtieth birthday.

Jake Daubert had just finished his fifteenth season in the majors, with Brooklyn and Cincinnati, and had a .303 lifetime average. He entered the hospital after the 1924 season for a routine operation to remove his appendix and gallstones. But complications developed, and Daubert died a week after the operation at the age of thirty-nine.

Benny Frey hurled eight big-league seasons, most of them for Cincinnati, when he suddenly developed an illness at the start of the 1937 season. He died at the age of thirty-one on November 1, 1937.

Tragedy struck the Washington Senators before their 1906 season. Joe Cassidy, who had been the Senators' regular shortstop for two seasons, died of an illness on March 25, 1906. He was only twenty-three.

● ● ●

Off-field violence has claimed the lives of a surprising number of players and former players.

Lyman Bostock, a twenty-seven-year-old outfielder for the California Angels, was shot to death shortly before the close of the 1978 season. He had been riding in a car on a trip from Gary, Indiana, to nearby Chicago. The bullets were intended for another occupant of the car.

Len Koenecke, a twenty-nine-year-old Brooklyn outfielder, died in September 1935 in a fight with a two-man crew of an airplane that he had chartered. During the fight, the plane wobbled at a dangerously low level above suburban Toronto. The pilot and co-pilot were later exonerated on grounds of self-defense.

Mystery still shrouds just what happened. The flyers testified that they each hit Koenecke with a fire extinguisher after Koenecke suddenly went berserk and tried to seize the plane's controls. Police reported that the ballplayer's body had been found in the front seat of the plane, half exposed and with his face battered.

● ● ●

Quarrels led to the death of several former players. Larry McLean, a catcher for the Cardinals, Cubs,

Reds, and Giants from 1903 to 1915, became embroiled in an argument with a bartender at a South Boston saloon on March 24, 1921. The barkeep pulled a rifle and shot the thirty-nine-year-old McLean dead on the spot.

John Levi, who was signed by the Yankees in 1924, was fatally shot by a woman in a Denver hotel on January 22, 1946.

Harry Otis, who pitched for Cleveland in 1909, also died of gunshot wounds. After quitting baseball, he became a New Jersey policeman and was one of three officers gunned down by a payroll bandit on May 24, 1923. He was thirty-seven.

Hi Bithorn, one of the Cubs' topflight pitchers in the early 1940s, was shot to death in a strange case in Mexico on December 29, 1948. Bithorn ran out of funds on an automobile trip from Chicago to Mexico City, where he planned to visit his mother.

He attempted to sell his car in El Mante, Mexico, about 300 miles from the capital city, but was unable to produce ownership documents. He was taken into custody by an El Mante policeman, and en route to the jail, the frightened Bithorn tried to break away. The officer shot him in the stomach with a 45-caliber pistol. The thirty-five-year-old Puerto Rico native had an 18–12 record with the 1943 Cubs and led the National League with seven shutouts.

Mystery was involved in the shooting death of Frank Grube, an all-American at Lafayette who later caught for the White Sox and St. Louis Browns for eight years. After retirement, he bought a New York City apartment building. On July 1, 1945, he chased six apparent vagrants away from the apartments. About an hour later, as he was talking with the apartment superintendent, he heard footsteps. He went out to investigate. He was wounded in the stomach by a shotgun blast and died the next day at the age of thirty-eight.

Several players have been victims of accidental shootings, including one in a weird incident involving a handkerchief. Mike Donovan, an American League infielder in the early 1900s, was killed on February 4, 1938, by his best friend, Joe Courtney, a former lightweight fighter. The two, serving as guards at a New York plant, went together one evening to draw their pay. Courtney removed a handkerchief from his pocket, and somehow it became entangled with his revolver. While he was trying to separate the two, the gun discharged, and the fifty-eight-year-old Donovan was struck in the head.

Thomas Coates, who had just been drafted by the Athletics, was killed when his shotgun accidentally discharged on October 11, 1909.

William Lee Hobbs, a former Cincinnati infielder, suffered a similar fate on January 5, 1945. He was fifty-one.

● ● ●

Ray Chapman was the only major leaguer to die in a game, but he wasn't the only major leaguer to die at a ballpark. Arthur (Bugs) Raymond, a talented but emotionally disturbed pitcher, wasn't a competitor at the time of his death. Although only thirty years old, he already had finished a career in the National League.

Under suspension by the New York Giants in 1912, Raymond was a spectator at a semipro game in Chicago on September 7, when he got into a fight with a fellow fan. Raymond suffered a fatal brain concussion when he was hit in the head by a brickbat.

● ● ●

Several suicides have shocked the baseball world.

Charles (Chick) Stahl, who had resigned as Red Sox manager only a few days before, killed himself by swallowing four ounces of carbolic acid at Boston's training camp at West Baden, Indiana, on March 28, 1907. He was thirty-four.

Arthur A. Irwin, an outstanding National League player for fourteen years and a manager for eight seasons in the 1890s, "either fell or was pushed" to his death from a steamer en route from New York to Boston on July 16, 1921.

Alvin (Jake) Powell, a hot-tempered outfielder for the Yankees and Senators between 1930 and 1945, ended his life in a grotesque manner. He was arrested by Washington, D.C., police on November 4, 1948, on a bad-check charge. The forty-year-old Powell was held in a Washington police station with a woman companion he said he was planning to marry later in the day.

Jake received permission from the police to talk with the woman in private. He suddenly pulled a 25-caliber pistol from his pocket and shouted, "Hell, I'm going to end it all!" He shot himself in the chest and then in the right temple.

Willard Hershberger, a twenty-nine-year-old who shared Cincinnati's catching duties with Ernie Lombardi, killed himself in his Boston hotel room on August 3, 1940, just a few weeks before the Reds clinched their second straight pennant. Hershberger, who borrowed a teammate's razor for his final act, reportedly had been distraught because the Reds recently had been losing most of their games when he caught.

● ● ●

Former major leaguers also have been victims of drowning and industrial accidents.

Will White, the first big leaguer to wear glasses and a forty-three-game winner for Cincinnati in 1879, died when a small boat overturned in Lake Muskoka, Ontario, August 31, 1911. He was sixty-two. Howard Freigau drowned after diving into a pool in Chattanooga, Tennessee, and striking his head. The twenty-nine-year-old Freigau was a National League outfielder from 1922 through 1928. William

(Duke) Kenworthy, who had played for the Senators and Browns, drowned near Eureka, California, on September 21, 1950.

Bob Unglaub, who managed the Red Sox in 1907 in the middle of an eight-year American League career, was crushed in an accident at a railroad shop in Baltimore, November 29, 1916. Carl Druhot, who pitched for the Reds and Cardinals in 1906–1907, suffered fatal injuries in a shipyard accident at Portland, Oregon, February 11, 1918.

• • •

Don Wilson, who pitched nine years with Houston, and his son died of carbon monoxide poisoning at their home on January 5, 1975. It was ruled an accident. Wilson, who had a 104–92 lifetime record, was only twenty-nine.

John (Nig) Grabowski, who had seven years' experience in the majors as a catcher with the Yankees, White Sox, and Browns, suffered a premature death in a fire at his home. The forty-six-year-old Grabowski carried his wife to safety when fire ravaged their home at Guilderland, New York, on May 19, 1946. He then tried to back his car out of the flaming garage and was engulfed in fire. He died four days later.

Harry Blake, a National League outfielder in the 1890s, perished in a Chicago lodging house fire on October 14, 1919. He was forty-five.

Forrest Cady, who caught for the Athletics and the Phillies and was Babe Ruth's receiver for the Red Sox, suffered a strange death in a Cedar Rapids, Iowa, hotel room on March 3, 1946. The fifty-seven-year-old Cady died of asphyxiation from a fire in his bed. The fire apparently had been touched off by a faulty heating pad.

Asphyxiation also was blamed in the death of fifty-four-year-old Fred Corey in a fire at Providence, Rhode Island, on December 21, 1912. From 1875 to

1885, Corey had played virtually every position for three teams in the old National League and American Association.

The Yankees' great second baseman Tony Lazzeri was only forty-one when he died of either "a heart attack or the effects of a fall." Lazzeri's body was discovered at the base of a flight of stairs in his San Francisco home on August 7, 1946. He may have struck his head against the banister while falling; during his playing days, Lazzeri suffered epileptic seizures.

● ● ●

Henry (Heinie) Reitz, a crack second baseman for the Baltimore Orioles from 1893 to 1897, was the first of nearly three dozen current or former major leaguers killed in automobile accidents. The forty-seven-year-old Reitz died in a 1915 crash.

Since then, auto deaths have claimed such greats as Hall of Famers Mel Ott and Carl Hubbell; Charles Irwin, a big leaguer for eleven seasons; Harry Wolverton, who managed the New York Yankees in 1912; Edward (Kid) Foster, an American League infielder for thirteen seasons; John C. Benton, who pitched seventeen seasons for the Reds, Pirates, and Giants; Jimmy Sheckard, a top player for the champion Cubs of 1906, 1907, 1908, and 1910.

One of the most promising catchers of the era, Walter Lerian, was an innocent bystander when he was killed on October 22, 1929. The twenty-six-year-old Lerian, who played for the Phils, died when a truck leaped the curb of a Baltimore street and pinned Lerian against a building.

Pirate pitcher Bob Moose, who had thrown a no-hitter against the Mets in September 1969, died in an automobile accident near Martins Ferry, Ohio, on October 9, 1976. Moose, who had a 76–71 lifetime record, died on his twenty-ninth birthday.

Chico Ruiz, who spent eight years in the majors

with Cincinnati and California, perished in a car crash near San Diego in February of 1972. He was thirty-four.

William M. Steele, who pitched for the Cardinals and Dodgers from 1910 through 1914, was killed by another mode of transportation: He was fatally injured when he was run over by a streetcar in Overland, Missouri, a St. Louis suburb, in October of 1949. He was sixty-four.

• • •

Outright stupidity brought an early death to Gus Sanberg, a catcher for Cincinnati in 1923 and 1924. Sanberg removed some gasoline from the tank of his own car in February 1930 to help a friend whose car had run out of fuel.

The good deed accomplished, the thirty-three-year-old Sanberg decided to see if he had left himself any gasoline in his car. Gus lit a match to check the tank. Burns from the explosion were fatal.

• • •

Two mass tragedies, both involving minor-league teams, have stunned the baseball world.

Nine players on the Spokane club of the Western International League were killed and six players injured July 24, 1946, when the team bus went out of control, crashed through a guard rail, and plunged down a 300-foot embankment in the Cascade Mountains of Washington. Two players escaped the calamity because they had received special permission to use a private car for the trip to Bremerton, Washington.

Miraculously, a third player who had been on the bus was saved because of a message that was delivered to him at the last stop just before the accident. Infielder Jack Lohrke was an option from San Diego of the Pacific Coast League, and the Padres tried to phone him with the news that he was being recalled.

Their call to Spokane came just minutes after the bus had pulled away, but a club official said the bus probably would make a rest stop at Ellensburg, Washington. The San Diego general manager phoned the Ellensburg bus stop and left a message for Lohrke to call. The message got through; Lohrke, who forever after carried the nickname Lucky, stayed behind to catch a bus to San Diego. (When he was in the military, Lohrke failed to report on time for a scheduled boarding of an Army transport plane. The plane left without him—and crashed.)

In 1948, manager George Treadwell and four of his Duluth players were killed when the team bus was involved in a flaming crash with an ice truck. The driver of the truck also was killed. Thirteen other players on the Northern League team were seriously injured. One of the few players who was able to continue his playing career was Mel McGaha, who later served short stints as manager of Cleveland and Kansas City in the mid-1960s.

MAJOR LEAGUER CHARGED WITH MURDER

At least one major leaguer has been charged with murder. Art (The Great) Shires, who played for the White Sox, Senators, and Braves during the late twenties and early thirties, was charged in the death of fifty-six-year-old W. H. Erwin, a former professional player, in Dallas, Texas. Erwin died on December 4, 1928, nine weeks after he and Shires got into a fight at Erwin's cleaning and pressing shop. Shires was later acquitted on grounds of self-defense.

THE STRANGE DEATH OF BASEBALL'S GREATEST HITTER

Ed Delahanty, perhaps the greatest baseball slugger of all time, was the only player to lead both major leagues in hitting. In the latter years of the nineteenth century and early part of this century, he was the most feared and famous batter in baseball. But when fans talk about great hitters of the past—Hornsby, Cobb, Ruth, Gehrig—Delahanty's name is seldom mentioned, even though he's a member of the Hall of Fame.

Perhaps that's because at the pinnacle of his sixteen-year major-league career, Delahanty drowned in the Niagara River near Niagara Falls—a death that has been shrouded in mystery since 1903. Even today, there is still no answer to the question whether Delahanty's death was an accident, suicide, or murder.

Ed broke into the majors with the Phillies at the age of twenty-one in 1888, and he soon established himself as a master hitter. Twice he was six for six in games, and in 1896—the height of the "dead ball" era—he hit four home runs and a single in one game.

In 1899 he led the National League in batting with a .408 average. In 1902 Delahanty jumped to Washington of the new American League, where he led the loop in hitting (.376) and doubles (forty-three) as well as scoring 103 runs and knocking in an additional 93.

Delahanty was off to an equally impressive season in 1903, when the mystery begins. He had a .333 average for forty-two games, when on June 25 he unexpectedly pulled himself from the lineup while Washington was at Cleveland. The thirty-five-year-old Delahanty continued to travel with the club but would not play. Then, on July 2 in Detroit, he mysteriously vanished. There was no trace of him for days.

His distraught wife finally received a telegram at their Cleveland home on July 7. It was from a railroad ticket agent in Detroit telling her that a man matching Delahanty's description had purchased a ticket July 2 on a Michigan Central train to New York.

At first there was speculation that Delahanty was going to return to the National League and play for the New York Giants. But that theory was discarded a few nights later, when Washington manager Tommy Loftus received word from the district superintendent of the Pullman Company. The report said that a man tentatively identified as Delahanty had been forcibly removed from a Michigan Central train at Bridgeport, Ontario, on the Canadian side of Niagara Falls the night of July 2.

Reportedly, the dispatch from the director said, the man had started to walk across the International Bridge to Buffalo and had fallen through an opening of the train bridge. During an investigation, the conductor of the train claimed that Delahanty had had five drinks of whiskey after leaving Detroit and had been so obnoxious and rowdy that he had to be put off the train. The conductor contended that at one point Delahanty had used an open razor to terrify persons in one of the sleeping cars. E. J. McGuire, Delahanty's brother-in-law, said that story was preposterous because Ed carried only a safety razor.

Sam Kingston, the night watchman on the bridge, told authorities that when Delahanty started to walk across the bridge, Kingston ordered him to return to shore. Apparently angry words developed between the two men, and Kingston said at first that some blows had been exchanged. Later he denied that there were any fisticuffs.

On July 9 Delahanty's body was found in the Niagara River downstream from Niagara Falls. One leg had been ripped off, apparently by the propeller of a sightseeing boat near whose landing the body was found. M. A. Green, a Senators official, identified the body. Delahanty had been carrying a large amount of cash and had been wearing some $2,000 worth of jewelry. The cash and jewelry were missing.

Delahanty's valise, containing a suit, a pair of baseball shoes, and a season pass to the Washington ballpark in the name of his wife, was found near the railroad tracks.

His relatives bluntly refused to accept a suicide theory. His mother, Mrs. James Delahanty, said her son was in excellent spirits when she last saw him June 25 in Cleveland. Family members also issued angry denials to reports that Delahanty could have been on a week-long drinking spree.

Whether Delahanty fell, was pushed, or jumped into the Niagara River will never be known. Nor will there ever be answers to why he suddenly pulled himself from the lineup or why he was traveling to New York. This strangest of deaths ever to befall a major league superstar will remain a mystery.

BOBO NEWSOM—MAYHEM IN MOTION

Pitcher Bobo Newsom suffered dozens of breaks—literally—during his twenty-year major-league career. No other player in the game suffered as many cuts, contusions, and broken bones as the fun-loving Newsom. He's also probably the only player ever sidelined by a mule kick. He was injured so many times that it borders on the miraculous that his major-league career extended from 1929 to 1953.

A few months before he was scheduled to play with the 1932 Cubs, Newsom's car skidded off a high embankment and plunged 225 feet. It would have meant instant death for most mortals, but Bobo escaped with only a broken leg.

While that leg was healing in a hospital, Newsom wrote cheery letters to Chicago officials, confidently assuring them that he was getting in shape for the '32 season. A couple of days after he was discharged from the hospital, Newsom, for some reason, decided to attend a mule auction. While he was looking on, one of the critters kicked his newly healed leg—and broke it again.

During his long career, Bobo suffered such injuries as another broken leg, a fractured kneecap, a skull fracture, a broken jaw, and a half-dozen or so "minor" fractures.

INJURIES END CAREERS

Hundreds of ballplayers have had their careers abruptly terminated or shortened because of injuries.

One of the sport's most tragic injuries ended the career of both the victim and the perpetrator. That was on the night of May 7, 1957, when Herb Score, one of the game's most shining lights, was struck in the eye by a fearsome line drive off the bat of Yankee Gil McDougald. Score, then in his third season with the Indians, suffered a broken bone and eye damage.

He was 16–10 in his first season in the majors and 20–10 in his sophomore year. But, after the injury, he never regained his pitching abilities. He slipped to 2–3 in 1958 and was 9–11 in 1959. He was traded to the White Sox, where he won only six of eighteen games before retiring from baseball at the age of twenty-nine in 1962.

The injury also caused the demise of McDougald's career. Hostile fans constantly rode the Yankee infielder about the accident. Finally, he couldn't take it any longer. At the end of the 1960 season, he gave up baseball at age thirty-two.

One particularly sad injury was the beaning of Boston's Tony Conigliaro, who had the potential to be one of baseball's all-time greats. Tony broke in with the Red Sox as a nineteen-year-old in 1964 and hit .290 with twenty-four home runs. The next year, he led the league in homers with thirty-two. The '66 season was another banner year for Tony, and so was the '67 season—until August 19, when he was bashed in the left eye by a pitch from Jack Hamilton.

Conigliaro never fully recovered, although he made a gallant effort to reclaim his old glory. After sitting out the 1968 season, he returned to hit .255 with twenty homers in 1969 and .266 and thirty-six homers in 1970. But problems from the old injury continued to flare, and he was traded to California in 1971, hitting only four homers with a .222 average in seventy-four games.

Tony disappeared from the majors after that, although he made one last comeback attempt with the Red Sox in 1975. After batting only .123 in twenty-one games, Conigliaro retired at the age of thirty.

Then, of course, there was the tragic automobile accident in which Hall of Famer Roy Campanella was paralyzed for life with a broken neck. Campanella's car skidded into a tree on an ice-slick highway during the winter that Brooklyn moved to Los Angeles for the 1958 season.

Pitcher Jim Lonborg's 22-9 record helped spur Boston to the American League crown in 1967. But he broke his leg during a skiing accident the next winter and saw only limited action in '68. He never regained his old touch.

Minnie Rojas, a California Angels relief pitcher, was permanently paralyzed in a 1968 auto accident. His wife and one of his children died in the crash.

One of baseball's greatest pitchers, Dizzy Dean, was sidelined by a freak accident in the 1937 All-Star Game. Dean, who had won eighty-two games for the Cards in the three seasons before 1937, suffered a fractured toe when he was struck on the foot by a line drive by Cleveland's Earl Averill.

Dean returned to pitching before the toe had healed properly; it forced a change in his pitching delivery that harmed that talented arm forever. The Cards traded him to the Cubs in 1938, but during the next four years, Dean earned only sixteen victories. Shortly after the start of the '41 season, he retired.

Los Angeles' brilliant pitcher Sandy Koufax was 25-5 in 1963, then followed with 19-5, 26-8, and 27-9

Pitcher Dizzy Dean trying out some bat work with the Chicago Cubs in 1938.

records. But every triumph was a painful one for Koufax, who suffered arthritis and circulatory problems—ailments that forced him to retire prematurely at the age of thirty after the '66 season.

Roger Metzger, who spent eleven years in the majors with the Cubs, Astros, and Giants, accidentally sawed the tips of his fingers off one hand with a power saw after the 1979 season. He tried to play in the 1980 season, but produced only two hits in twenty-eight games.

At least three big leaguers have survived wounds inflicted by female hands. During 1963 spring training, Yankee relief pitcher Marshall Bridges made friendly overtures to a woman at an Elks Club in Fort Lauderdale. The woman pulled a pistol from her purse and shot Bridges in the leg. Bill Jurges, who spent seventeen seasons in the majors with the Giants and the Cubs from 1931 to 1947, was stabbed in the side by a woman, but he quickly recovered. Eddie Waitkus, a former Cub who had just been traded to the Phillies, was seriously wounded when a crazed woman admirer shot him in a Chicago hotel room in 1949. He missed the rest of the '49 season but recovered to play six more seasons in the big leagues.

An off-season hunting accident in 1938 near his hometown of Greenville, Texas, cost Monty Stratton his right leg and a successful pitching career with the White Sox. A movie, starring James Stewart, dramatized Stratton's courageous recovery . . . how he came back as a coach with the White Sox and as a minor-league pitcher, stumping onto the diamond on an artificial leg.

Old-time pitcher Mordecai Brown lost two fingers in a farming accident, but it didn't prevent him from becoming a Hall of Famer. Dubbed "Three Finger" Brown, he was able to use his remaining fingers to put an unusual hop on the ball—good enough to win 239 games.

Charlie Bennett, a long-time catcher for Detroit and Boston in the National League, was traveling in Kansas after the 1893 season. But he tarried at one stop too long and saw his train pulling out of the station. He rushed to leap aboard but slipped, and both of his legs were mangled by the wheels.

Boston lost the services of Ted Williams for the rest of the season in 1950, when the great slugger broke his elbow after crashing into the outfield wall during the All-Star Game.

Joe DiMaggio was constantly bothered by an injury to his heel, and he was once sidelined when a trainer put a heat lamp on it, then forgot all about it—until Joe's foot was nearly baked.

THE PLAYER WHO BIT HIMSELF IN THE POSTERIOR

Baseball players have come up with some of the darnedest ways of inflicting self-injury. But no one will ever top Clarence Blethen, a Red Sox pitcher during the 1920s.

Blethen wore false teeth, but whenever he pitched, he'd remove his teeth as a ploy to look more menacing to opposing batters. Blethen seemed to think the idea worked—until one day when he slipped his teeth into his back pocket in a game with Detroit.

Early on, when batting, Blethen reached first against the Tigers, before the next batter cracked an infield shot. Blethen slid into second in an effort to abort a double play. Trouble was, the instant his posterior touched the ground, it forced the teeth in his back pocket to clamp down—hard—on his rear end!

MORE SELF-INFLICTED MAYHEM

There have been other injuries nearly as bizarre. Take the case of Jimmy Johnston, a Brooklyn outfielder who broke his leg while standing still! Johnston, a journeyman performer during the teens and twenties, was standing in his position one afternoon, when an easy fly came floating in his direction. Instead of moving a few steps to catch it, Johnston crumpled to the ground and lay motionless—while the ball rolled to the fence. It turned out that one of Johnston's feet was planted in a slight depression in the ground. When he started to move his body toward the ball, his foot remained locked in the ground—and his leg snapped into two pieces.

Steve Dillon, who pitched briefly with the New York Mets in the 1960s, was sprinkling hair tonic on his head at spring-training camp. He leaned his head back a bit too far—and was sidelined with a sprained neck.

Sailor Bill Posedel, a relief pitcher for the old Boston Braves, suffered a broken jaw in the bullpen. He was limbering up in Philadelphia on the last day of the 1938 season. After delivering a pitch, he paused to take a look at the game. He didn't notice the relief catcher's return throw—which struck him square in the jaw.

Warming up for a turn at bat, Baltimore's Dick Williams held the bat behind his back, one hand at each end as he flexed and twisted. Suddenly, there was a pop, and Williams was sidelined for weeks with a pulled shoulder muscle.

Catcher Earl Battey of Minnesota, in his haste to fling off his mask to pursue a foul, missed the crossbar and jabbed a finger in his eye. He was forced to leave the game.

Wade Boggs of Boston lost his balance in 1986 while removing his cowboy boots. He fell, striking his ribs against the side of a sofa. He was out for a week.

A weird coincidence in 1970 involved the Phillies' two catchers, Mike Ryan and Tim McCarver. Each broke his hand—in the same inning of the same game!

Jack Coombs almost ruined his pitching career—and nearly lost his life—because he caught his spikes in the pitching rubber and twisted his leg during the 1911 World Series. Despite excruciating pain, Coombs continued to pitch for five more innings before giving up. That night, he was taken to a Philadelphia hospital, where he contracted typhoid of the spine and spent the next year flat on his back.

In the mid-1960s, Bob Lee of the Los Angeles Angels took a swing at an abusive fan—and missed. Instead, he hit a railing and broke his hand.

Perhaps this isn't a legitimate injury, but in 1974 the

Cubs' Jose Cardenal asked permission to sit out a couple of games. He claimed one of his eyelids was stuck open.

Lonny Frey, Cincinnati's second baseman, was forced to sit out the 1940 World Series with a broken foot. A water cooler in the dugout had tipped over on it.

Sam Mele of the Red Sox had to leave a game in the third inning early in the 1947 season because of a painful sacroiliac condition. Sam had aggravated the condition the night before when his roommate, Dom DiMaggio, climbed into bed and it collapsed, prompting Mele to laugh so hard that it . . . well, you guessed it.

Baltimore's Jim Palmer suffered a pinched nerve in his neck in 1984, when he took a quick look over his shoulder at a runner on first base.

Vern Ruhle of the Astros injured a finger on his pitching hand in 1980 when he grabbed for a towel in the dugout. The towel had a thumb tack in it.

Yankee pitcher Lefty Gomez came to bat one day and swung his bat to knock the dirt out of his spikes. Instead he whacked his ankle and was forced to leave the game.

Cleveland pitcher Ray Caldwell apparently is the only major leaguer ever struck by lightning during a game. Caldwell had a 2–1 lead over the Philadelphia Athletics on August 8, 1910, when lightning started flashing from thick black clouds floating over the ballpark.

Suddenly, a bolt struck Caldwell, who slumped to the ground. Frantic teammates gathered around him, and in a couple of minutes he regained consciousness, immediately demanding to know who had hit him! He recovered quickly enough to finish—and win—the game.

And in the Most-Distasteful-Injury Department, the

winner is Morrie Arnovich of the Phillies. A large beetle flew into his mouth one day while he was chasing a fly ball. Arnovich had two choices: stop and cough up the large insect, or gulp it down and continue after the ball. Arnovich chose the latter, certainly one of the greatest contributions a team member has ever made to his club!

A ROTTEN MOTHER'S DAY GIFT

One of baseball's most unusual injuries—as far as timing is concerned—involved a spectator: the mother of Cleveland pitcher Bob Feller.

In May of 1939, when Feller was achieving superstar status with the Indians, the White Sox staged a special combination Mother's Day and Feller Day celebration in Chicago. Bob's mother and father, along with half of the residents of Feller's hometown of Van Meter, Iowa, traveled to the Windy City for the special event.

Before the game, Feller promised his mother that he would win especially for her. He was well on the way to achieving that promise by the third inning. The Indians had a 6-0 lead, and Feller could see his mother beaming with delight from her front-row seat.

But then Feller delivered one of his blazing fastballs to Marv Owen, Chicago's third baseman. The ball was fouled into the stands and struck Mrs. Feller above the left eye, shattering one of the lenses of her glasses. Feller knew that it was his mother who had been struck; he stood stark still on the mound while she was rushed from the park to a hospital.

Shaking, Feller managed to finish the game (he won it), then rushed to the hospital, where he learned that six stitches had been required to close the wound around his mother's eye and that she had suffered a mild concussion.

THE NIGHT THE CARDINALS WERE NEARLY WIPED OUT

A manager's worries over his team's sleeping accommodations once saved the St. Louis Cardinals from being virtually wiped out in a railroad wreck.

The Cardinals had played in Philadelphia on July 10, 1911, and took a train from there to board Pullmans (sleeping cars) on the Federal Express of the New York, New Haven, and Hartford Railroad for an overnight trip to Boston.

When the team arrived in Washington, Roger Bresnahan, a former catching star who was manager of the Cards, threw a fit when he discovered that the Pullmans reserved for the Cardinals were only a couple of cars behind the engine. He protested that the noise from the engine would disturb the slumber of his charges, who were scheduled to play the Braves the next afternoon. The conductor finally promised to move the Cardinals' cars at the first opportunity, when the train reached the yards in New Jersey.

At about 4 A.M., only an hour or so after the change had been made, the train soared off the rails and plunged down an eighteen-foot embankment just west of Bridgeport, Connecticut. Fourteen persons were killed and forty-seven were seriously injured. All of the dead and injured were in the front part of the train, where the Cardinals' cars had been!

The only day coach on the train had replaced one of the Cards' Pullmans. It was crushed and splintered more completely than any other car, and most of the victims were in its twisted wreckage.

The Cards' Pullmans at the back of the train were undamaged. Most of the players didn't learn about their luck until after the accident; they had slept right through the switching.

Cardinals players aided in the rescue work for

more than three hours. They could have reached Boston on another train in time for the game, but sympathetic Boston officials postponed the game.

DODGERS ESCAPE FIERY TRAIN CRASH

Members of the Brooklyn Dodgers escaped injury in a fiery train crash during World War II. The Dodgers were en route from St. Louis to Chicago, when their train crashed into a gasoline truck during the early morning hours near Joliet, Illinois.

The truck spewed flaming gasoline onto the train, but all passengers escaped injury because the momentum of the train carried it past the accident site. The engineer and fireman, however, lost their lives.

BASEBALL EXECUTIVES ESCAPE DEATH

Wild Bill Donovan, a former pitching great, manager of the Yankees from 1915 to 1917, and boss of the Phillies in 1921, was killed in a railroad accident in 1923. But, miraculously, scores of other baseball dignitaries escaped serious injury or death in the accident.

Forty-seven-year-old Donovan, who had been managing New Haven, was killed when he and other baseball officials were en route to Chicago for the annual minor-league meetings. The train derailed after crashing into another train near Forsyth, New York.

George Weiss suffered only minor injuries, although he occupied the berth next to Donovan. Weiss, then owner of the New Haven club, later gained fame as general manager of the Yankees.

Among the passengers in the front section of the train were John A. Heydler, president of the National League, dozens of minor-league officials, and sportswriters. None received more than slight injuries.

Heydler was cited for his efforts in rescuing injured passengers and in helping recover several bodies.

MISFORTUNE HAUNTED TINKER, EVERS, CHANCE

Good luck produced the first of the Tinker-to-Evers-to-Chance double plays—but in later years misfortune haunted all three members of baseball's most famous double-play combination.

The debut of Tinker-Evers-Chance was a bizarre one indeed. A grass-searing grounder struck shortstop Joe Tinker's toe and flipped right into the hands of second baseman Johnny Evers, who then rifled the ball to first baseman Frank Chance.

Although these three men were the darlings of the baseball world during the first decade of this century, when they helped the Cubs to National League pennants in 1906, 1907, 1908, and 1910, their luck began turning sour when their careers were still going strong. Tinker and Evers, who never did care much for each other, got into a fight and refused to speak a word to each other for years.

Chance was beaned late in his career with the Cubs, and for the rest of his life was tormented by persistent headaches. In 1913, he signed a contract to manage New York's American League team and was expected to revive what was then one of the worst teams in baseball. But he was repeatedly embroiled in arguments with the team's owners and top star, Hal Chase, and was fired before the season was over in 1914.

It was nine years before Chance had an opportunity to return as a major-league manager, at Boston in 1923. The Red Sox finished dead last, and Chance was exiled again. In 1924 Charlie Comiskey, his team still fragmented by the expulsion of the eight players from the Black Sox scandal, hired Chance as manager, with Tinker as his top assistant.

But at spring training, Chance developed breathing difficulty that soon was diagnosed as acute tuberculosis. During the summer, Chance, who had carried the nickname Husk, saw his athletic body wither from nearly 200 pounds to less than 100 pounds. On September 14, he died in a California sanatorium.

Evers's troubles began with a nervous breakdown before the start of the 1911 season. Later in life, he battled financial ruin and still later was crippled by a stroke.

Evers did manage to recover from his breakdown to play the last forty-seven games of the 1911 season. After his playing days, he was manager, coach, and scout for the White Sox, Giants, and Braves. He even served briefly as general manager of Albany, New York, of the International League.

Evers earned some $200,000, but poor investments—including one in a sporting goods store he operated in Albany—reduced him to near-pauper status. He was forced to take a job as superintendent of a city-owned athletic field in Albany in 1942. Less than a year later, he suffered a stroke that paralyzed his right side and caused a partial loss of his voice. He spent the last four years of his life confined to a wheelchair.

For a time it appeared that Tinker would escape the jinx. After retiring from baseball, he cashed in royally on the great Florida real estate boom of the 1920s and earned a modest fortune. Then tragedy struck. His first wife suddenly died in Orlando, Florida. Later Tinker remarried—and his second wife died of illness.

When the Great Florida Boom went bust, Tinker was wiped out. He tried a comeback with a hotel and a billiards parlor, but both ventures became casualties of the Great Depression.

In 1936, Tinker suffered a prolonged serious illness. When he eventually recovered, he was nearly penniless and was forced to take a job as a beer salesman. During the last decade of his life, he continued to be plagued by a variety of illnesses, including an infected foot that developed complications and eventually forced amputation of his left leg.

The Tinker-Evers-Chance misfortune also affected Harry Steinfeldt, who was a standout at third base when the Cubs' double-play combination was at its peak. Steinfeldt developed a mysterious illness during 1913 and died of "paralysis" in Bellevue, Kentucky, in August 1914. He was only thirty-seven.

• • •

Tinker, Evers, and Chance probably owe their fame more to a poem than to their double-play success. The three executed only fifty-four double plays between 1906 and 1909. The Philadelphia Athletics executed a record 217 double plays during the 1949 season alone. But in 1910 columnist Franklin P. Adams of the New York *Evening Mail* wrote a poem that repeatedly used the key phrase "Tinker to Evers to Chance."

All three players were inducted into the Hall of Fame. Steinfeldt, the fourth member of the Cubs' famous infielding quartet, never made it to the Hall. It has been suggested that one of the prime reasons was that he wasn't named in Adams's poem.

INDEX